Memoirs Of Madame De Motteville On Anne Of Austria And Her Court, Volume 1...

[Françoise Bertaut] de Motteville

MEMOIRS

OF

MADAME DE MOTTEVILLE

Volume I.

The Cour de France Edition

LIMITED TO TWELVE HUNDRED AND FIFTY NUMBERED SETS, OF WHICH THIS IS

No. 534

Madame de Motteville

MEMOIRS

OF

MADAME DE MOTTEVILLE

ON

ANNE OF AUSTRIA AND HER COURT.

WITH AN INTRODUCTION BY

C.-A. SAINTE–BEUVE.

Translated by

KATHARINE PRESCOTT WORMELEY.

ILLUSTRATED WITH PORTRAITS FROM THE ORIGINAL

IN THREE VOLUMES.

VOL. I.

BOSTON:

HARDY, PRATT & COMPANY.

1902.

University Press

JOHN WILSON AND SON, CAMBRIDGE, U.S.A.

CONTENTS.

CHAPTER III. — 1643–1644.

CHAPTER VIII. — 1647.

CHAPTER IX. — 1648.

CHAPTER X. — 1648.

CHAPTER XI. — 1648.

CHAPTER XII. — 1648.

LIST OF

PHOTOGRAVURE ILLUSTRATIONS.

FAC–SIMILE LETTER.

INTRODUCTION.

By C.-A. SAINTE-BEUVE.

LET us repose awhile with Madame de Motteville, the writer of these judicious Memoirs, — with that wise and reasonable mind which saw very closely the things of her day, and estimated and described them in such perfect proportion and with an accuracy so agreeable. When the Memoirs of Madame de Motteville appeared for the first time, in 1723, the journalists and critics of that day, while praising their tone of sincerity, deemed that they gave too many minute details, too many little facts. This was the opinion of not only the " Journal de Trévoux " and the " Journal des Savants," but it was that of Voltaire himself. We no longer think so. These little facts, belonging to an old and vanished society which they represent to us with absolute truth, please us and fasten our attention: at a short distance they might seem superabundant and superfluous; at a greater distance they become both new and interesting. And besides, while Madame de Motteville, keeping to her woman's rôle and telling nothing that she does not know of her own knowledge, never attempts to penetrate cabinet secrets (though she divines some of them very well indeed), she pictures to the life the general spirit of all situations and the moral character of the personages. It is this lasting side that time has more clearly brought forth, placing her henceforth in a rank both distinguished and well-established.

Madame de Motteville, born about 1621, her maiden name being Françoise Bertaut, was the niece of a bishop-poet,

illustrious in his day and still remarkable for sentiment and
elegance; the same Bertaut whom Boileau praised for his
reserve, and Ronsard judged to be "too virtuous a poet."
I remark at once on this basis of virtue, which seems to
have been inherent in the race. Madame de Motteville had
a younger sister who was called from her infancy Socratine,
on account of her austerity, which ended by making her a
Carmelite. This austerity, much softened and adorned in
the elder sister, deserved in her the name of reason and
good sense; and it was thus that those who knew her only
by reputation spoke of her. "Mélise may pass for one of
the most sensible *précieuses* of the island of Delos," says the
"Grand Dictionnaire des Précieuses."

Mademoiselle Bertaut had received a very careful and
very literary education. Her father, Pierre Bertaut, was
gentleman-in-ordinary of the king's bed-chamber. Her
mother, who came of a noble family in Spain and had
lived her youth in that country, was noticed by Anne of
Austria in the early days after the queen's arrival in France.
Knowing Spanish as her own language, she was employed
by the queen for her family correspondence and treated as
a friend. She profited by this favour to *give*, as they said
in those days, meaning to attach to the queen's service, her
daughter, then seven years old (1628). But Cardinal Richelieu, always uneasy about the queen's surroundings and
anxious to cut off her communications with Spain, removed
the little girl,—an act to which Anne of Austria strongly
objected. To all her complaints "they answered," so Madame
de Motteville tells us, "that my mother was half Spanish,
that she had much intelligence, that already I spoke Spanish
and might resemble her." Madame Bertaut accordingly
took her daughter, now ten years old, to Normandy, where
she completed her education with care. The young girl

still received an annual payment of six hundred *livres* from the queen, and in 1639 she was thought worthy, for her beauty and good reputation, to be married to M. Langlois de Motteville, president of the Chamber of Accounts of Normandy, who made her his third wife. "This was an ill-assorted marriage," says the "Journal de Savants" (January, 1724); "the president was eighty years old, and the wife only eighteen. It is said that she wearied of her half of the bed, so that sometimes after the goodman went to sleep she made her waiting-maid take her place, and the old man never found it out." If this detail, stated by a grave journal, is correct, it was the liveliest piece of giddiness of Madame de Motteville's life. Her nature, calm and unimpassioned, seems never to have suffered from such a marriage. "In the year 1839, having married M. de Motteville," she says, "I found much comfort, with an abundance of everything; and if I had been willing to profit by the friendship he had for me and receive the advantages he could and would have given me, I should have been rich after his death." But she neglected these views of self-interest, and, like all others exiled from Court, she thought only of the hope held out by the coming death of the cardinal, at which time she expected her return to favour. On the death of the cardinal and that of the king, one of the queen's first acts was to recall all those who had been dismissed on account of their love for her, and Madame de Motteville was among them. She was henceforth attached to the queen, less as woman-in-waiting (which was her title) than as one of the persons of her daily intercourse and intimacy. Wise, discreet, and punctual, of a gentle but playful mind, a curiosity both serious and readily amused, with an observing eye that did not seek to be piercing or to look deep, but contented itself with seeing clearly that which went on about her, she spent twenty-two very varied years, some of which were shaken by violent storms. Faithful and devoted, without pretending to be heroic, she was able to reconcile the timidities of her sex with the obligations and duties of her position, and pass at Court through the breakers of many reefs, visible and invisible, without being turned from her way, continuing always within the rules and delicacies of scrupulous integrity — woman in many points, but the most reasonable of women, a genuine person, yet at the same time amiable. She seems never to have thought of remarrying, and never to have known a tender weakness. In that agreeable discussion which she holds by letter with La Grande Mademoiselle on the conditions of a perfectly happy life she says: "I was only twenty years old when I regained my liberty, which has always seemed to me preferable to all the other good things that the world esteems; and by the way I have used it I seem to be a fit inhabitant of the village of Randan," — a village in Auvergne where the widows do not marry again. The title of dowager, which she gained so young, did not terrify her. She enjoyed friendship and conversation; but she could also enjoy, if need were, "the sweets of solitude, which are books and revery." A true and practical religion, which did not exclude but on the contrary brought her back to philosophical reflection, sustained and strengthened her in virtue and prudence. It was thus that this soul, equable and temperate, passed through life, without great lustre, without inward distresses, and constantly ripening.

We at once ask ourselves, as we do of all women, whether Madame de Motteville was beautiful, and it appears that she was. "Her portrait, which is at Motteville," says the "Journal des Savants," "represents her as a very pretty brunette." The only engraved portrait which I have seen of her, and which every one may see at the Cabinet des

Estampes, shows her to us with her hair dressed in the fashion of Anne of Austria, no longer in her first youth, the face full, with a double chin, and a gentle, tranquil expression. The lower part of the face, however, is scarcely agreeable, and the whole together has nothing that claims marked attention. It is in her mind that we must seek for the delicate and charming traits that distinguished her.

The principal figure around whom Madame de Motteville's narrative unfolds itself is that of the queen, Anne of Austria, her mistress. The author does not pique herself on being either a politician or an historian; she is a woman who relates that which she has seen with her own eyes or learned from the best-informed persons. Very sensible and very safe as she was, the most honourable men among the initiated and the talented (such as de Retz calls the Estrées and the Senneterres) liked to talk with her. She was usually in the cabinet, that is to say, the royal withdrawing-room; she makes it her centre, and dwells more willingly on the scenes there presented to her observation. Nevertheless, she does not neglect, as occasion offers, more extended narratives, such, for instance, as the episode on the English Revolution, which she gathered from the lips of the Queen of England herself and made into a separate narrative. She also enlarges on the revolution in Naples, which took place about the same time. "This is a fragment which I let drop as I go my way," she says of one of these chance episodes: "it will find its place with others of the same nature; and as it will not be treated with more order or connection it will also not have more value." The sound judgment of Madame de Motteville, which led her to consult as to these remote matters none but good witnesses and also made those most worthy of confidence like to speak of them openly with her, gives to these accessory parts and to these *hors-d'œuvres* more interest than she ventures to claim.

She begins by an abridged narrative of the queen's life from her arrival in France to the death of Louis XIII. and the Regency. But the original part of these Memoirs is that which starts from the latter period and treats only of what passed within sight of the writer. When she returns to Court in 1643 Madame de Motteville describes to us the different personages on the stage, the divers cabal interests; she shows herself to us in the midst of those great intrigues as a simple spectator seated in a corner of the best box and perfectly disinterested. "I thought only of amusing myself with what I saw; as at a fine comedy played before my eyes in which I had no interest." "Kings' cabinets," she says elsewhere, "are theatres in which are being played continually the pieces that all the world is thinking about: some are simply comic; others are tragic, the greatest events of which are caused by trifles." Present at all these things with a clear-sighted mind and a spirit never bitter, and at first taking interest in them merely to escape tedium, she had, very early, a resource that came to her from her family —that of writing; the moments that other women took for cards or promenades, she spent in locking herself in and making notes of all she had seen and heard, to be used at a later day.

The first period of the regency of Anne of Austria is exhibited and clearly shown by Madame de Motteville in a manner that makes us present with her. All the old friends of the queen have returned, after an exile more or less long; each of them expects the same favour as before, and they do not at first perceive that the Anne of Austria whom they had left oppressed by Richelieu, without children, and Spanish at heart, was now a mother, devoted to the interests of the young king, and a queen wholly French. Neither do they perceive that her heart is already won by Mazarin, and that she has chosen him, from affection and laziness, as the minister who is to release her from business and make her reign. Madame de Senecé, Madame de Chevreuse, Madame de Hautefort on returning to Court have therefore much to learn, much to divine. Many of these exiles of other days no sooner think they have again grasped Fortune than they provoke to their own detriment her caprice and inconstancy. "Here, then, is the Court, very grand and beautiful, but much embroiled," says Madame de Motteville, who cannot help enjoying the spectacle. "Each is thinking of his own designs, his own interest and cabal. The cardinal, of a suave, shrewd mind, goes about working to win to himself all parties." But a goodly number, feeling sure of their ground, resisted all his advances. Madame de Motteville shows us, in this interior view, the unexpected reverses from which resulted new downfalls for the presumptuous and for those who played the "Important." Apropos of Madame de Hautefort, whose firmness without gentleness and "mind attached to her senses" harshly resist the queen, Madame de Motteville lets us see the whole of her own court morality, a temperate but not relaxed morality. "We may give our advice to our masters and our friends," she thinks, "but if they are determined not to follow it we ought to enter into their inclinations rather than follow our own, when we do not see essential evil in them and when the things themselves are not important."

The quality of Cardinal Mazarin's cleverness, his dissimulation, the grace and delicacy of his play, that cabinet spirit in which he excelled and which "set going so many great engines" are rendered with fidelity and to the life by a person who, without reason herself to speak well of him,

has the merit of appreciating equitably his superior points.
Many of those whom Mazarin dismissed were friends of
Madame de Motteville; she does not abandon them when
they fall; she visits, consoles, and even tries in some cases
to defend them to the queen. By this sincerity of action
she does herself harm with the minister; but the queen has
enough elevation of heart to forgive her all such proofs of integrity and, after a first coolness, to bear no resentment to her.

If Anne of Austria were more interesting than she appears
to us in history, we might adopt from Madame de Motteville
the various portraits she has made of her which are full of
noble beauty and majesty. The waiting-woman (for here
Madame de Motteville is somewhat that) shows us her royal
mistress with admiration and love from the moment she
wakes and rises and is given her chemise to that of her
supper and *coucher*. Her widow's mourning became the
queen, and she lost something by quitting it. She was at
that time forty years old, "an age so dreadful for our sex,"
says Madame de Motteville; but she triumphed over it by
a stately appearance as sovereign and mother.

All the portraits given by Madame de Motteville are fine
and made almost without intention. In the troubles which
soon arose she shows us qualities in the queen which it
would be unjust to refuse her amid her faults; she had
courage and pride; "the blood of Charles V. gave her a
lofty dignity," and boiled in her veins. To such descriptions of Anne of Austria, a little partial but not false, we
must always add, and hear, the "sharp little voice" she had
when angry, the tone of which Retz has so well conveyed.

The Queen of England, magnificently lauded by Bossuet,
is pictured more familiarly by Madame de Motteville, who
knew her well; and this time it is she who gives to that
figure, solemnized in the funeral oration, the touch of reality.

On the occasion of the arrival of a Swedish ambassador (September, 1646), Madame de Motteville shows us the first idea received in France of Queen Christina, and, while making herself the echo of that extraordinary eulogy, she adds a touch of light and gentle irony, as sometimes happens with her. "Fame," she says, "is a great talker, she is fond of passing the limits of truth; but truth has much force; it does not long leave a credulous world in the hands of deception. Some time later, it was known that the virtues of this queen were middling; she had no respect for Christians; and if she practised morality it was more from fancy than feeling."

Thus speaking, Madame de Motteville, who is always essentially a woman, gently avenges her sex, outraged somewhat by the brusque and fantastic manners of that eccentric queen.

"Fame a great talker" reminds me of one of the graces of Madame de Motteville's style; a simple style, rather incorrect in its arrangement of sentences, retouched perhaps in various places by the editor, but excellent and wholly her own in the essentials of language and expression. She has many of those pleasing metaphors which brighten the texture. Wishing, for example, to say that kings never see evils and danger until at the last extremity, because they are hidden from them by a thousand clouds, "Truth," she remarks, "which poets and painters represent naked, is always dressed up in a hundred ways before kings; and never did a worldly woman so often change her fashions as truth when she enters a royal palace." Apropos of the cardinal's hat promised for years to the Abbé de la Rivière, MONSIEUR'S favourite, and suddenly claimed by the Prince de Condé for his brother the Prince de Conti, she says that "Discord has flung a crimson apple into the cabinet." Pointing to

Mazarin, so adroit in turning to account the very excesses of hatred and accusation, in neutralizing and making his own profit from them, she says : " Cardinal Mazarin does with insults what Mithridates did with poisons, which instead of killing him came at last by constant usage to nourish him. The minister, in like manner, seems by his adroitness to make good use of public maledictions; he employs them in getting credit with the queen for suffering in her defence." We feel in these passages, and in the whole current of Madame de Motteville's style, a natural and poetic imagination, without much sparkle, but such as became the niece of the amiable poet Bertaut. In certain places we find some wealth of imagery in " flowers," " roses," " thorns," some trace of the bad taste of the Louis XIII. period; but these are only here and there ; her natural good sense usually reigns in her language as it does in her judgment and thought.

Madame de Motteville is a contemporary of Corneille, and has a little of the tone of the romances of that period in her language. Speaking of Cinq-Mars, she calls him " that amiable criminal;" in relating the downfall of those whom fortune deserted she is touched by " so many illustrious unfortunates;" though still young she slightly regrets the olden time. Speaking of the old Maréchal de Bassompierre, whom the young men laughed at, she says, after praising his generosity, his magnificence, and his courteous manners: " The relics of the old maréchal are worth more than the youth of some of the most polished men of these times" (1646). In Corneille's plays she liked especially the lofty morality and the noble sentiments which had purified the stage. When Italian comedy was introduced under Mazarin's auspices she took but little pleasure in those musical plays. " Persons who understand them esteem them highly," she says; "as for me, I find that the length of the play diminishes the pleasure, and I think that verses, repeated naturally, represent conversation more easily and touch the mind better than song delights the ear." All this shows a right mind and a noble heart, rather than a nature inclined to tenderness or passion. Italian comedy, played before the cardinal, excited the enthusiasm of certain courtiers, such as the Maréchal de Grammont and the Duc de Mortemart, who seemed enchanted by the very names of the minor actors, and "all together, in order to please the minister, uttered such great exaggerations when they spoke of them that Italian comedy became wearisome to persons who were moderate in speech." Madame de Motteville was one of those moderate persons, and she gives us in those words the tone of her own soul. Thus, when I say she was by taste somewhat a contemporary of Corneille, the reader sees in what sense it must be understood, and how she corrected all exaggeration of it.

Though she likes to recall and repeat the following gallant lines of her uncle, —

> "And constantly to love rare beauty
> Is the sweetest error of earth's vanities, — "

her heart was more fitted for friendship than for love; she was made, in all ways, for correct and regulated sentiments, for happy equanimity, and she expresses a desire for them more than once. From her beautiful Normandy she had gained a love of nature and of country life; but she could not enjoy it on a hasty journey. "The country," she says, "is beautiful with repose and solitude only when we can taste the innocent pleasure that the beauty of Nature affords us in woods and on the shores of rivers." She says elsewhere, speaking of kings: "I think those happy who know

them only through the respect due to their name, who can
enjoy the quiet, tranquil life of a good citizen with means,
who have enough to live on and are not poisoned by ambition. That is where all reasonable souls should seek for true
happiness, — obscure, it is true, but tranquil and innocent."
This desire for private life reappears in her frequently, with
a tone of sincerity that cannot be misunderstood.

She likes, in these Memoirs of hers, to moralize, to
give serious reflections which she enforces by agreeable
quotations; she is fond of citing Spanish or Italian poets,
sometimes Seneca, but oftener Holy Scripture. These reflections have been thought too long and too frequent, which
may be true of the latter part of the Memoirs; but as a
general thing she knows how to mingle them with the cir-
cumstances that inspired them. In certain very fine pages
on the character, schemes, and talents of Cardinal Mazarin
she shows him to us (during a stay he made in Paris,
May, 1647) as shutting himself up to work, and leaving the
greatest men in the kingdom waiting in his antechamber
unable to reach him. Murmurs resounded on all sides;
but the door opened, the minister came out, and all were
silent:

"When he got into his coach to go away, the courtyard
of the Palais-Royal was filled with *cordons bleus*, great seigneurs, and persons of that quality, who, by their eager
manner, seemed only too happy to have looked at him
solely from a distance. All men are by nature slaves to
fortune; and I can say that I never knew a person at Court
who was not a flatterer, some more, some less. The self-
interest that blinds us misleads and betrays us on occasions
which concern ourselves; it makes us act with more sentiment than intelligence; quite often it happens that we are
ashamed of our weaknesses; but they are not perceived

except through wise reflection, which we all owe to ourselves, but which does not come until the occasion to do
better has passed."

She knows what the grand airs of independence assumed
by those whom favour rebuffs too often signify; she under-
stands the showy pride which melts at the first advance and
turns to meanness. Mazarin, who cannot use her, as he
wished, for a creature of his own beside the queen, cavils
at her, makes her sometimes uneasy, and keeps her on the
qui vive: that is his system when he is not sure of people.

"As he did not know my intentions, and judged me by
the opinion he held of the universal corruption of the world,
he could not keep himself from suspecting that I was mixed
up in many things contrary to his interests. He told me
one day that he was convinced of this because I never told
him anything of others; I listened to the malcontents,
and must therefore be in their confidence."

And, in truth, more than one malcontent was not afraid
to confide in Madame de Motteville, even where there was
no intimacy, and they spoke to her "as to a person who had
the reputation of knowing how to hold her tongue." This
was precisely what displeased Mazarin and made him complain of her. "That reproach," she adds, "shows his natural distrust and how unfortunate we were in living under the
power of a man who loved double-dealing and with whom
integrity had so little value that he thought it a crime."
These complaints of the cardinal, which did not fail to
transpire, she endeavoured to offset by certain kind words
of the queen which counteracted the impression before
others; "for at Court," she remarks, "it is easy to dazzle
spectators; we must never give them the pleasure of knowing we are not as fortunate as they imagine, or as unfortunate as they desire."

In all her remarks on the Court, that "delightful and wicked place" which was often justly hated, but "always naturally loved," I fancy as I read Madame de Motteville that I am listening to Nicole, but a feminine Nicole, softened and more agreeable.

Nevertheless, we meet with many very fine expressions of vigour and moral energy. At a ball given by Cardinal Mazarin during the carnival of 1647 she describes to us, one after another, the principal beauties and queens of the festival; after which she makes the supernumeraries defile before us, and they are by no means the least pretentious or the least noisy. "The queen's maids-of-honour, Pons, Guerchy, and Saint-Mégrin, tried to make a few natural conquests by the pains they took to embellish themselves in all sorts of ways; happy if, among so many lovers, they could have caught husbands suited to their ambition and the license of their desires." That is only a piquant stroke; but presently, speaking more particularly of Mademoiselle de Pons, beloved by the Duc de Guise, now on his way to conquer Naples for her sake, and yet, for all that, not content or satisfied with such a prize, she says: "That soul, *gluttonous of pleasure*, was not content with an absent lover who adored her and a hero who, to deserve her, sought to make himself a sovereign. Ambition and love combined did not have charms enough to fill her heart; to satisfy her she must needs go promenading on the Cours, where she received the incense of all her new conquests." A soul *gluttonous of pleasure!* it is a sense of honest decency which here conveys to Madame de Motteville's style that expression of disgust.

Her habitual tones are much more restrained; acrimony does not touch her decent pen. Near as they are to the queen, she and her companions are deprived by the avarice of the cardinal of many of the practical and efficacious

results of favour, but she confines herself to jesting about it
with light and smiling irony. There is nothing in these
Memoirs of Madame de Motteville that recalls those other
Memoirs, so distinguished but so bitter, of Madame de Staal-
Delaunay, lady-in-waiting to the Duchesse du Maine; the
situation however was very different. Madame de Motteville was in a great and real Court, beside a queen who,
with a mind of ordinary compass (though accommodating
and agreeable), had a noble and generous heart and paid for
services with esteem. If one must find an historical parentage for Madame de Motteville, I find it more in the Memoirs
of the wise chamberlain Philippe de Commines, whom she
likes to quote, recalling at times the results of his sound
and judicious experience.

Her own Memoirs become more serious and take a loftier
historical character the farther they advance into the period
of civil agitations and the troubles of the Fronde. Madame
de Motteville judged them rightly, and while ascribing to
herself only the rôle of a timid woman, she makes reflections which one could wish had been made at the time by
many men. The long conversations in private which she
had with the Queen of England had enlightened her as to
the real tendency of perils which often, in their beginning,
seem no more than a gust. Noting with vigorous justice
the illusion of the Parliament people, and their insatiable exactions which caused them to reject all preliminary offers of
compromise and conciliation, she boldly declares that "the
corruption of men is such that to make them live according
to reason they must not be treated reasonably, and to make
them just they must be treated unjustly." She points to
men of property who, by obstinately shouting against taxa-
tion and those who abused it, were aiding turbulence and
lending support to malcontents, which often happened.

"Men of property, without considering that an evil is some-times necessary, and that, in this respect, all the ages have been about equal, hoped through disorder to attain to some better order; and that word *reformation* not only pleased them as a good principle, but it also suited those who courted evil through the excess of their folly and ambition." There are moments when all things concur for disorder and ruin, and when sedition is in the very air. "The star," says Madame de Motteville, "was at that time terrible against kings."

The first scenes of the Fronde are related by her in a manner that does not pale before even the narrative of Car-dinal de Retz. The latter gives us the scene in the rue du Palais-Royal when he enters it, and of the interior of the archbishop's palace. Madame de Motteville shows us the interior of the queen's cabinet, where she finds herself, at first, the only person who is seriously alarmed. The first day of the Barricades was almost wholly spent in joking her. "As I was the least valiant of the company, all the shame of that day fell upon me."

For a person belonging to that interior she comprehends very clearly and at once the nature of the revolt in the town, and the disorder so quickly and so well organized. "The bourgeois," she says, "who had taken arms very willingly to save the city from pillage, were no better than the populace, and demanded Broussel as heartily as the scavengers; for, besides being *infected with a love of the public welfare,* which they reckoned to be theirs personally, . . . they were filled with joy in thinking themselves necessary to some-thing." These words, "infected with a love of the public welfare," have often been quoted; but we should see in them only a simple little jest of Madame de Motteville; she knew what she was saying in speaking thus and in characterizing as disease and pestilence the false love which had seized that seditious populace for a moment.

Madame de Motteville is not a blind royalist; she believes in the right of kings, but also in the justice which is its law, and which God, she thinks, often inspires in kings, and has done so almost always in this kingdom of France. Her ideal of a monarch is Charles V. On the day when Parliament relied on I forget which ordinance of Louis XII. to demand that " no one shall be put in prison without being brought twenty-four hours later before his native judges," she cannot help remarking that this article guaranteeing individual security, as we should say, " was agreeable to all France. The love of liberty," she adds, " is strongly imprinted in nature. The wisest minds, which, until then, had disapproved of the doings of this Assembly, could not in their hearts, hate this proposition; they blamed it apparently, because it was impossible to praise it before the world, but in point of fact they liked it and could not help respecting such boldness and wishing it success." We see that Madame de Motteville would have made a fairly liberal royalist; but this woman of intelligence and good sense, who was present at such terrible scenes, and relates them, is never the dupe of grand words nor of appearances; she mingles with them observations such as do honour to historians and are not disavowed by politicians. " When subjects revolt," she says, " they are pushed into it by causes of which they are ignorant, and, *as a usual thing, what they demand is not what is needed to pacify them.*" She points out to us these very magistrates (the parliament), who had been the first to stir up the people, amazed to find it turning against them and not respecting them. " They knew themselves to be the cause of these disorders, but they could not have remedied them had they wished to do so, for when the

people meddle with ordering there is no longer any master;
each man for himself endeavours to be one." We may look
at home to-day, and ask ourselves if this is not still our
history.

But I remind myself that I chose the subject of Madame
de Motteville in order to distract my mind for a moment —
mine and my reader's if possible — from the painful spectacle of our present dissensions [Dec. 1, 1851], and I do not
wish to fall back to them by allusions which they supply
but too freely.

Madame de Motteville ran some danger in Paris during
the first Fronde. Not being able in the early days of 1649
to follow the fugitive queen to Saint-Germain, and wishing
to rejoin her soon after, she was arrested, with her sister, at
the Porte Saint-Honoré by a furious mob, and was forced to
take refuge on the steps of the high altar at Saint-Roch,
where some of her friends, hastily summoned, came to her
rescue. She joined the queen a little later and quitted her
again at certain times; for this distinguished woman was
not, as she tells us humbly, an amazon or a heroine; it was
with difficulty that she rose above the terrors or even the
inconveniences of her sex. Present or absent, however, her
fidelity never failed. When peace was re-established, she
resumed beside the queen the habits of her regular, gentle,
serious life, which suited her so well. Her virtue, her delicate integrity in that world of treachery and ambush, exposed her, even to the last, to certain cavillings, over which
her prudence and calmness, supported by the esteem of the
queen-mother, enabled her to triumph. Religion took deeper
and deeper hold on a soul made to welcome it and naturally ordained to it. This enlightened and submissive religion has dictated to her in these Memoirs certain pages,
which are as charming as they are solid and sensible, on

the quarrels of the period, the disputes of Jansenism and Molinism, in which women were as eager as others to mingle. " It costs us so dear," she says, alluding to Eve, " for having sought to learn the knowledge of good and evil, that we ought to agree that it is better to be ignorant of it than to know it; especially as we women are accused of being the cause of all evil. . . . Whenever men talk of God and the hidden mysteries I am astonished at their boldness, and I am delighted not to be obliged to know more than my *Pater*, my *Credo*, and the Commandments." Madame de Motteville follows exactly the line that Bossuet traced in such matters. This whole page should be read; the author crowns it with very noble Italian verses, which prove that while submitting her mind she by no means renounced a reasonable self-adornment and embellishment. This rare person, this honest woman of so much judgment and intelligence, died in December, 1689, in her sixty-eighth year. She can be appreciated at her full value only by accompanying her throughout the whole course of her Memoirs, following her in her development and continuity; quotations and analysis give but a very imperfect idea of their slow, full, tranquil, and engaging character.

SAINTE-BEUVE.

TRANSLATOR'S NOTE.

THESE Memoirs are somewhat abridged; chiefly in the parts relating to matters that did not come under Madame de Motteville's personal observation; such, for instance, as the period before she became the daily companion of Anne of Austria, the military details of the wars of the Fronde, etc.

PREFACE.

KINGS are not only exposed to the eyes but to the judgment of all the world; very often their actions are good or bad according only to the different sentiments of those who judge them by their passions. They have the misfortune to be censured with severity for things about which they might be blamed, but no one has the kindness to defend them for other things which might justly obtain some excuse. All who approach them praise them in their presence through base self-interest, in order to please them; but each man, with sham virtue, joins in judging them severely when absent. Moreover, their intentions and their sentiments being unknown and their actions public, it often happens that, without wronging equity, they may be accused of faults which they never intended to commit, but of which they are nevertheless guilty, because they have been deceived, either by themselves, for want of knowledge, or by their ministers, who, slaves to ambition, never tell them the truth.

It is this that has led me to write in my leisure hours, and for my amusement, what I know of the life, habits, and inclinations of Queen Anne of Austria, and to repay, by the simple recital of what I recognize in her, the honour she did me in giving me her familiarity. For, though I do not pretend to be able to praise her in all things, and, in accordance with my natural disposition, I am not capable of disguise, I am, nevertheless, very sure that historians who have not known her virtues and her kindness, and who will speak of her only in accordance with the satirical talk of the public, can never do her the justice that I would fain be able to do her if my incapacity and my want of eloquence did not take from me the means of doing it.

Therefore, what I now undertake is not with any fixed design of correcting their ignorance or their malice; that project would be too great for a lazy woman, and too bold for a person like me who dreads to show herself and would be unwilling to be thought an author. But I do it for my own satisfaction, out of gratitude to the queen, and to review once more (if I live), as in a picture, all that has come to my knowledge concerning the things of a Court, — which is certainly very limited, for I do not like intrigue. But I shall add nothing. That which I put upon paper I have seen and I have heard, and during the whole Regency (which is the period of my attendance on the princess), I have written, without order, from time to time, and sometimes daily, what seemed to me most remarkable. In doing this I employed the time that ladies are accustomed to give to cards and promenades, because of the hatred I have always felt to the useless life of the people of the great world. I do not know if I have done better than others; but at least I know well that, to my thinking, one cannot do worse than to do nothing.

MEMOIRS

OF

MADAME DE MOTTEVILLE.

———◆———

I.

1611—1630.

KING LOUIS XIII. was but nine years and eight days old when he came to the crown; but King Henri IV. had left him a kingdom so peaceful and flourishing, with such good troops in his armies, such able ministers in his councils, and such large sums in his coffers, that if the queen, Marie de' Medici, had been willing to follow the system established by that great prince in the State, her regency would have been far more glorious and the rest of her life much happier. But, having allowed the Marquis d'Ancre, whom she made marshal of France, to take too great authority, he advised her to dismiss the servitors of the late king, and particularly those great men who had grown old in the highest offices and managed the most important negotiations, to put in their place others who were wholly dependent upon her.

This drew upon her the hatred of all the princes of the blood, and of the other princes and great seigneurs, whom she treated with such haughtiness that they retired from Court; and the treaties of Sainte-Ménehould and Loudun, which the marshal had made, having no effect, the number of malcontents increasing daily, he resolved, in order to break

up the measures he saw were preparing against him, to arrest
the Prince de Condé, who, as first prince of the blood, would
probably be the leader of the party now beginning to form
itself. At the same time he sent orders to the two armies
intended to act outside the kingdom, in execution of the
great designs of the king who had raised them, to hold
themselves ready to sustain the royal authority confided to
him [the Maréchal d'Ancre] in case it was attacked in consequence of the arrest of the prince. He also raised a third
army, to be ready to march more promptly against the first
malcontents who ventured to declare themselves.

So bold an action as this and such great preparations confirmed the queen in the high opinion she had of him whose
advice she blindly followed, and made her believe she would
soon be mistress of the Court and of all France without opposition. It was this that ruined her, as well as the man
she had chosen for her first minister. For, as she was persuaded that none could resist her, she imagined she had no
need to treat any one with caution, not even the king her
son; and she took no heed that he too had a favourite with
as much ambition as her own, who, insinuating himself daily
more and more, worked so strongly to detach the king from
the tenderness he had for his mother that in the end he
made him resolve to part from her altogether. This favourite was de Luynes, who, during the time he was the young
prince's page, had found means to make himself so agreeable
and so necessary to all his pleasures, exercises, and amusements, particularly those of all kinds of hunting where few
persons liked to follow him, that the freedom in which he
lived with the king raised him at last to the dignity of
connétable.

The French nobles, naturally attached to the princes of
the blood, having taken up arms in the provinces, were daily

swelling the party of the Prince de Condé, while disorder reigned in Paris, where the populace pillaged the house of the Maréchal d'Ancre, against whom they made loud outcries as the author of the violent manner of the queen's governing, and the bad employment, robbery, and squandering of the treasure amassed by Henri IV. Riots became daily more frequent, and no one having the force or the desire to quell them, the populace at last attacked the marshal as he was leaving the Louvre, April 24, 1617, — the *bravi* who everywhere accompanied him, giving him no succour, nor the guards either (who were not far off when he drew his sword intending to defend himself), for they thought that the Marquis de Vitry, their captain, who appeared at that moment, was coming to his rescue. Instead of that, he came to arrest him, so that it remained doubtful whether his death was due to the fury of the people, or to his own resistance to the king's orders.

Since his majority the king had manifested on so many occasions his intention of taking cognizance of public matters that, the queen having now retired to Blois, he was not long in recalling the chancellor, de Sillery, and in setting the Prince de Condé at liberty. This was not enough to really pacificate the kingdom which all these changes had disturbed. But as I have not undertaken to describe the life of that unhappy princess, I shall not speak of the war undertaken by those who took her side. My purpose is only to note what may concern Queen Anne of Austria, who began to be spoken of during the subsequent negotiations for a general peace which her marriage was to give to all Europe.

I shall therefore merely say here that the Grand-duke of Tuscany, being naturally obliged to act towards maintaining Queen Marie de' Medici's former influence with the king (who, though attaining his majority, was still willing to share his authority with her), and having great interest in the tranquillity of France, which could not be shaken without Italy and Spain being disturbed, directed the Marquis Borri, his ambassador, to be the first in the conferences held with the Spanish ministers at Madrid to suggest a double marriage between the two princes and the two princesses of France and Spain.

The result was that the Duc du Maine went to Spain and the Duc de Pastrana came to France. The espousals of Philip IV., son of Philip III., King of Spain with Madame Élisabeth of France [daughter of Henri IV.] were solemnized at Burgos, and those of King Louis XIII. with Anne of Austria, Infanta of Spain, at Bordeaux in 1615. The Duc de Guise, who had conducted Madame Élisabeth to the middle of the little river of Bidassoa, which separates the two kingdoms, took leave of her to let her pass on to Fonta-rabia, while he himself conducted the Infanta of Spain to Saint-Jean de Luz, where the Duc de Luynes gave her a letter from the king, to which, it is said, he brought back an answer in her own handwriting. It was supposed that the army of the Huguenots would oppose her journey, and it is true that it was so near to that of the king that it seemed to flank it; but this only served to make them see his strength, and to render the entry of the Infanta into France the more imposing.

I know from my late mother, who had henceforth the honour to approach the princess familiarly (though she was not her servant), that she was handsome and very amiable. I have heard my mother say that the first time she saw her she was seated on cushions, according to the Spanish custom, among her ladies, of whom she had a great number, dressed in the Spanish fashion in a gown of green satin, embroidered in silver and gold, with large hanging sleeves, fastened with great diamonds serving as buttons, on the arms; she wore also a closed ruff and a little cap upon her head of the same colour as her dress, in which was a heron's feather which enhanced by its blackness the beauty of her hair, which at that time was very handsome and worn in large curls.

The young king was also very handsome and very well made, and his dark beauty did not displease our young queen. She thought him very agreeable from the beginning; and though he stuttered, and the fatigues of hunting, his long illnesses, and his natural gloom changed him infinitely towards the end of his life, I still believe, from the way in which I have heard the queen speak of him, that she would have loved him much if the misfortune of both, and that fatality which seems inevitable for all princes, had not disposed otherwise; for the king, making for himself a grievous destiny, did not love the queen as much as she deserved. He spent his life in hunting beasts and allowed himself to be governed by favourites; so much so that he and the queen lived together with little intercourse or happiness.

All the Spanish ladies who came with our young queen were soon taken from her, which caused her great pain. Only one remained, named Donna Estefania, whom she loved tenderly because she had brought her up, and was, as we say in France, her first bed-chamber woman. My late mother, who had lived many years in Spain (whither she had been taken at six years of age by her grandmother, the second wife of the Sieur Saldagna, who had no children, to obtain an inheritance of which she had promised her the chief share), was a great comfort to Donna Éstefania in the first years of her life in France, during which she took no pleasure except in things that reminded her of Spain.

My mother formed at the outset a great friendship with this lady, who, beginning to feel infirm, needed to lay her cares on some faithful person who not only spoke Spanish but could also read and write it, and who knew the Spanish Court; and the queen herself, finding all these requisites in my mother with much intelligence and charm, made no difficulty in placing confidence in her, not only for the innocent, though secret, correspondence which she maintained with her brother, the King of Spain, but also to console herself with her for the grief she could not disguise at the great favour of the Duc de Luynes, who had the audacity, so it was said, to propose to the king to repudiate her and marry a relation of his wife, afterwards the Princesse de Guémenée, whom we knew as the handsomest woman of the Court.

But if this thought ever came into his mind, it could only have remained there a moment as an absurd vision; for the Duchesse de Luynes, who was on very good terms with her husband, was not long without being liked by the queen, who, although in the beginning she could not endure her on account of her own aversion to the duke, did accustom herself to her for the sake of the good terms she was thus enabled to have with the king, who liked the duchess, and for the hunting and riding parties she was now invited to join.

Thus she did enjoy certain periods of pleasure without other bitterness than that of becoming pregnant several times, as she believed, and miscarrying for having ridden too hard in hunting. From which we may judge that if her Court lacked prudence it was not without enjoyment, since youth and beauty had sovereign rights there.

The Duc de Luynes having died in 1621, his little empire ended with him; and Queen Marie de' Medici, being reconciled to the king, the peace between mother and son destroyed that between husband and wife; for the queen-mother, being convinced that, to hold control over the young prince, the young princess must not be on good terms with him, intrigued with such perseverance and success in creating misunderstandings between them that from that day forth the queen, her daughter-in-law, had neither influence nor comfort. All her consolation was the part which the Duchesse de Luynes, now remarried with the Duc de Chevreuse, a prince of the house of Lorraine, took in her sorrows, which she tried to soften by the amusements she proposed and by communicating to her, as much as she could, her own gay and lively humour, which turned the most serious things of the greatest consequence into matters for jest and laughter — *a giovine cuor tutto è giuoco.*

Some years went by without my being able to explain how they were passed, knowing nothing but what the queen herself told me later, amusing herself sometimes by relating stories of them. I can say, however, that she was loved, and that, in spite of the respect which her majesty inspired, her beauty did not fail to touch certain men who openly showed their passion.

The Duke of Buckingham was the only one who dared to attack her heart. He came, on the part of the King of England, his master, to marry by proxy Madame, the king's sister. He was well-made, handsome in face; he had a lofty soul, was magnificent, liberal, and a favourite of his king, so that he had his wealth to spend, and all the crown jewels to adorn him. It is not astonishing that with such amiable advantages he had high thoughts and noble but dangerous and blamable desires, or that he had the happiness to make the beautiful queen admit that if a virtuous woman could love another than her husband, he would have been the only one who could have pleased her. The praises

that I give him I heard from the queen herself, for he was
the person in the world of whom I have heard her say the
most good. It is, no doubt, to be presumed that his regard
was not unwelcome, and that his vows were received with
a certain amount of complacency. The queen, making no
secret of it, had no difficulty in telling me later (wholly
undeceived then about such dangerous illusions) that, being
young, she did not comprehend that fine conversation, otherwise called polite gallantry, in which no pledges were given,
could be blamable any more than that which Spanish ladies
practise in the palace, where, living like nuns and speaking
to men only in presence of the King and Queen of Spain,
they nevertheless boast of their conquests and talk of them
as a thing which, far from injuring their reputation, adds
to it. She had in the Duchesse de Chevreuse a friend who
was wholly given up to these vain amusements; and the
queen, by her counsels, had not avoided, in spite of the
purity of her soul, taking pleasure in the charms of that
passion which she accepted with a certain complacency, for
it flattered her glory more than it shocked her virtue.

Much has been said of a walk she took in the garden
of a house where she lodged when she went to conduct the
Queen of England to Amiens. But this was most unjust,
for I know from herself, who did me the honour to confide
it to me without reserve, that she only wished to walk in
that garden because the king had forbidden every one to
enter it, and, as difficulty increases desire, this gave her a
very strong wish to go there; so that, after getting the keys
with much trouble from the captain of the guard, she walked
there one evening with Madame de Chevreuse and her little
Court. The walk was taken in presence of her whole suite,
which accompanied the princess as usual. I have seen persons who were present and who told me the truth. The

Duke of Buckingham

Duke of Buckingham was there and wanted to talk with her. Putange, the queen's equerry, left her for a few moments, thinking that respect required him not to listen to what the English lord was saying to her. Chance led them to a turn of the path where a palisade hid them from view. The queen, at that moment, surprised to find herself alone, and apparently startled by some too passionate sentiment from the Duke of Buckingham, cried out, and calling to her equerry, blamed him for leaving her.

By that cry she showed her wisdom and her virtue, preferring the preservation of her inward innocence to the fear she must have had of being blamed; for that cry, reported to the king, would certainly cause her much embarrassment. If on this occasion she showed that her heart could be susceptible of a tenderness that invited her to listen to the romantic speech of a man who loved her, it must at the same time be admitted that a love of purity and her virtuous feelings surmounted all the rest, and that she preferred a real and true credit, unmixed by any sentiment unworthy of her, to a reputation suspected, after all, of little.

When the duke took leave of the queen-mother, who had also come to conduct her daughter, the Queen of England, beyond Amiens, the queen did me the honour to tell me that when he came to kiss her gown, she being in the front of the coach with the Princesse de Conti beside her, he screened himself with the curtain to say a few words to her and to wipe the tears that were falling from his eyes. The Princesse de Conti, who laughed at goodness, and was, as I have heard say, very witty, said as to this, speaking of the queen, that she could assure the king of her virtue; but she could not say as much for her cruelty, because no doubt the tears of this lover, which she had seen (being seated beside the queen), must have touched her heart, and she suspected that her eyes at least looked at him with some pity.

The Duke of Buckingham's passion led him to do another very bold action, about which the queen informed me and the Queen of England afterwards confirmed to me, having heard it from himself. This celebrated foreigner, after starting from Amiens to return to England, conducting Madame Henriette de France to her king and to reign over the English, being full of his passion and goaded by the pain of absence, wanted to see the queen again, if only for a moment. Though they had almost reached Calais, he made a plan to satisfy his desire by feigning to receive news from the king his master which obliged him to go to the French Court.

Leaving the future queen of England at Boulogne, he returned to see the queen-mother and negotiate this pretended affair, which was only a pretext for returning to Court. After discussing his chimerical negotiation, he went to the queen, whom he found in bed and almost alone. This princess knew by letters from the Duchesse de Chevreuse, who was accompanying the Queen of England, that he had returned. She spoke of it before Nogent, laughing, and was not astonished when she saw him. But she was surprised when, with much freedom, he threw himself on his knees before the bed and kissed her sheet with transports so excessive that it was easy to see his passion was violent, and one of those which deprive such as are touched by them of their reason. The queen did me the honour to tell me she was embarrassed; and this embarrassment mingled with vexation caused her to remain for some time without speaking. The Comtesse de Lannoi, then her lady-of-honour, wise, virtuous, and elderly, who was beside her pillow, not willing to allow the duke to remain in such a state, told him with much severity that it was not the custom in France and that she wished him to rise. But he, not abashed, argued with the old lady, saying that he was not a Frenchman and was not bound to observe all the laws of that State. Then, addressing the queen, he said the most tender things in the world to her. But she only answered with complaints of his boldness, and, without perhaps being very angry, ordered him to rise and leave the room. He did so; and after seeing her again the next day in presence of all the Court, he departed, fully resolved to return to France as soon as possible.

After the English ambassador had crossed the sea, the two queens returned to the king who awaited them at Fontainebleau. All these things relating to Buckingham were told to him to the disadvantage of the queen, so much so, that several of her servants were dismissed. Putange, her equerry, was exiled; Datal, La Porte, and the queen's doctor were treated in the same way.

The Queen of England told me afterwards that in the beginning of her marriage she had some distaste to the king, her husband, and that Buckingham fomented it, telling her freely that he would set them against each other if he could. He succeeded so far that, from a feeling of vexation, she wanted to return to France to see her mother; and as she knew the passionate desire the English duke had to see the queen again, she spoke to him of her design. He entered into it with ardour, and powerfully helped her to obtain the permission of the king, her husband. The princess, knowing this, wrote to the queen-mother asking her to think it well that she should bring the Duke of Buckingham with her, because without him she could not make the journey. She was refused both by the queen her mother, and the king her brother; and her project, in consequence of this desire of the duke, could not take effect. This need not astonish us; the rumour of his sentiments was an invincible obstacle. As the king had some tendency to jealousy, the queen-mother giving him as much as she could to disgust him with the queen (served in this by Cardinal Richelieu, whom she had brought into public affairs), the Duke of Buckingham could never afterwards obtain permission to return to France.

This man, who, from all descriptions given to me, had as much vanity as ambition, embroiled the two crowns in order to get back to France by the necessity of a treaty of peace, after he had, as he intended, made a great reputation by the victories he expected to win over our nation. On this basis he brought a powerful naval force to the help of the Rochelle people then besieged by King Louis XIII., showing publicly the passion he had for the queen and making a glory of it. But this ostentation was punished at last by no success, and the shame of having ill succeeded in all his designs.

Madame de Chevreuse, who followed vehemently all her inclinations and loved the Duke of Holland, a friend of the Duke of Buckingham, having now returned from England, saw with some satisfaction the arrival of Buckingham's fleet and his return to France with what at first appeared to be a high reputation. She did not cease to talk of it to the queen. The mistress and favourite both hated Cardinal Richelieu because he was the creature of the king and the queen-mother, who had put him in the ministry. They found nothing more agreeable than to annoy him, all the more because the queen was persuaded that he did her ill service with the king. She made therefore no difficulty in listening with pleasure to the wishes Madame de Chevreuse expressed for the success of the English. She often told me this herself, wondering at the error, into which the gayety and folly of innocent youth, which did not yet know the full extent to which virtue, reason, and justice bound it, had led her.

The Duchesse de Chevreuse was no doubt the cause of this blindness, which was not in reality as criminal as it seemed, because the intentions and sentiments of the soul are what make good or evil in us. But in the days when the queen became more enlightened she regretted it. Madame de Chevreuse told me afterwards, in relating the follies of her youth, that she had forced the queen to think of Buckingham by always talking of him and removing what scruples she had by dwelling on the annoyance thus given to Cardinal de Richelieu. I have also heard her say, with much asseveration on this point, that it was true that the queen had a noble soul and a very pure heart; and that, in spite of the clime in which she was born, where, as I have said, the name of having a lover is the fashion, she had had all the trouble in the world to make the queen take a liking to the fame of being loved.

The queen herself spoke of these things with so free and honest a simplicity that it was easy to see she had never had in herself other than slight imperfections. Indeed, they served to make her know in later days what she owed to God for having maintained her in true purity, when vanity made her swerve from the maxims so virtuous a princess wished and was bound to observe. Her misfortune was in not being loved enough by the king her husband, and in being as it were forced to amuse her heart elsewhere by giving it to ladies who made a bad use of it, and who, during her first years, instead of leading her to seek occasions to please the king, and to desire to be esteemed by him, estranged her from him as much as they possibly could in order to possess her more completely.

It is believed that Cardinal de Richelieu had in reality more love for the queen than hatred, and that, seeing she was not inclined to wish him well, he did, either for revenge or from the necessity of thus using her, do her harm with the king. The first signs of his affection were the persecutions he inflicted on her. They were visible to the eyes of all; and we shall see that this new manner of loving lasted till the end of the cardinal's life. There is no apparent ground for thinking that this passion, so vaunted by poets, caused the strange effects they asserted in his soul. But the queen related to me that one day he spoke to her in too gallant a manner for an enemy, and made her a very passionate speech, which she was about to answer with anger and contempt, but the king entering the room at that moment, his presence interrupted her reply; and since that instant, she had never dared to return to the cardinal's harangue, fearing to do him too much favour by showing that she remembered it. But she answered him tacitly by the hatred she always had for him and by the steady refusal she gave to his friendship and his assistance with the king. Those who had the most influence with her and who did not like the cardinal did not fail, in order to draw her to their party, to strengthen her aversion. That aversion won her many adherents, for Cardinal Richelieu was hated; but by this conduct, though it was just fundamentally, she placed herself much worse with the king; we can judge from her sentiments and those of the minister whether there was reason for it.

The queen and many private persons who had felt the harsh effects of this minister's cruel principles had cause to hate him; but, besides the fact that he was beloved by friends because he esteemed them much, envy certainly was the sole cause for the public hatred, because in truth he did not deserve it; for, in spite of his defects and the justifiable dislike of the queen, it must be said of him that he was the greatest man of our time, and that past ages had none who could surpass him.   He had the principles of illustrious tyrants; he ruled his designs, his thoughts, his resolutions by reasons of State and the public good, which he considered only so far as this said public good enhanced the authority of the king and swelled his treasury.   He wished to make him reign over his peoples and to reign himself over his king. The life and death of men touched him only according to the interests of his grandeur and fortune, on which he thought those of the State depended wholly.

Under this pretence of preserving the one by the other he made no difficulty in sacrificing all things to his private preservation; and though he wrote "The Life of the Christian," he was very far indeed from gospel principles.   His enemies were the worse for his not following those principles, but France profited; like those fortunate children who enjoy here below a prosperity for which their fathers toiled, procuring for themselves perhaps eternal woe.

Not that I wish to make an evil judgment of that great man; it must be owned that he enlarged the borders of France, and by the taking of La Rochelle diminished the power of heresy, which was still considerable in all the provinces where the remains of the old war kept it alive. His great vigilance in discovering cabals that were formed at Court, and his speed in smothering them, enabled him to maintain the kingdom.   He was, moreover, the first favourite who had the courage to lessen the power of princes and grandees, so damaging to that of our kings, and — in the desire perhaps to govern alone — to destroy whatever was opposed to royal authority, defeating those who tried by ill-offices to remove him from royal favour.

The queen was amiable, the king inclined to piety, and if the policy of the minister had not put obstacles in the way of their union it is very likely that Louis XIII. would have attached himself to the friendship of the person in the world most capable of it from the sweetness of her nature, and most worthy of it for her goodness and beauty. Some have said that the king never had any inclination for her, and the queen herself believed this, because she judged by the indifference he showed to her; but I know from one of the king's favourites,[1] inferior in power to Richelieu, but who, nevertheless, had enough share in the king's inclinations to know all such private matters, that he thought her beautiful, and one day, making him a confidence in respect to her beauty, he said that he dared not show her tenderness lest he should displease the queen his mother and the cardinal, whose counsel and services were more important to him than to live pleasantly with his wife.

The enemies of the queen, the better to succeed in making the king hate her, used against her strongly the intercourse she kept up with Spain. The slightest mark of affection that she gave her brother the King of Spain, they magnified into crime against her husband. She had some reason to fear being repudiated, and for all consolation, she hoped, after the death of her aunt, the Infanta Isabella-Clara-Eugenia, to be sent to govern the Low Countries, whither my late mother, who always passed for a Spaniard on account of her name, Luisa de Saldagna, which she had borne in Spain, was resolved to take me. The inheritance from the Dame Du Faï and that from my late uncle the Bishop of Séez not proving as good as they imagined, the pension of six hundred *livres* which the queen had given

---

[1] On the margin of the manuscript is written "Duc de Saint-Simon." This was the father of the author of the Memoirs.

me since 1622, when I was only seven years old, and the brevet she gave me in 1627, which bound me, indispensably, to follow her fortunes, were very welcome, but they gave occasion to Cardinal Richelieu, who knew that the queen had great confidence in my mother, and who saw that she was beginning to take pleasure in conversing with me in Spanish, to make the king send me an order to retire from Court. The queen could not refrain from complaining that they took from her even a child, for I was then only nine or ten years old. My late mother, seeing that the matter concerned her as much or more than it did me, took me to Normandy; but the queen paid my mother, when she could, the pension she had given me.

In the year 1639, having married Monsieur de Motteville, president of the Chamber of Accounts of Normandy, who had no children and much property, I found comfort with an abundance of all things; and if I had chosen to profit by the friendship he had for me and receive the advantages he could and would have given me, I should have found myself rich at his death. But, being wholly occupied by the hope that every one had in those days of the approaching death of Cardinal Richelieu, which would give us the opportunity to return to Court, I was very glad to make a journey there in the same year (1639), believing that, being married and settled in Normandy, my presence could no longer give anxiety to Cardinal Richelieu. I went, therefore, without any scruple to pay my duty to the queen, who received me very well and gave me letters as one of her ladies, with a brevet of two thousand *livres* pension; and the late Monsieur de Motteville, as well as my father and mother, having died shortly after Cardinal Richelieu, I prepared to establish myself with my sister in Paris, where my brother was finishing his studies. The order the queen gave me was far more agreeable than the one which obliged me to quit her. She received us with much kindness, and said the same day to one of my mother's friends that the children of her friend had come back, and she was very glad to see them.

Having thus returned to the Court, which I had left so young, I tried to recall in my memory the state in which it then was, to compare it with that in which I now found it. I do not know if the regency gave a grander and more majestic air to the queen than that she had when unfortunate, but she seemed to me more amiable than formerly, and as beautiful as any of those who formed her circle.

At the time when I was sent away she wore her hair in the fashion of a round coiffure, transparently frizzed, and with much powder; after that she took to curls. Her hair had grown rather darker in colour, and she had a great quantity of it. Her features were not delicate; having even the defect of too thick a nose, and she wore, in Spanish fashion, too much rouge; but she was fair, and never was there a finer skin than hers. Her eyes were perfectly beautiful; gentleness and majesty united in them; their colour, mingled with green, made her glance the more vivid and full of all the charms that Nature gave them. Her mouth was small and rosy, the smile admirable, and the lips had only enough of the Austrian family to make them more beautiful than many that claimed to be more perfect. The shape of her face was handsome and the forehead well-made. Her hands and arms were of surpassing beauty, and all Europe has heard their praises; their whiteness, without exaggeration, equalled that of snow; poets could not say enough when they wished to laud them. Her bust was very fine, without being quite perfect. She was tall, and her bearing lofty but not haughty. She had great charms in the expression of her face, and her beauty imprinted in the hearts of those who saw her a tenderness which did not lack the accompaniment of veneration and respect. Besides these perfections, she had the piety of her mother, Queen Marguerite of Austria, dead in the odour of sanctity, who, having had the care of her daughter's education, had imprinted in her heart the sentiments that filled her own; this it was that produced in her that great inclination to virtue which drew to her the grace, that God gave her throughout her life, to prefer it to all things else.

The Court was at this time full of beautiful women. Among the princesses, she who was the first of them was also the first in beauty [the Princesse de Condé]. Without youth, she still excited the admiration of all who saw her. Her gift of beauty she shared with Mademoiselle de Bourbon, her daughter, who was beginning, though still young to reveal the first charms of that angelic face which later was to have such fame, — a fame followed by grievous events and salutary sufferings.

I leave the Cardinal Bentivoglio, who has published in his writings the praises of Madame la Princesse, to tell of her adventures and of the passion King Henri IV. had for her; I desire only to bear witness that her beauty was still great when in my childhood I lived at Court, and that it lasted to the end of her life. We praised it during the regency of the queen, when she was over fifty, and praised it without flattery. She was fair and white, her eyes blue and perfectly beautiful. Her bearing was lofty and full of majesty, and her whole person, her manners being agreeable, always pleased, except when she prevented it herself by a rude pride full of acerbity against those who ventured to displease her; then she changed entirely, and became the aversion of those to whom she showed it. We like,

naturally, whatever flatters us ; never can that which despises
and affronts us be agreeable. *E ritrosa bella ritroso cuor
non prende.*

After Madame la Princesse, such as I represent her, the
Court had many beautiful women. Madame de Montbazon
was one of those who made the greatest stir. She had
extreme beauty with an extreme desire to please; she was
tall, and in her whole person we felt an air of freedom,
gaiety, and hauteur. But her mind was not as fine as her
body; her lights were limited to her eyes, which imperiously
demanded love. Her forehead was so well modelled and
perfect that she always wore it uncovered without giving it
any added charm by the arrangement of her hair; the out-
line of her face was so handsome that, to let it be seen, she
wore her hair in very few curls. Her lips were not full;
and for this reason her mouth seemed rather less prominent
than was necessary to make her beauty quite perfect. She
had fine teeth, and her neck was shaped like those the great
sculptors represent to us in Greek and Roman beauties. She
claimed universal admiration, and men paid her that tribute,
ever vain, imperfect, and often criminal in its results and
effects. I desire, nevertheless, to doubt, in the matter of
gallantry, that which one ought never to believe, and which
does not appear in evidence. But to show the character
of her mind as to this, she told me one day when I saw
her during the regency and praised before her one of my
friends for being virtuous, that all women were equally so,
and (with a laugh at me) she let me understand that she
did not think much of that quality.

Madame de Guémenée, her daughter-in-law, was also one
of the handsomest women at Court, and did not yield to her
in the quantity of her lovers, or in valuing that sort of good
which ladies imagine to be great triumphs. She had a very

handsome face, all the features of which were equally perfect. I heard the queen say, long afterwards, that on ball
days when this one and that one was striving who should
be most beautiful, she and Madame de Chevreuse, fearing
Madame de Guémenée, did what they could by many inven-
tions to prevent her from effacing their beauty; and that
sometimes when she arrived in a state to cause jealousy to
those most perfect they would go in concert to tell her she
was not looking well. On which, without consulting a
mirror, she would go away quite terrified and hide herself;
by which artifice they often escaped the shame of not being
the handsomest woman present.

In the rank of those who were younger than Madame
de Chevreuse, Madame de Montbazon, and Madame de
Guémenée, was Madame la Princesse Marie [de Gonzague],
with whom Monsieur, the king's brother, had been in love,
and whom the queen, his mother, Marie de' Medici, had put
away for some time in the forest of Vincennes, fearing that
he would marry her. She was afterwards married to the
King of Poland. There was also Mademoiselle de Rohan,
who was very beautiful; she seemed to wish to make profession of extreme virtue and great pride, both of which she
maintained until the time of the regency, when we beheld
her pride change to passion, and her virtue, as I shall tell
elsewhere, forced her to marry a gentleman of quality [Henri
Chabot], but much inferior to those she might have chosen.

There were other handsome women, particularly Mademoiselle de Guise, estimable in all things and whose beauty
was great and perfect. Mademoiselle de Vendôme was also
a fine woman. They deserve, with many others, a panegyric
in their favour, but I shall pause only on Mademoiselle de
Hautefort, who made, as soon as she came to Court, a
greater effect than all the other beauties of whom I have

spoken. Her eyes were blue, large, and full of fire, her teeth white and even, and her complexion had the fairness and glow which belong to a blond beauty. The number of those who loved her was great; but their chains were often made heavy to bear; for though she was kind she was not tender,— severe, rather than hard, and naturally satirical.

As soon as the king saw her he had an inclination for her. The queen-mother, to whom she had been given as maid-of-honour, seeing this little spark of fire in the soul of a prince so shy of women, tried to light rather than extinguish it, in order to gain his good graces by such compliance. But the piety of the king made him attach himself so little that I heard this very Mlle. de Hautefort say later that he never talked to her of anything but dogs, birds, and hunting; and I have known her, with all her virtue, when telling me this history, laugh at him because he dared not come near her when conversing with her. This passion was not strong enough to bring him as often to the queen-mother's apartment as he would have come had he been really in love with one of her ladies; instead of making her Court more gay and gallant, it only diminished the influence of the queen and increased that of the queen-mother. The latter was the absolute mistress of France, and her happiness seemed to be without a flaw; but now came a change, which ought to show to all the world that no creature is safe from the blows of fortune, and that crowned heads, in being above those of other men, are the most exposed.

II.

1630 — 1643.

THE queen-mother, having raised Cardinal Richelieu, her favourite after Maréchal d'Ancre, to the dignity of prime minister, she considered him her creature and believed she would always reign through him; but she deceived herself, and gained cruel experience of the little fidelity to be met with in those who have unbounded ambition. I do not know what grounds of complaint she had against him, and few persons have known them; I have only heard say that, not being satisfied, she desired to ruin him, supposing it to be an easy thing to do, and that no one could object if, being mistress of her work, she destroyed it when she saw fit.

But that which seems to us right when we wish it, is often not according to the impenetrable will of God, who does not choose that human judgment should be followed by events that would authorize it. I knew from the queen, who, not liking Cardinal Richelieu, was glad to know all that was doing against him, when I put her on the topic, that on a journey to Lyon when the king was so ill that he thought himself dying and the cardinal thought himself lost, the queen-mother (who was beginning to no longer defend him against those who did him ill turns with her in order to get his place) requested the king to dismiss him; and that this prince after promising that he would and agreeing to send him away whenever she wished, begged her to let him stay a little longer on account of the plans he had about Italy; so that Queen Marie de' Medici, satisfied with this willingness, would not press her son to dismiss him immediately for fear of inconveniencing his affairs, and contented herself with his promise to do so whenever it pleased her.

By this kindness which deprived her of happiness for the rest of her life, she enabled the cardinal to get her sent away herself, though the mother and mother-in-law of the greatest kings in Europe. Marie de' Medici had given a queen to Spain, a sovereign to Savoie, a queen to England, and a king to France; but all these dignities which environed her could not guarantee her from disaster. The Court having returned to Paris, she pressed the king to fulfil his promise, and, as she supposed the affair to present no difficulty, she was astonished to find that the king resisted it. He not only asked for time, but he urgently entreated her to forgive Cardinal Richelieu.

The queen-mother, surprised and angry at the proposition, burst out against her son, shed tears, and reproached him, neglecting nothing that might win her the victory in this battle. But, far from succeeding, she found that her son and judge was in collusion against her with her enemy, and was *quasi* on his side. Cardinal Richelieu entered the room where they were together, to plead his cause in concert with the king. The queen-mother, all in tears and provoked that he had come into that room against her will, called him a traitor, told him it was true that she complained of him to the king, and railed against him with the strong feelings that always accompany great affronts and great hatreds. She did the same to his niece, the Duchesse d'Aiguillon, who entered towards the end of the conversation, treating her with the utmost contempt.

But the cardinal, without showing surprise, threw himself at her feet and asked pardon on his knees, doing, so they say, all that he could to obtain it. The queen-mother, incensed against her son for having refused her, and full of wrath against the servant whom she believed unfaithful, would not pardon him. Nor would she pardon the king himself, who knelt before her and seemed in great trouble. Finding himself refused, without any plan of what came later but with a sense of grief for the quarrel, the king went off to Versailles to reflect on what he had better do.

The cardinal, quite overcome, not knowing whether he ought to abandon all, took counsel with Cardinal de la Valette; after which he followed the king, and served his own purposes so adroitly by the advantage that personal presence gives, that he made himself in a short time, or rather in a few hours, master of the king's mind. It was then determined to arrest the Keeper of the Seals Marillac; and there is little doubt that Cardinal Richelieu began on this day to premeditate what was done later at Compiègne against the queen-mother, his benefactress. This day, so terrible in its effects and its changes, has since been very famous, because many persons who agreed with the queen-mother in wishing the dismissal of Cardinal Richelieu, were duped in all their hopes and suffered for them. [This was the celebrated " Day of the Dupes," November 11, 1630.]

Queen Marie de' Medici, by remaining in Paris at her house of the Luxembourg and not following the king, ruined her cause completely. She abandoned it in this way to the artfulness of her enemy, and ruined at the same time the great seigneurs of the kingdom, who, hating the cardinal, had made common cause with her. It was said that the whole cabal had held certain councils against the cardinal in which each member had given his opinion; and later he treated these persons according to the manner of their advice: Maréchal de Marillac, who was said to have advised that he be killed as soon as the king abandoned him, he put to death very unjustly; Maréchal de Bassompierre, who had proposed imprisonment only, was put in prison himself, where he stayed twelve years; and so with the others, as the maréchal, whom I knew later during the queen's regency, confirmed to me. This was the first cause of all the many persecutions and exiles which made, during this century, so large a number of illustrious unfortunates. Monsieur, the king's brother, Gaston de France, who was ever at the head of all these cabals, was, with good reason, at the head of this one on account of the queen his mother.

Some time after this "day of the dupes" the Court went to Compiègne, the two queens in the best understanding on account of the hatred they united in feeling for Cardinal Richelieu, and also because their fates began to be alike. The king, having the intention to arrest the queen his mother, was very restless; although he had done the same thing before, the influence of nature, which he now had to conquer at an age when he knew his duty better, weakened at times his resolution and made it uncertain. On the other hand, the minister, impatient to avenge himself, to satisfy and secure himself, turned many schemes over in his head; while the queen-mother, ill-treated by her son, and little confident of succeeding in her designs, was far from tranquil in soul.

A few days after their arrival, the day on which the destiny of so many great personages was to be fulfilled, a knock was given very early in the morning on the door of the queen's [Anne of Austria's] chamber. Hearing the sound she woke, astonished, and called her women to know if, by chance, it could be the king at her door. He alone had the right to treat her with such familiarity. In that instant, having herself opened her curtains and seen that it was scarcely daylight, she was troubled by a thousand thoughts that passed through her mind. As she always doubted, and with reason, of the king's good-will, she fancied they had come to bring her some fatal news which, at the least, might exile her from France. Regarding this moment as one which might decide her whole life, she strove to gather up her strength to meet the blow with as much courage as possible. She had by nature a firm soul and a sufficiently resolute mind, and I do not doubt what she did me the honour to tell me afterwards when relating these particulars, that, the first moment over, she resolved without much difficulty to receive with submission whatever Heaven ordained for her.

She bade them open the door, and her first waiting-woman returning to tell her it was the Keeper of the Seals who asked to speak with Her Majesty from the king, she was fully confirmed in her first belief. This apprehension was, however, soon removed by the speech of the envoy. He told her that, for certain reasons which concerned the welfare of the State, the king was obliged to leave his mother in that place under guard of Maréchal d'Estrées, and that he begged the queen not to see her, but to rise and come to him at the Capucins, where he had already gone to await her.

At this news the queen was much surprised, as any one who loved justice and right reason would be; but she was comforted to find that the matter only touched her through the compassion she must feel for the queen, her mother-in-law. She replied to the king's commands by prompt obedience, and rose as quickly as she could to go to him. But not without first going to see the disgraced queen. She thought the king would pardon her that small disobedience, which pity alone induced her to commit; but, by the advice of the Marquise de Senecé, her lady-of-honour, she sent to the unhappy queen-mother, to express the desire she had to see her and speak to her on a matter of importance, though, for certain reasons, she dared not go to her unless she first sent to ask her to do so.

The queen-mother, knowing nothing of this decision, although, in the position she felt herself to be in, she feared a return of all the evils she had already borne, sent Mademoiselle Catherine, her first waiting-woman, at once to do what the queen requested, a slyness asked solely to satisfy the king. The queen took only a dressing-gown and went in her night-dress to the queen-mother, whom she found sitting up in her bed. She was hugging her knees, and, not knowing what to think of this mystery, she cried out as the queen entered: "Ah! my daughter, either I am dead or a prisoner. Will the king leave me here? What does he mean to do with me?" The queen, touched by compassion, flung herself into her arms, and though in the days of her favour the queen-mother had sometimes ill-used her, the position she was now in effaced such memories; she wept for her downfall, she felt it, and showed a sincere regret for the king's decision, which she told her, and also the order for imprisonment.

The two princesses parted, satisfied with each other and both much touched at seeing themselves the victims of Cardinal Richelieu, their common enemy. This was the last time they saw each other, for the queen-mother, alarmed at an imprisonment in Compiègne, escaped during the night [July 19, 1631] and went to Flanders, where the Infanta Clara-Eugenia, granddaughter of Charles V. and aunt of the queen, received her and treated her well. She received in the same manner Monsieur, the king's only brother, Gaston de France, who, after having threatened Cardinal Richelieu, went to share with his mother the kindness of that great princess.

The queen, having satisfied by this pitying visit what she owed to one who so shortly before had seemed to have absolute power, went to the Capucins to meet the king, who was awaiting her in order to take her back to Paris. There, he made her a present of Mademoiselle de Hautefort, of whom I have already spoken, whom he had taken from the queen-mother; also of Madame de la Flote, Mademoiselle de Hautefort's grandmother, as lady of the bed-chamber. Some time later he gave the beautiful granddaughter the reversion of that office, in order that she might have the title of " Madame." The king, in presenting her to the queen, said that he begged her to like her and to treat her well for his sake. She was then without lady of the bed-chamber; since the dismissal of Madame Du Farges, whom she liked, she had never been willing, from vexation and revenge, to fill her place; but she was now constrained to accept all that the king chose to give her, for this was no time to say, "I will not." She received both ladies with the best face in the world, and though such presents do not usually please wives very much, it is nevertheless true that the queen loved Madame de Hautefort for herself, and that that beautiful and virtuous girl, esteeming the noble qualities of the queen, and sufficiently disgusted with the king's temper, gave herself entirely to her, and was faithful to her through all her troubles. The king, some years later, angry at this change, wished to harm her; he ceased to love her much when she began to love the queen, and when he saw that she was entirely devoted to her, he ceased to love her at all. His resentment went so far at last that he dismissed her, and sent her back to her province, where she was when he died.

After the great stroke at Compiègne, the king, to soften in some way the bitterness the people felt against him for the imprisonment of his mother, and for rigours enforced against many private persons, treated the queen, his wife, rather better, and saw her oftener; this pleased the people, because she was much loved. Cardinal Richelieu, to conciliate her, brought back Madame de Chevreuse from Lorraine where she had passed her exile; no doubt that lady promised him all he wanted of her. The cardinal, in spite of his severity against her, had never hated her. Her beauty had charms for him, but as she was allied with the queen and contraband with the queen-mother, ambition, which always carries the day over friendship, had forcibly removed her from the good graces of the minister. But after he had himself quarrelled with his benefactress, wishing to be reconciled with the queen and to gain alliance with her through her favourite, he brought the latter back to Court.

After all this the king, following his natural inclinations, abandoned himself wholly to the power of the cardinal. He found himself reduced to the most melancholy, most miserable life in the world; without suite, without Court, without power, and consequently without pleasure and without honour. In this way several years of his life were passed at Saint-Germain, where he lived like a private person, and while his armies were taking cities and fighting battles he was amusing himself by snaring birds. This prince was unhappy in every way; he did not love the queen, but on the contrary felt a coldness to her, and he was the martyr of Madame de Hautefort, whom he loved in spite of himself, and whom he could not resolve to send away from Court, though accusing her of laughing at him with the queen. Moreover, he had scruples about his attachment to her, and did not approve of himself. Jealous of the grandeur of his minister, though it came only from the part which he himself bestowed, he began to hate him when he saw the extreme authority he assumed in his kingdom; and not being able to live happily either with or without him, he never was happy at all.

The queen accustomed herself to her solitude as best she could, leading a pious and private life, and living only on news which her attendants and her friends brought to her. She made a few little intrigues against the cardinal, or at least desired to make some that might ruin him. He only laughed at them, and his power increased through the need the king had of his counsels. He made all France adore him and obey the king, making his master his slave, and that illustrious slave the monarch of a great kingdom!

Amid such gloomy humours and dark fancies it would seem that a great passion could find no place in the king's heart. Nor did it after the fashion of men who find pleasure in it; for this soul, accustomed to bitterness, had no tenderness beyond that of feeling the more for his own pains and sorrows. But at last, weary of suffering, he dismissed, as I have said, Madame de Hautefort, and turned his inclinations to a new object whose brunette beauty was not so dazzling, but who, with beautiful features and much charm, had also great sweetness and strength of mind. La Fayette, maid-of-honour to the queen [Louise Motier de La Fayette], amiable and proud both, was the one he loved; and it was to her that he unbosomed himself most about the cardinal, and the vexation that his power gave him.

As this young girl had an upright heart she did not fail to keep the secrecy she owed to the king. She strengthened him in his aversion from the regard she felt for him, thinking him dishonoured by too basely allowing himself to be governed by the minister. The cardinal did his best to win her over, as he did all persons who approached the king; but she possessed more courage than the men of the

Court, who had the baseness to tell the cardinal whatever the king said against him.   They feared, if they were faithful, to lose benefits, and their interests seemed to them something better than integrity.   They feared also that the king, ever timid, would betray them, and they wished to be the first to betray.   But a young girl had a finer and firmer soul than they; she resolved to do right, and had the courage to despise ill-fortune through a secret resolution which she made in her heart to become a nun.

The king, finding in her as much security and virtue as beauty, respected and loved her; and I know that he had thoughts about her that were far above the common affections of mankind.   The same sentiment which made this generous girl refuse all relations with Cardinal Richelieu also made her live under some reserve with the queen. Not that she did her any ill-offices, as her rival, Madame de Hautefort, tried to persuade the queen she did — she was too virtuous for that; and the queen knew, later, the goodness and generosity of her whole conduct.   But the fact is she liked the king, and said so openly; for a pure and honourable friendship can be owned without shame.   And truly, the virtue and propriety of the king, which equalled that of the most modest woman, controlled him strictly; so that she felt she ought to repay that virtuous affection by great fidelity to his confidences.   I am assured that she was the only person who ever had such feelings towards him, and consequently the only one who could have made the happiness of his life.

An attachment so great and so perfect could not fail to please the king and displease the queen, though the latter was used to the misfortune of not being loved by her husband.   This deprivation of a happiness she desired and thought her due, in whatever way it was seasoned to her, did not fail to seem to her very hard and disagreeable. La Fayette, avowing openly that she loved the king, and in the manner he seemed to wish, might have made the happiness of his life. But the king was not fated to be happy; he could not keep his treasure. It was said that the cardinal made use of his piety to deprive him of it, and that, not being able to have La Fayette in his own pay, he used her confessor to give her scruples as to her compliance to the king, which idea was so shrewdly managed by the confessors of both that the love of God triumphed over human love; La Fayette retired to a convent, and the king resolved to permit it. The truth is, that God destined her for that happiness, in spite of the malice and false arguments of the Court people. Père Caussin, confessor of the king, has himself written in his Memoirs (which the Comte de Maure, to whom he confided them, showed me) that instead of adhering to Cardinal Richelieu, as he was supposed to have done, he advised her, in view of the innocent intentions with which he credited her, not to make herself a nun; thinking that he would himself use her to inspire the king to recall the queen-mother, and govern the kingdom himself.

But she, who was urged by Him who gives the will and the power to do, did not hesitate long between God and His creatures. Perhaps also she saw with some vexation the intrigue that was forming against her, and pride mingled with virtue had some share in her retreat. It was even suspected that her relation, Madame de Senecé had tried to give her over to the cardinal. I do not know the ground or the details of this accusation; I know only that she begged the king's confessor to go to him and ask permission that she might quit the Court and enter a convent. Père Caussin describes in his memoirs the pains he took to examine into the vocation of La Fayette, and to give the king the advice he asked of him. He states that the king seemed much afflicted at the resolution of the virtuous young girl, and threw himself back into the bed from which he had risen when the father began to speak to him, weeping, and complaining that she wanted to leave him; but at last, having conquered the tortures of his grief by his piety, he made him this answer: "It is true she is very dear to me; but if God calls her to religion, I will put no hindrance to it."

This permission being once obtained, she was seen to leave the Court suddenly, in spite of the tears of the king and the joy of her enemies, which, as she told me afterwards, were the only things to conquer. It needed great strength of mind to put herself above that weakness, for though the king was not gallant, the ladies of the Court were none the less glad to please him. Among others, Madame de Hautefort was far from sorry at her retirement; she was not ashamed to be thought her rival; and there was no prude who did not aspire to be loved by the king as he had loved La Fayette — for everybody was convinced that the passion she had for him was not incompatible with virtue. When she parted from him she talked to him long before all the company in the queen's room, where she went as soon as she had received his permission to leave. No change appeared on her face; she had the strength not to give a single tear to those which the king shed publicly. After quitting him, she took leave of the queen, who could not like her; she did this with gentleness and the satisfaction a Christian must have in seeking God, wishing to love but Him on earth, and to desire only eternity.

The king was not long without going to see her at the convent of the daughters of Sainte-Marie, in the rue Saint-Antoine, which she had chosen for her life-long place of

rest and the haven of her salvation.   The first few times he
went there he stayed so long before her grating that Cardinal Richelieu, thrown into fresh alarms, resumed his intrigues to detach the king wholly from her.   He succeeded
finally and found means to take from his master the consolation of sharing his griefs with the only person he had
found discreet and faithful enough to confide in, and one
with a spirit that was soft and pleasant enough to soothe
them.   It was to the king as cruel a deed as that of a rob-
ber on the highway who takes from a traveller his all; for
the greatest of the blessings of life is the love of a faithful
friend; and if my uncle, the Bishop of Séez, says in his
poems, with the approval of everybody, that to love a young
beauty is "the sweetest error of earth's vanities," it is even
more true to say that to love solidly as the king loved La
Fayette was the sweetest of all innocent pleasures.

I cannot, however, refrain, while on the subject of this
pure and beautiful love between a prince so pious and a girl
so virtuous, from relating a strong proof of the corruption
which may always be met with in attachments of feeling
which count themselves pure.   I heard this from La Fayette herself who, being at Chaillot [where she founded the
Convent of the Visitation] and my friend, talked with me
confidentially.   She told me that in her last days at Court,
before she had fully resolved to enter religion, the king, so
wise and so constant in virtue, had, nevertheless, certain
moments of weakness in which, ceasing to be modest, he
had pressed her to consent that he should place her at
Versailles, to live under his orders and to be wholly his; and
that this proposal, so contrary to his usual sentiments, having
alarmed her, was the cause of her resolving more quickly
to leave the Court and take vows upon herself which must
remove from his mind all sentiments of that nature.

For some time nature struggled against grace, but grace was at last victorious. Otherwise the king would never have consented so easily that she might enter a convent; but as soon as she was there, he had no pain in seeing her in a nun's dress, nor had she any in seeing him before the grating; both were far away from a desire to maintain an intercourse for which they might have scruples. But in order to have peace with his minister, he consented to lose this one satisfaction that remained to him, and he left her to give herself entirely to Him who gives to all according to their actions, contenting himself with now and then sending a priest from Saint-Germain to bring him news of her. I know that this piety brought him to certain thoughts of inward retreat; and though he still went sometimes to see her, it was to talk over designs known to none but herself, which would have astonished Europe had they been executed. But God was satisfied with his intention, and, to reward him for the sacrifice he wished to make to Him, He granted the prayers of his subjects by taking from him those melancholy thoughts which prevented his living well with the queen, who at last became pregnant. It is even said that La Fayette was a secondary cause of the queen's pregnancy. Having stayed with her too late to return to Saint-Germain as he intended, he was constrained to go to the Louvre and share the bed of the queen, who had come to Paris for affairs of no importance; and it is said that this gave us, September 5, 1638, our present reigning king, Louis XIV.

In the beginning of this pregnancy the king showed much satisfaction and even tenderness for the queen's person. But this comfort lasted but a short time, and when she was delivered it was necessary to urge him to approach her and kiss her.

All France supposed that after giving to the king a

dauphin the queen would have some influence, but as the minister was not on her side, and she was too generous to seek him, she remained in the same condition as before. As an increase of favour, however, God gave her a second son, Philippe de France, on the 21st of September, 1640, for which the king, as I have heard the queen say, showed far more pleasure than at the birth of the first, because he did not expect the great happiness of being father of two children, he who had feared he might have none at all. But it is a strange thing that the dauphin was only three years old when he began to cause him grief and umbrage. The queen did me the honour to tell me that one day, after a hunting party, the little prince, seeing his father in a night-cap, began to cry and was frightened, not being accustomed to see him thus, and the king was angry as if it were a matter of the greatest consequence, complaining to the queen and reproaching her for bringing up her son to aversion for his person, and roughly threatening to take away from her both her children. But when the king started for a journey to Narbonne he had with him his equerry Cinq-Mars, a man whom Cardinal Richelieu had given him as a favourite after the loss of La Fayette. Whether it was by Cinq-Mars' advice or of his own motion, he spoke to the queen in another manner. Bidding her farewell, he said quite cordially that he begged her to take good care of his children, and not to quit them — which she religiously obeyed. Besides the interest that she had in their preservation she fastened all her pleasure to the agreeable occupation of seeing and caressing them.

December 4, 1642, Cardinal Richelieu died gloriously in Paris at his own house, with the tranquillity of a private individual, and in the arms of his king, whom he made his heir in many things. He received all the sacraments. He

died, laden with honours and glory, in the lustre of many
virtues and the shame of great defects, of which cruelty
and tyranny were the chief. It may be said of him that
he acquired a great reputation by procuring the good of the
State and the power and grandeur of his prince. The
harshness with which he treated the queen-mother, his mistress and his benefactress, during her exile, lessens by a
great deal the eulogy that is due to his memory; and his
cruelty towards many private persons makes him infinitely
blamable. He died finally with the aspect of a saint, not
having lived in all things the life of a Christian. I have
heard it said that he asked a bishop if he could die in peace
without having made restitution of the property he had
taken from the public and from private persons, sometimes
unjustly; and the bishop, accustomed to flatter him, having
answered yes, that the great benefits he had done to France
rendered his own legitimate, he begged him to give him that
opinion in writing; and that writing he put very carefully
under the pillow of his bed, as if to serve as justification
before God of his iniquities. What seems to me strange
is that a man more able and possessing more knowledge
than the man on whom he laid the burden of his scruple,
should be willing to deceive himself in a matter where he
alone could be the judge, and his own conscience the most
faithful instructor he could consult.[1]

He seemed so content with having triumphed over his
enemies that his chaplain could not refrain from urging
him to forgive them; to which he answered that he had
never had any enemies but those of the State. He had
written books on the Education and on the Perfection of
Christians; therefore he ought to have known in what they
consisted. Nevertheless the Bishop of Nantes, Cospean,

---

[1] On the margin is written: " This is not a certain thing."

nany
ielty
that
the
The
nis-
 a
his
ly
ot
e
e
l

Philippe de Champagne

Cardinal de Richelieu

esteemed for his virtue and piety, who was afterwards Bishop of Lizieux, having gone to see him at the close of his life, said aloud, as he left the room after conversing with him, that his tranquillity astonished him. And they say that Pope Urban VIII., hearing of his death and of his life, remarked, with a great exclamation: *Ah! che se gli è un Dio, ben tosto lo pagarà ; ma veramente se non c'è Dio, è galantuomo.* ("Ah! if there is a God he will soon pay for it; but truly if there is no God, he is an able man.") An Italian friend of mine, whom I asked if that were true, told me it was true, and it was not surprising, for the good pope often jested and said witty things, but all the same he was a great man and had virtue — which does not accord very well with such jokes.

The queen, after this death, which did not afflict her much, began to foresee her coming power by the crowd that now surrounded her. It was not because the king showed her more consideration. The cardinal had worked with such care to destroy her in his mind that she could never obtain a better place there; and the prince himself was by nature so gloomy, and at this time so crushed by his woes that he was no longer capable of any feeling of tenderness for one whom he had never been accustomed to treat well. But, serenity having returned to the faces of the courtiers, and this change giving hope and consequently joy to all, they began to consider the queen as the mother of two princes and the wife of a sickly king. She was nearing the period of a regency which would surely be a long one; so that now she was regarded as a rising sun from which each in particular expected to receive in his turn a favourable influence.

The king, though ill, attended to all business, and publicly announced that he would have no other governor. He sent pardons to criminals, opened the prisons, suffered exiles to return, and did all that was needed to persuade his people that the late cruelties had not been done by himself and that his inclinations were far removed from them. All this mildness and calm caused the present reign to be blessed and the late severity detested; but it did not last long, for the king died shortly after. He had called to the ministry Cardinal Mazarin, an Italian by birth, but half Spanish from the years he had passed in Spain, and a friend of Cardinal Richelieu. It is to be supposed that he would have gained power over the king had the latter lived, for he knew how to please when he chose.

This was the state of the Court when France lost the king. He was still young, but so broken by fatigues, worries, remedies, and hunting, that, feeling he could not live any longer, he resolved to die well in order to live eternally. He did it in a manner that was quite extraordinary. No one ever showed such constancy in suffering, such firmness in the certain thought of his end, or such indifference to life. He had always been unhappy because he had subjected himself to others, following the passions of his favourites rather than his own sentiments. This submission had led him to commit faults for which he repented within himself.

There is reason to think that the innocent passions he had felt for Madame de Hautefort and La Fayette had caused him nothing but grief and a few moments of weakness which God had given him the grace to surmount; for he always appeared to fear God, and they both believed him very scrupulous, — worthy in that of great praise if in other things he had shown the same strength.

It was in his last days, in view of the judgments of God, that he repented keenly for having failed in keeping one of His first commandments. Cardinal Richelieu was no longer with him to maintain the exile of the queen-mother as necessary to the State; and, examining himself sincerely on that matter, what he had done against her now seemed to him as terrible as it really was. He openly asked pardon of God for it with great signs of a true repentance, and he did apparently all that a good Christian is bound to do, with sentiments of piety and marks of perfect faith. He had said to Chavigny at the beginning of his illness that he felt a cruel distress for two things: first, for having ill-treated his mother, who had lately died [Marie de' Medici died at Cologne July 3, 1642], and secondly, for not having made peace.

Towards the end of the king's illness, when M. de Chavigny saw that the doctors considered the king had no hope of escaping, he took upon himself to warn him of the state in which he was; which he did, while softening the harshness of the news as much as possible. Nevertheless, he represented to him with strength and courage that although he was a great prince he was on an equality with the least of men in death, and ended by saying it was time for him to think of quitting life. The king embraced him, and said, as he pressed him in his arms, that he thanked him for that good news, and assured him that he had never felt such joy in life as he received in hearing he was about to lose it. He made him withdraw that he might think of his conscience and his affairs; then, after passing half an hour alone, he recalled him and said, "M. de Chavigny, let us now think of business." They then made the plan of his will, in which he declared the queen regent. Madame de Chavigny told me that her husband, who had more share in this than Cardinal Mazarin, could have had Monsieur, the king's brother, appointed, the latter having requested him to do so; but he held good for the queen, thinking he could thus serve his own interests better, in which he was much mistaken. The queen did not like him, and those about her had already resolved on his downfall.

After this, the queen entered the council, and the king made the chancellor read the declaration, the plan of which had been written by Chavigny and adopted by the king. It was read in presence of the parliament and of the nobles of the kingdom. The king required the queen to swear that she would observe it inviolably. This she was obliged to do; but she did it with an intention contrary to the king's wishes as to certain persons, some of whom had gained his hatred, others his friendship. The king had wished to put in a clause that the Keeper of the Seals, Châteauneuf, and Madame de Chevreuse should be forever removed from the Court, as dangerous persons, whose minds were always to be feared. He was dissuaded by those who wished to please the coming regent, and who dared no longer act except in harmony with her. When the reader of the declaration came to the place where this was omitted the king, who was then moribund, fearing those two persons as favourites of the queen, rose in his bed and said aloud, "That is devilish, that!" [*Voila le diable, cela!*]

Séguin, the queen's head doctor told me that two hours before the king's death, as he passed before his bed, he made him a sign with his head and eyes to come to him, and holding out his hand said in a firm voice: "Séguin, feel my pulse, and tell me, I beg of you, how many more hours I have to live; but feel it carefully, for I should be glad to know the truth." The doctor, seeing his firmness, and not wishing to disguise a truth which he saw would not frighten him, said, quite coolly: "Sire, your Majesty may have two, or three hours at the most." On which the king, clasping his hands and turning his eyes to heaven, said softly, without showing any alteration whatever, "Then, my God, I consent, with all my heart." And shortly after he closed his eyes forever, May 14, 1643, aged forty-two years only.

The queen seemed sincerely afflicted. She went at once to the little dauphin, or rather the king; whom she saluted and embraced with tears in her eyes as her king and child. It may be said that she and all France did right to weep for the king, who, according to his lights and his sentiments, might even then have governed his kingdom gloriously. He had defects which effaced him from the hearts of his subjects and of all his family; but he had also great virtues, which, for his misfortune, have never been sufficiently known; and the subjection of his will to that of his minister had smothered all these nobler qualities. He was full of piety and zeal for the service of God and the grandeur of the Church; and his greatest joy in taking La Rochelle and other places was the thought that he would drive all heretics from his kingdom and purge it in this way of the different religions which spoil and infect the Church of God.

He was, as I have heard his most intimate favourites say, one of the best soldiers of his kingdom. He knew war, and he was valiant. I know this from those who in their youth were with him in danger, when he seemed not to fear it. He loved the officers on service, and this was the only matter he did not abandon to his minister. He himself knew the men of true courage, who had done fine actions, and he took great care to reward them. His keenest vexation against the cardinal was that he often wanted to command his army in person, and the cardinal, fearing to let him go among such a crowd of his own enemies, always opposed it and prevented it by a thousand contrivances.

He had much intelligence and knowledge; Cardinal Riche-

lieu himself said of him on several occasions that in his
council he was always of the right opinion, and often found
expedients in the most embarrassing matters.   I have heard
the Duc de Saint-Simon, who was with him on the day he
quarrelled with the queen-mother, say that he would not
give up Cardinal Richelieu when she asked it, from a principle of justice, because he was convinced that he had not
been unfaithful to him; that it was the Maréchal de Marillac and the Maréchal de Bassompierre and several others
who, having formed a cabal with the Princesse de Conti
against Cardinal Richelieu, wanted, for their own private
interests, to use the queen-mother as a buckler against him;
and that the king, knowing the services he had rendered him,
thought himself obliged to uphold him; but that never had
he any thought of injuring the queen his mother to save
the cardinal; on the contrary, his design was to keep his
minister without failing in respect to her; and that the first
thing that alienated him from her was her urging him to
dismiss the cardinal, and, having gone upon his knees before
her to soften her, that she had no regard to his submission
or to his prayers.   It was this that caused him some vexation, so that he went to Versailles, where the cardinal, by
the advice of friends, followed him.   At first the minister
wished to retire, but the king said to him: " No, Monsieur
le Cardinal, I will not allow it; you have done no wrong to
the queen my mother; if you had, I would never see you
again; but knowing that all these things are being done by
a cabal, and that you have served me well, I should not be
just if I abandoned you."

Other persons of that time have also assured me that he
never had any plan for what happened afterwards at Compiègne.   But soon after this [Day of Dupes] the cardinal
made him understand that he must break up the cabal which

was instigating the queen-mother to embroil the State; and for that purpose she must be arrested for some little time, after which, her party being dead or imprisoned, it would be easy to bring her back again.   But, the queen-mother having escaped to Flanders (which was, they say, arranged by the cardinal himself), it was easy for him to disguise the truth from the king her son, and persuade him that her absence was necessary for the peace of his kingdom.   That is what may be said to excuse the greatest fault which the king committed; for as to the death of the Maréchal d'Ancre, there was never any sign that he ordered it, or the indignities that accompanied it, which must be attributed to the little discretion of those who had the order to arrest him, to the resistance offered by the attendants of the maréchal, and to the hatred that the people had to him.   Consequently, that matter did not prevent the king from obtaining the title of Just.   Nor has any one ever doubted that he was brave, and that he knew how to take an army into battle as well as any of his generals.   But, besides these great qualities so necessary to great kings, he knew many things to which melancholy minds are wont to devote themselves, such as music and the mechanical arts, for which he had great skill and a peculiar talent.

III.

1643—1644.

WE now come to the regency of the queen [May 15, 1643], where we shall see, as in a picture, the various revolutions of fortune; of what nature is that climate called the Court; its corruption, and how fortunate should they esteem themselves who are not fated to live there. The air is never sweet or serene for any one. Even those who, apparently in perfect prosperity, are adored as gods, are the ones most threatened by tempests. The thunder growls incessantly for great and small; and those whom their compatriots regard with envy know no calm. It is a windy, gloomy region, filled with perpetual storms. Men live there little, and during the time that fortune keeps them there, they are always ill of that contagious malady, ambition, which kills their peace, gnaws their heart, sends fumes to their head and often deprives them of reason. This disease gives them a continual disgust for better things. They are ignorant of the value of equity, justice, kindliness. The sweetness of life, of innocent pleasures, of all that the sages of antiquity counted as good, seem to them ridiculous; they are incapable of knowing virtue and following its precepts, unless chance may happen to remove them from this region. Then, if they can by absence be cured of their malady, they become wise, they become enlightened; and no man can be so good a Christian or so truly a philosopher as a disillusioned courtier.

On the morrow of the death of King Louis XIII., King Louis XIV., the queen, Monsieur le Duc d'Anjou, the Duc

Frans Porbus

Anne of Austria

d'Orléans, and the Prince de Condé quitted Saint-Germain to come to Paris. The body of the late king was left alone at Saint-Germain, without other surroundings than the people, who flocked to see it out of curiosity rather than tenderness. The Duc de Vendôme remained there to do the honours, and the Marquis de Souvré, gentleman of the bedchamber on service, to do his duty. Of all the people of quality who were paying their court the night before, not one remained to pay respect to his memory; they all ran after the regent.

The queen had many on her side in the parliament; among them its president, Barillon, who had been at all times attached to her person. All were of opinion that the queen should not be satisfied with a restricted regency as provided by the king, and that she ought to make use of the parliament to render her mistress of everything.

She liked the proposal extremely, for it put her in a position to break her chains and dismiss those persons whom the king had appointed to take part in all deliberations. Chavigny and his father [President Bouthillier] were the ones she particularly desired to remove, as the creatures of Richelieu and hated by those who were now the most powerful about her. On the other hand, the parliament desired to find occasion to recover the authority it had lost under the late king; and the able men of this assembly esteemed it fortunate that the queen (who thought that the late king had not treated her properly in his will) should wish to use them to receive from their hands the sovereign power which the king had seemed to take from her by ordaining that, in the council of regency, affairs should be determined by a plurality of votes. She herself could scarcely endure that restraint, and those who hoped to have a share in her confidence wished her to have the power to dismiss some of those who were appointed, in order that they might take their places.

The offers of the parliament gentry to annul the declaration of the king in its present form were accepted. I have since heard Cardinal Mazarin say that the queen did them too much honour in putting them above the king's wishes and giving them the power to ordain a thing of so much consequence. She went to parliament, where, with the consent of Monsieur, Duc d'Orléans, and the Prince de Condé, she was declared regent, without the appointment of a council. The queen was in deep mourning, and took with her the king, who was still in his bibs and was carried by the Duc de Chevreuse, his grand chamberlain, and accompanied by the Duc d'Orléans, his uncle, and the Prince de Condé, first prince of the blood, the dukes and peers, the marshals of France, and the whole council.

The chancellor, Séguier, made an harangue that was worthy of the esteem he had acquired; and, after exalting the virtues of the queen, he thanked Heaven for having given to France a regent from whom they might hope to gain a general peace and the repose of the State. He then called for votes on the clause of the regency. Monsieur, uncle of the king, promptly and without hesitating, gave his in its favour; declaring that of his own will he made over to the queen all the power which, as only brother of the late king, he could have claimed in the kingdom in order that her regency might be more absolute and her will unlimited. The Prince de Condé said, in his turn, that since Monsieur so desired it he consented. I have heard the queen say, as to that consent, that it was by no means as frank as that of Monsieur, and that she noticed on his face a repugnance to give it; and also that the difficulty he seemed to have in resolving to do so made her feel more obligations to Monsieur, whose power would have been much greater had hers been limited, which it would have been had he voted as the Prince de Condé wished.

As she knew the opposition of the one, she must also have felt the yielding of the other; which, in truth, was surprising, seeing that it is not natural to give up so easily one's share in a great benefit. Many persons ascribed it to weakness, and this weakness to the selfish interests of his favourite, the Abbé de la Rivière, who was accused of detaching him from ambitious sentiments in the hope of making his own private fortune through the benefactions of the queen, rather than by leading his master to great projects — for which he may have thought him incapable, for the soul of that prince was not turned to things heroic. However that may be, the two lions were tamed, and Monsieur contented himself with the station of generalissimo of the armies of France, — very different in that from the king his father, Henri le Grand, of whom it was said that never was there a better king nor a worse prince of the blood. Indeed the great qualities that make a great king do always prevent the first prince of the blood from being peaceable and without faction.

As soon as the queen saw herself independent and absolute mistress, she dismissed Chavigny from the council, and took the finances from his father, Bouthillier, to give them to President de Bailleul, whom she knew to have much integrity, without knowing if he had any talent for that office. At the same time she sent to Rome to ask for a cardinal's hat for the Bishop of Beauvais, recalled the Duchesse de Chevreuse from exile, and did favours to many private persons without regarding the just measure that the great are bound to examine, but which she did not duly observe because as yet she did not know the value of her liberalities, while every one hastened to ask favours of her boldly and refusal gave her too much pain to inflict.

The Duc de Vendôme, and his whole family, had so far gained more than any one by the king's death; and particularly his youngest son, the Duc de Beaufort, for the queen during the last days of the king's illness had confided to the latter the care of her children. The fame of this confidence had attracted so many persons to him that he seemed for a time to be master of the Court.

The queen had intended to take the government of Havre from the Duchesse d'Aiguillon and give it to the Prince de Marsillac, a friend of Madame de Chevreuse and Madame de Hautefort, who was very handsome, had much wit and many ideas, and whose extraordinary merit destined him to cut a great figure in the world. The duchess, Richelieu's niece, who had played a great part during the ministry of her uncle, now commanded in Havre, and that government was left to her by consent of the late king, to hold it for her nephews.

This lady, who by her fine qualities surpassed ordinary women in many ways, was so well able to defend her cause that she almost convinced the queen that it was necessary for her service to leave her in that important place, telling her that having none but enemies now in France, she could have no safety or refuge, except under the protection of her Majesty, who would always be her mistress, while, on the contrary, the Prince de Marsillac to whom she was giving the government was too clever, too capable of ambitious designs, and might at the least affront join some cabal; it was, therefore, important for the good of the service that she should keep this place safe for the king. The tears of a woman who had once been so proud arrested the queen in the first place, and then, after reflecting on these reasons, she thought it best to leave things as they were.

The complaints of the Prince de Marsillac were many; he murmured publicly against the queen, and, on the first occasion that presented itself, he let her see that he felt her change, and was resolved to abandon her interests and take others in revenge, which was in part the cause of all our woes.

The Bishop of Beauvais did not maintain public affairs with the force and capacity a prime minister ought to have; the queen, drawn from a life of great idleness, and by nature lazy, felt herself completely overwhelmed by so great a burden. She was not long without seeing that she needed help, and that it was impossible for her to govern a State as large as France, or distinguish all alone the interests of the people and those of the nobles, which are two very different things; it is certain, moreover, that a long time was needed to examine that question, which would harass the greatest minds if they were not accustomed to toil, and had no knowledge of public business.

That which gave the greatest trouble to the queen was the desire she had to satisfy, as far as she could, those who demanded justice for the losses they declared they had borne under the ministry of Cardinal Richelieu, who came in great numbers and were very difficult to content.

In this interval of disgust and embarrassment, Cardinal Mazarin, appointed by the late king as one of the council, was lucky enough to be fated, and then chosen by the queen, to fill that place. She had not dismissed him, because she had no dislike to him; and as he was very able he had won the favour of the Prince de Condé, who did not like the Vendômes, and he had put into his interests the Duc d'Orléans' favourite, the Abbé de la Rivière, who was not of their party.

At the same time he acquired as friends those who were

servants of the queen without being of the Vendôme cabal;
such as the Marquis de Liancourt, the Marquis de Mortemart, Beringhen, and Lord Montague, an Englishman whom
the queen had known in the days of Buckingham, and
who retained a familiarity with her. The first two were
recommended by the regard the late king had felt for them,
and the last two by the confidence the queen reposed in
them. They were all former courtiers who esteemed Cardinal Mazarin, having known him long before in France
with Cardinal Richelieu, and they now gave all their attention to persuading the queen of his ability. They had not
much trouble in succeeding, for the queen was already disgusted with the Bishop of Beauvais, so much so that by
her own inclination she was quite disposed to make use
of the cardinal, whose wit and person pleased her in the first
conversation she had with him. During the life of the late
king she had quite often signified, in speaking of Cardinal
Mazarin, that she esteemed him, and to those in whom she
confided she declared she was not sorry to see him in order
to inform herself about foreign affairs, of which he had a
perfect knowledge, and in which the late king had employed
him. Following, therefore, her personal sentiments, the
advice of some of her best servants, and the desire of the
Duc d'Orléans and the Prince de Condé who declared they
esteemed him, she willingly gave him her confidence, yielded
her authority to him, and allowed him to acquire within
a few days the highest degree of favour in her heart, while
those who believed they possessed it solely never imagined
that he dared to even think of it.

This insinuating process was so easily carried on in the
soul of the queen that the cardinal became in short time
master of the council, the Bishop of Beauvais diminishing
in power in proportion as that of his competitor increased;

the new minister beginning from this time to come every
evening to the queen, and hold long conferences with her.
His gentle, humble manner, beneath which were hidden his
ambition and his designs, made the opposite cabal have
almost no fear of him; they regarded him at first with the
assumption that favour inspires. But the fickle creature to
whom under the name of Fortune pagans burn incense,
desiring, as usual, to mock at those who follow her, abandoned them all to give herself wholly to a foreigner, and
raise him suddenly from the first rung of the ladder to
the highest a private individual could reach, above all the
princes and grandees of the kingdom.

While these intrigues were tangling in the cabinet, God
was favourably taking part in our affairs in the field. The
Prince de Condé had a son, the Duc d'Enghien. He had
married in spite of his father a niece of Cardinal Richelieu,
and commanded the armies when the king died. At the
beginning of the regency he won a battle before Rocroy,
which strengthened the good fortune of the queen, and was
the first of the fine actions of that young prince, then twenty-
two years of age, so brave and with so great a genius for
war that the greatest captains of antiquity can scarcely be
compared with him. The late king, a few days before his
death, dreamed that he saw him giving battle and defeating
the enemy at the very spot. This is a matter worthy of
wonder, which ought to cause respect for the memory of
the king, who, dying amid sufferings, and quitting the world
with joy, seems to have had some light upon the future.

This victory, won at the beginning of the queen's regency,
was a good omen for what might follow, and, by making
her feared without, put her in a position to manage all
things within the kingdom. But the princes of Vendôme
and the Bishop of Beauvais were growing uneasy. They

now wished to oppose the new-comer, Cardinal Mazarin, and drive him away as an interloper, not liking that any one should share the influence they had with the queen. But they were not able to succeed, and what they did only served to ruin them.

I have heard it said by Maréchal d'Estrées, uncle of the Duc de Vendôme and brother of the Duchesse de Beaufort whom Henri IV. had thought of marrying, that Cardinal Mazarin, in the early days of the regency, not knowing which side to turn, tried at first to join that cabal, as the one best established in the mind of the queen, and that he asked him, the maréchal, to be his negotiator; and as he was interested in the fortunes of these princes, being their nearest relative, he did his best to attach them to Cardinal Mazarin, whom he had known in Rome when he was sent there as ambassador. He thought him a great politician and a great courtier, and liked him, in consequence, doubly, believing that his ability and his shrewdness of mind would infallibly raise him to favour. It depended, therefore, solely on the Vendôme princes whether or not he joined their fortunes; but they refused his friendship, from the hatred they felt to everything connected with Cardinal Richelieu. They could not help seeing, however, that he was a man to fear, not only for his ability, but for his charming manners which might make him beloved by the queen.

The Vendôme princes having thus missed their opportunity and refused alliance with Cardinal Mazarin, the fortunes of that minister took a turn, but only to rise the faster and show the inconstancy of the things of this world. I know from the queen that one evening in the early days of her power she asked Lord Montague, who often spoke to her of Cardinal Mazarin, whether she could trust him, and what his natural temper was; and that Lord Montague having told her, in his praise, that he was the opposite in all things of Cardinal Richelieu, that answer seemed to her such great eulogy, through the hatred she had to the memory of the dead man, that it helped her much in determining to use him. And after she had taken this resolution it was so fully confirmed daily that it soon became immovable; and he, as prime minister, took the habit, as I said before, of coming every evening to converse with her. These conferences began from that time to be called " the little council." He remained a long time with the queen, all the doors being open to the place where she was. He related to her the various foreign affairs of which he had been master during the lifetime of the late king, having made himself (before becoming cardinal) capable of serving her well through the many high offices he had filled, whether in foreign affairs and in the interests of various princes, the King of Spain, and the Duc de Savoie, or through the services he had given to France (which made him a cardinal) and the lessons he had derived from that able minister Cardinal Richelieu — whom would to God he had more closely resembled in certain ways.

It is not astonishing that the queen followed his advice. The great reputation he had acquired in Italy, where, by a flourish of his hat, he was able, though at that time only *il Signor Giulio,* to stop the armies on the point of combating, won him that of cardinal; and the great affairs he had negotiated with Cardinal Richelieu made the latter conceive so high an esteem for him that, intending to make him his successor, he had given him all the instructions necessary to serve France, binding him firmly to carry out his principles and perfect them.

Every one knew that Cardinal Mazarin had been named in the declaration of the late king as prime minister, because

Cardinal Richelieu, before dying, had assured the king that
he knew no one more capable than he of filling the place.
And this declaration the queen made use of to obtain
approval for her own choice of him.   I know, as to that, that
this lucky minister, being persuaded of his luck by that
which he had already found in all phases of his life, said
to one of his friends (the Maréchale d'Estrées), while the
decision was pending, that he was not troubled on that point,
but merely that he did not as yet see how to *spiegar le vele*
più larghe (put on all sail).

Here, then, was Cardinal Mazarin, his favour already con-
spicuous through the crowd that was beginning to surround
him.   He replaced Chavigny in the ministry, being unable
not to keep his word or refuse his obligations to those who
had placed him near the queen, but he held him aloof from
his confidence.   He confirmed the queen in the inclination she had to allow the Duchesse d'Aguillon to retain
Havre, and he prevented her from ruining the relatives of
Cardinal Richelieu by telling her that they, having no protection but hers, would doubtless be the ones who would
serve her best.   He did his duty in sustaining those who
were left of a great man to whom he owed his grandeur.
But, besides this reason, it was shrewd policy, seeing that he
had this troop of courtiers on his shoulders, to make powerful friends of those who held offices and possessed the
highest dignities in the kingdom.   In this he succeeded so
well that in spite of the opposition of the queen's former
friends, she relinquished the intention she had had of dis-
missing Cardinal Richelieu's followers, and the hatred she
had seemed to feel so strongly against them in the early
days of her regency.   She passed easily to the greatest
gentleness towards them, and, by her authority, they almost
all became her confidants and were well-treated.

This change, which was in the first place a counsel received and given from political maxims, readily became in the queen's soul a Christian principle, which her virtue and clemency made her value; and as she was capable of being deceived under a semblance of good, it is to be believed that Cardinal Mazarin, without being generous, advised her to act generously, intending to weaken the impulse of her heart towards hatred as well as towards friendship, so that, becoming indifferent to revenge, she might be more susceptible to the impressions he wanted to give her for his own interests. The queen, thinking his advice to be good and sincere, followed it without objection and even with some satisfaction, believing that she combined the good of the State with the pleasure of conquering herself in her resentment.

The favour of the cardinal was therefore more and more established in the mind of the queen, and the Vendôme party became truly alarmed by it. They made every effort to oppose it and to bring the queen back to her first feelings. But opposition has this quality, it excites the desire and the will to resist and combat. The queen was determined to defend and maintain her minister by force of reason. She openly declared that she chose to make use of it, and said to all those who spoke to her, that his policy was sound in advising her not to enter upon any plans of vengeance, unworthy of a Christian and royal soul; and she freely showed to certain of her servitors that she should be very glad if they accommodated themselves to her inclination and will. Then, paying but little attention to the Bishop of Beauvais, she showed by all her actions that she had given her entire confidence to Cardinal Mazarin.

He was capable of pleasing by his adroit mind, shrewd and clever at intrigue, and by a manner and behaviour full of gentleness, far removed from the severity of the preceding reign and well-suited to the queen's natural kindness. It has been thought that he was not worthy of her esteem; but it is true, nevertheless, that he had laudable qualities which were fitted to repair the defects that were in him, although, increased by envy, those defects made him hated and despised by the people and by many honourable men. The queen had reason to esteem the beauty of his mind, his capacity, and the signs he gave her of his moderation. She readily believed that he was virtuous in all things because he had no apparent vice or evil qualities that she could then perceive; and although she judged him rather too favourably, the infinite difference between him and the Bishop of Beauvais renders the queen praiseworthy for her discernment.'

The Court being in this state, favour was still unsettled; for, to the eyes of the public it did not seem as fixed as it really was, on account of the great stir which the princes of Vendôme still made. But this disturbance no longer had much force except through the unbridled audacity of the Duc de Beaufort, who, young and well-made, with many friends and a haughty demeanour, seemed to live in the fashion of favourites. Nor could it be imagined that the queen would so quickly abandon those whom, up to that time, she had liked and treated with so many marks of sincere friendship. Cardinal Mazarin had only just dawned into her good-will; she gave him, apparently, no more favourable treatment than she did the Duc de Beaufort, who spent whole days beside her, entertaining her gayly and with the freedom that smiling fortune inspires in the favoured. But the need of being served, and the pains the minister took to show that he was sincere and full of kindness, made the entire conquest of her confidence at all moments easy to him. The duke, his competitor, mingled what he had of good and praiseworthy with many defects; his youth deprived him of experience, his natural intelligence was very limited, he talked boldly and talked ill; it is not surprising, therefore, that so many bad points produced much that was not advantageous to him.

About this time an affair happened which disclosed the intrigues of the Court, and was the cause of Cardinal Mazarin's finding himself, soon after, completely established in the power and eminence that he desired. It was by a special providence of God that the very things which mischief-makers tried to use to overturn the Court were actually what brought it into order, — at the cost, however, of a few worthy persons.

Women are usually the originating causes of the great convulsions of States, and wars which ruin kingdoms and empires proceed nearly always from the effects produced by their beauty or their malice. The Duchesse de Montbazon, who, in our time, held the first rank for beauty and gallantry, being the mother-in-law of the Duchesse de Chevreuse, belonged with the latter to the Vendôme cabal, not so much out of interest for her daughter-in-law, but because the Duc de Beaufort was her lover. Consequently, both these ladies were opposed to the Princesse de Condé, who liked neither the one nor the other, and who favoured the cardinal because of her hatred to Châteauneuf, the Keeper of the Seals.

Besides these contending interests, there was another very strong one between Madame de Longueville, daughter of the Princesse de Condé, and the Duchesse de Montbazon. This young and beautiful demoiselle de Bourbon had been forced by the prince her father to marry the Duc de Longueville, who was the greatest seigneur, by reason of his vast property, whom she could have married. He followed in precedence the princes of the blood; but he could not consider himself wholly worthy of her, because of his birth, and because of his age, and also because he was in love with Madame de Montbazon. These two ladies, therefore, with many reasons not to like each other, had strong inclinations to do each other harm; and the perfect beauty of Madame de Longueville, her youth, and her natural grandeur led her often to look down upon her rival with contempt.

It happened one day that, Madame de Montbazon being at home in her house with a great company, one of her young ladies found a letter in the room, and picking it up carried it to her mistress. The letter was in a woman's handwriting and was tenderly addressed to some man whom she did not hate. As such matters are usually the talk of all companies and preferred to all else, the subject of laughter thus afforded to Madame de Montbazon's company was not neglected. From gayety they passed to curiosity, from curiosity to suspicion, and from suspicion they ended by deciding that the letter had fallen from the pocket of Coligny, who had just left the room, and who, it was whispered, had a passion for Madame de Longueville. This princess had a great reputation for virtue and prudence, although she was suspected of not hating adoration and praise.

Those of Madame de Montbazon's company who first said, after her, that this letter was from Madame de Longueville, did not really believe it. It was then only an amusing story which each told secretly to friends, merely to divert those who had not heard it. But it was not long in reaching the ears of the Princesse de Condé, who, with her proud and vindictive nature, resented it keenly, and it is impossible to say to what lengths she might not have carried her wrath and indignation. Madame de Longueville, who did not feel the matter less, but was more self-controlled, thought it advisable not to make a stir. The jealousy she felt of Madame de Montbazon, being proportioned to the love she had for her husband, did not carry her so far but what she thought it best to overlook the outrage; for it was of such a nature that she desired to smother it rather than make it the occasion of a solemn vengeance.

The Princess, her mother, was actuated by other great interests. She knew how to profit by her advantage in having entered the house of Bourbon; and being unable to restrain herself she made this quarrel a State affair. She came to see the queen and complained loudly of Madame de Montbazon. The Court was divided. The women, who had respect for the princess and little esteem for her enemy, ranged themselves on her side; while nearly all the men went over to Madame de Montbazon; as many as fourteen princes were said to have gone to see her. This glory, with the pleasure of avenging herself on Madame de Longueville, who had married the lover she hoped to make her husband as soon as her present one, who was very old, was dead, were matters that gave much joy to a malicious woman who desired no other reputation than that of making a brilliant appearance and of having many lovers.

But all the abettors of her vanity were soon after compelled to desert her from the fear they had of the young Duc d'Enghien, who, when he heard of the anger of the princess his mother, showed plainly that he meant to support the interests of his sister with much warmth. That fear made them all withdraw quickly, for he alone was worth the fourteen other princes put together. Among this number must be excepted, in the matter of esteem, M. de Nemours who had just married Mademoiselle de Vendôme, an amiable prince and one of great worth.

The queen, who had always liked the Princesse de Condé, was much disposed to favour her; she was mother of the Duc d'Enghien who had just won a battle and was already making himself feared; it was necessary to conciliate her in every way lest the peace of the regency be troubled. These considerations carried the day against all the rest. The thing in itself was compelling, and the right on the side of these persons obliged her to protect the fame of Madame de Longueville, who, besides her birth, had noble qualities, whose reputation had never yet been attacked, and who was very amiable personally.

She was at this time pregnant, and had gone to La Barre, a country-house near Paris, to escape the first annoyance of this affair and to rest. The queen went to see her to comfort her and promise her protection. After the opening speeches of civility, the Princesse de Condé took the queen into an inner room where mother and daughter threw themselves at her feet and asked justice for the outrage Madame de Montbazon had done to them. This they did with such feeling and tears that the queen, having done me the honour to tell me these particulars on her return from Barre, said to me that the princesses had made her pity them and she had promised they should be entirely justified. Which was done with all requisite ceremony, and in a manner that satisfied them.

The Duc de Beaufort, the great supporter of Madame de Montbazon, was beginning to fall from his first favour, which had dazzled every one. In spite of his love for Madame de Montbazon, the queen now favoured the Princesse de Condé and Madame de Longueville. He asked for the admiralship; it was refused him because Cardinal Mazarin had previously induced the queen to give it to the Duc de Brezé, nephew of Cardinal Richelieu. The latter was already in possession and deserved it, but the office would have been taken from him had it not been for the cardinal.

This change in the queen's mind was very displeasing to the opposing cabal, but it keenly affronted the Duc de Beaufort personally. He was amazed to be refused a favour he had expected and which he openly said the queen had promised him. His resentment made him resolve to get rid of the minister, who was beginning to brave him on all occasions; and the minister, seeing plainly how these people wished his downfall, determined to use the anger of the Princesse de Condé to drive them out and ruin them, if he could.

That which proceeded from the malignity of Madame de Montbazon, seeking as much to gratify her private passion as to do harm to those who supported Cardinal Mazarin, served the cardinal usefully in getting rid of his enemies and in annihilating the cabals against him. As he had more intelligence than they, and that sort of cabinet intelligence which can work so many machines, it was easy for him to use these petty events to further his great designs. He was insinuating; he knew how to employ his kindness to his own advantage; he had the art of charming men and of making himself beloved by those to whom fate subjected him; just as he had that of making himself hated and despised by those who were dependent on him, because he had the essential defects of great baseness of soul, avarice, and insincerity. I have heard it said by a person who knew him intimately in Rome (the Maréchale d'Estrées) that when his fortunes were only moderate he was the most agreeable man in the world; which made me conclude that we ought not to feel surprised if he was able to please a great queen and two princes like Monsieur and the Prince de Condé (to whom he at first deferred in all things), while at the same time he made himself disliked by all France with many signs of contempt and hatred.

The queen, to pacify these little disturbances, which she regarded as trifles, ordered that the Duchesse de Montbazon should go to the Princesse de Condé and not only make excuses to her, but also public reparation for what had been said either by her or by those who were at her house. The speech she was to make for this purpose was written out in the little salon at the Louvre on the tablets of Cardinal Mazarin, who was apparently working to pacify the quarrel to the satisfaction of both parties. I was present on the evening that all these important trifles were discussed; and I remember that I wondered in my soul at the follies and the silly preoccupations of that society. I saw the queen in the large cabinet and the Princesse de Condé, excited and terrible, with her, making a crime of lèse majesté out of the affair. Madame de Chevreuse, involved for many reasons in the quarrel of her mother-in-law, was with the cardinal composing the speech that Madame de Montbazon was to make. Over every word parleys were held. The cardinal, playing the go-between, went from one side to the other to settle their differences, as if this peace were necessary to the welfare of France and to his own in particular. I never saw, as I think, such complete mummery; for the thing in itself was nothing at all; such things, and worse, happen every day not only to private persons, princes, and princesses, but to kings and queens. Crowned heads are, in every way, the most exposed to the injustice of evil tongues; the most reasonable among them endeavour not only not to feel it, but not to punish it; they know, and ought to know, that it is an irremediable evil. There is no place in the world where tongues are more licentious or minds more unchained in judging ill and speaking ill of sovereigns than our France.

Every one declaims freely against king and ministers, every one takes upon himself to censure them freely, and no one thinks it improper. But fate chose that in this particular affair the license thus practised should have results of the greatest consequence.

It was finally settled that the criminal duchess should go the next morning to the princess; where she was to say that the talk made about the letter was false, and the invention of malignant minds;[1] and that, for her part, she had never thought it, knowing too well the virtue of Madame de Longueville and the respect which she owed to her. This speech was written out in a little note attached to her fan in order that she might say it word for word to the princess. She did this in the haughtiest and proudest manner possible; making a grimace which seemed to say, "I scoff at all I say."

The Princesse de Condé, after this satisfaction, entreated the queen to permit that she might never be in the same place with the Duchesse de Montbazon, which the queen granted readily. She was glad to do her that kindness, thinking the matter of no great consequence, though difficult to execute. It happened, some days later, that Madame de Chevreuse gave a collation to the queen in Regnard's garden at the end of the Tuileries. The queen, wishing to take the Princesse de Condé with her, assured her that Madame de Montbazon would not be present because she knew she had taken medicine that morning. On this assurance the princess risked accompanying her. But when the queen entered the garden she was told that Madame de Montbazon was already there,

---

[1] I ought to say here that it was known for a certainty that this letter found in Madame de Montbazon's salon was written to Maulevrier by a lady [Madame de Tonquerolles, author of Memoirs of no value], who was very unworthy of being compared to Madame de Longueville. (Author's note.)

assuming to do the honours of the collation as mother-in-law of the lady who gave it.

The queen was much surprised; she had promised security to the princess and was greatly embarrassed at the luckless encounter. The Princesse de Condé made a motion to retire in order not to trouble the fête; but the queen retained her, saying that she herself must remedy the matter inasmuch as it was on her word that the princess came. To do this without an uproar, she sent to beg Madame de Montbazon to pretend to be taken ill and to withdraw, in order to relieve her from the embarrassment in which she found herself.

But that lady, knowing the cause of her little banishment, would not consent to flee before her enemy, and was stupid enough to refuse this compliance to one to whom she owed much more. The queen was offended at such resistance; she would not allow the Princesse de Condé to go away alone, but she herself, declining the collation and the promenade, returned to the Louvre, much irritated at the little respect Madame de Montbazon had shown to her. As kings are usually far above those who offend them, they can easily avenge themselves. The next day the queen sent a command to Madame de Montbazon to absent herself from Court, and to go to one of her country-houses. This she did at once, to the great regret of her friends, and even to that of the Duc d'Orléans, who, having loved her in former days, still remembered that fact. He could offer no remedy, however, for the queen was angry. She had reason to be so, and her minister thought it expedient, even more for his own interests than because of the affront offered to her.

This dismissal was immediately followed by that of the Duc de Beaufort and of the whole troop of "the Importants." The intimacy he had with the exiled duchess, the anger he showed in finding that the cardinal had taken his favour from him, the hatred that the Prince de Condé, the princess, and Madame de Longueville felt against the whole cabal, but above all, the necessity which the cardinal felt to ruin him, led finally to his disgrace, caused the disaster of his life, and strangled the great hopes he had conceived, with some reason, of his future fortunes. He was unlucky enough to be unable to accommodate himself to the inclinations of the queen, who had always shown much friendship and confidence in him. In fact it was that which spoilt him; wishing to possess that favour for himself alone, he could not endure to share it with another, to fail towards those he desired to place in the first rank, or to submit himself to the authority of a foreigner who was no friend to him. Consequently, being allied to those now out of favour, he was dragged down by them; and, by his fate and that of others, he fell, and found himself reduced to a most deplorable condition.

He was suddenly accused of intending to assassinate Cardinal Mazarin, and the queen became convinced that he had twice thought of doing so. What I know of my own knowledge is that certain friends of the Duc de Beaufort did not altogether deny it to me; and it is true that on the morrow of that day the rumour was strong at Court that an intention existed to murder Cardinal Mazarin. On this rumour, a great many persons came to the Louvre; and the queen seemed to me very ill-pleased with the Duc de Beaufort and the whole cabal of " the Importants." She said to me, when I went up to her and asked the cause of the tumult, —

" You will see before twice twenty-four hours go by how I avenge myself for the ill-turns these evil friends have done me."

As I was then without interests and without passion, and was by nature rather discreet, I kept in my own heart, very secretly, what the queen had done me the honour to tell me, and waited, very attentive to observe and see the result of the two days of which the queen had notified me. Never will the memory of those few words be effaced from my mind. I saw at that moment by the fire that blazed in the eyes of the queen, and by the things that actually happened on the morrow and even the same night, what a royal personage is when angry and able to do whatever she wills.

That same evening the Duc de Beaufort, as he returned from hunting, met, on entering the Louvre, Madame de Guise, and Madame de Vendôme, his mother, with Madame de Nemours, his sister, who had been with the queen all day. They had heard the rumour of assassination and had seen the emotion on the face of the queen. For this reason they did all they could to prevent the duke from going up to her, telling him that his friends were of opinion that he ought to absent himself for a few days and see what would happen. But he, not disturbed, continued his way, and replied to them, what the Duc de Guise had said before he was killed, "They will not dare." He was bold, and still intoxicated with the belief of his favour. He had seen the queen in the morning, or on the evening of the preceding day, when she spoke to him with her usual sweetness and familiarity, so that he never imagined that his fate could change so readily. He therefore entered the queen's presence in this perfect security.

He found her in the great cabinet of the Louvre, where she received him amiably, and asked him a few questions about the hunt, as if she had no other thought in her mind. She had learned to dissimulate from the late king, her husband, who had practised that ugly virtue with more per-

fection than any other prince in the world. But finally,
after fulfilling with fine acting all that policy required of
her, and the cardinal having entered during this suave conversation, the queen rose, told the cardinal to follow her,
and went, as if to hold the little council, into her own room.
The Duc de Beaufort then, intending to leave by the little
cabinet, found there Guitaut, captain of the queen's guards,
who arrested him and commanded him in the name of the
king and queen to follow him. The prince, without seeming
astonished, looked at him fixedly, and said, " Yes, I am
willing; but it is, I acknowledge, rather strange." Then
turning to Madame de Chevreuse and Madame de Hautefort,
who were in the room and conversing together, he said to
them, " Mesdames, you see that the queen has ordered my
arrest."

No doubt they were much surprised by the affair and
pained by it, for they were friends of his; as for him, I
think that vexation and anger filled his soul completely.
He never imagined that after the service he had rendered
the queen in her misfortunes she could ever resolve on
treating him so ill. He was not a man disillusioned of the
things of this world, nor one who could make the solid judgment that a reasoning mind would have made; he was a
man of intelligence in many things, but strongly attached to
the false glory that goes with favour; consequently, he was
ill-pleased to find himself deceived and his finest hopes betrayed; but as he was a man of courage, he put a good face
on his misfortune.

The next day, very early, the prisoner was taken to the
forest of Vincennes. They gave him one of the king's valets
to serve him, and a cook. His friends complained that
his own servants were not given to him, but the queen, to
whom I spoke of it at their request, assured me it was not

the custom.   Commands were sent to M. and Madame de
Vendôme, and M. de Mercœur, elder brother of the Duc de
Beaufort, and other of "the Importants" to leave Paris instantly, on which they retired to their country-places.   M. de
Vendôme at first excused himself on the ground of being
ill; but to hasten his departure and make it more comfort-
able, the queen sent him her own litter.

The downfall of the Duc de Beaufort was followed by
that of the Bishop of Beauvais, who could not hold out
against a competitor as powerful as Cardinal Mazarin.   The
hat which had been asked for him was countermanded.
He seemed to quit the Court without regret, and went to
find in his diocese of Beauvais a better master than the best
and greatest kings of this world can ever be; and there he
lived a saintly life for the rest of his days.   This was a matter of which one cannot speak without blaming the queen,
because she might have made the bishop a cardinal without
keeping him as minister.   He was a worthy man, very pious
and very peaceable; so that he could have lived at her
Court beside her, without suspicion that his intrigues would
ever trouble the State.   He deserved much from her (she
even owed him a great deal of money), and was very faithful to her.   The money, no doubt, was paid, but his fidelity,
which was worth more than the wealth of the Indies, was
very ill rewarded.

Madame de Chevreuse, disgusted at seeing all her friends
exiled and ill-treated and her own influence lessening day
by day, complained to the queen of the little consideration
she showed to her old servants.   The queen requested her
not to interfere, but to leave her to govern the State and
choose what minister she pleased and manage her affairs in
her own way.   She advised her, as she did me the honour to
tell me, to live pleasantly in France, not to mix herself in

any intrigue, but to enjoy under her regency the peace she had never had in the days of the late king. She represented to her that it was time to find pleasure in retreat and to regulate her life on thoughts of the other world. She told her that she promised her her friendship on that condition; but, that if she chose to trouble the Court and meddle in matters in which she forbade her to take part, it would force her, the queen, to send her away, and that she could promise her no other favour than that of being the last person dismissed.

Madame de Chevreuse did not take these remonstrances and counsels in the spirit that is practised in convents; she did not believe that charity and a care for her salvation were their principal motive. It is not in a Court that such merchandise is sold in good faith; nor is it there received with humility. Thoughts of retreat from the world do not enter hearts from human motives; on the contrary, nothing makes minds so rebellious as preachments against their grain. This one had precisely that effect; and as the queen received no satisfaction from her answer or her conduct, the displeasure increased on her side, and Madame de Chevreuse, aware that the good-will of the queen was lessening towards her every day, was not surprised when at last she received an order to go to Tours or to one of her country-houses.

She left the Court and was several days in her own house; but, unable to stay quietly in retreat, she started in disguise, with Mademoiselle de Chevreuse, her daughter, intending to go to England, but was taken ill and remained in the island of Guernsey, where she suffered much misery. From there she went to Flanders, where the poor Duc de Lorraine, banished as he was, received her most kindly for the second time, and assisted her much. Cardinal Mazarin said, to excuse himself for her dismissal, that she had too much love for Spain, and wanted so urgently to have peace made for the advantage of Spaniards that he could never acquire her friendship.

I have heard it said, by those who knew her intimately that no one ever understood so well the interests of all princes, or talked of them better, or had more capacity to disentangle great affairs; but it never seemed to me from her conduct that her ideas were as great as her reputation. As she had intelligence and experience among foreigners it is to be believed, without saying too much in her favour, that she may have been capable of giving advice as to the peace; but we may also say of her with justice that those who examined what seemed good in her found many defects. She was vague in speech, and much occupied by chimeras which her inclination for intrigue suggested to her. It is also to be presumed that her judgments were not always regulated by reason, but that her passions contributed to form them. The queen and her minister had some cause therefore to fear her. I heard her say of herself (one day when I was praising her for having played a part in all the great affairs which had happened in Europe) that ambition had never touched her heart, and that pleasure alone had led her; that is to say, she had been interested in the affairs of the world solely in relation to those she loved.

In the person of Madame de Hautefort we shall now [1644] see the fate of the whole group of "the Importants" accomplished. The queen had quitted the Louvre, where her apartment did not please her, and had taken up her abode in the Palais-Royal, which Cardinal Richelieu when dying had bequeathed to the late king. In the beginning of her residence there she was very ill with a dreadful jaundice, considered by the doctors to come solely from vexations and sadness. The vexations she received from the many complaints made against her government troubled her; the management of public affairs brought her much embarrassment; and the pain she felt in being forced to cause unhappiness made so great an impression on her mind that her body, sharing these sufferings, felt them too much. Her sadness being dissipated after a while, and her illness also, she determined to think of nothing but enjoying the rest she gave herself by laying upon her minister the cares and the business of the State, believing that henceforth she would be as happy as she was powerful.

Madame de Hautefort, who had never been able to conquer the hatred she felt for Cardinal Mazarin, was the only person who now troubled the calm of the queen's soul, not only because she could not endure the minister, but because her self-sufficient mind, turning to piety, began to take up sentiments that made her stern, rather annoying, and too critical. All that the queen did displeased her; and as she still retained something of her old familiarity with her, she was constantly saying rough things and showing plainly that she did not approve of her conduct in any way. The queen could not endure this behaviour, and the cardinal, who desired the dismissal of the lady, did not fail to embitter the queen's mind against her. So that her lectures on generosity were considered to be tacit reproaches; and such conduct, lacking all prudence, caused her finally to lose the good graces of one who, up to that time, had treated her as a dear friend.

One day in the year 1644, having, as usual, had the honour of passing the evening with the queen up to midnight, we left Madame de Hautefort talking with the princess in perfect freedom and with the pleasure that her presence and the favour she did us in allowing us to be

with her always gave us.   The queen was just about to go
to bed and had only her last prayer to say when we left her
and retired, Mademoiselle de Beaumont, the Commander
de Jars, my sister, and myself.   At this moment Madame
de Hautefort, always thinking of doing good, supported
(while they were removing the queen's shoes and stockings)
the application of one of her women who spoke in favour
of an old gentleman, long her servant, who needed some
favour.   Madame de Hautefort, not finding the queen very
willing to help him, said, making her meaning plain by
disdainful smiles, that she ought not to forget her old
servants.

The queen, who was waiting for an occasion to dismiss
her, contrary to her usual gentleness took fire at this, and
said, much displeased and very angry, that she was tired
of her reprimands and very much dissatisfied with the
manner in which she behaved to her.   As she said those
important words she threw herself into her bed and ordered
her to close the curtains and say no more to her.   Madame
de Hautefort, astounded at this thunderbolt, fell upon her
knees and, clasping her hands, called God to witness her
innocence and the sincerity of her intentions, protesting
to the queen that she believed she had never failed in
serving her, or in her duty to her.   She went to her room
after that, deeply moved by the incident, and I may say
much afflicted.   The next day the queen sent her word
to leave the palace and take with her her sister, Mademoiselle d'Escars, who had always been in service with the
queen.

I was never more astonished than when I heard in the
morning, at my waking, this history of what had happened
in the short time after we had left Madame de Hautefort
with the queen, which had brought such results upon her.

It may be said in her defence that her good intentions
made her excusable; but the best things are on a level
with the worst when they are not wisely done, and virtue
taken askew has often caused as much evil as its contrary.
As I respected hers, though I saw its imprudence, I went
to see her in her chamber. She seemed to me fairly strong
under her misfortune — if misfortune it is to leave a Court.
After a conversation of an hour, during which she justified
herself to me as best she could, I went to find the queen, to
whom I related the visit I had just paid, excusing the lady
with as much judgment as possible.

The queen, with feeling, did me the honour to say that
I was wrong not to enter into her just reasons for complaint; that I hardly knew Madame de Hautefort and
already my kindness made me excuse her, though I ought
to see very plainly that she was to blame. Besides these
reproaches to me, she said to Beringhen, shortly after, that
she was sorry to see me so quickly engage in friendship
with Madame de Hautefort, having but lately returned
to Court, and that I ought to have no better friend than
herself.

This complaint was very kind, coming from a great queen
who certainly, if I may dare to say so, was my best friend
and the one I loved most truly. But as the heart cannot
be seen, the queen was for some time rather cold to me,
and that did me some harm with the minister, who believed
I was against his interests because I seemed to take the
part of a dismissed person who was so opposed to him.
Nevertheless, I had entered no cabal, my intentions were
upright; pity alone had made me act.

I did not refrain from returning that evening to Madame
de Hautefort, who, from having wished to seem strong,
had so restrained her grief and weakness within her heart

that she nearly died of them. Her illness was so violent that she could not leave her room, in spite of the commands she had received. We found her — Commander de Jars, Mlle. de Beaumont, my sister, and myself — in a pitiable state. Her heart, which had not sighed all day, renouncing at last the pride with which she strove to fill it, was now so choked, so wrung, so abandoned to her resentment that I can truly say I never saw anything like it. She sobbed in such a manner that it was easy to see she had much loved the queen, that her dismissal was hard to bear, and that she had not foreseen it.

We consoled her as best we could; and heartily wished that the queen was capable of softening, and forgiving her. But the next day, being rather better, and relieved by two bleedings which they had to give her during the night, she left the Palais-Royal to the regret of every one. For, as disgrace without wrong-doing has this property, that it kills envy in the souls of enemies and moves them readily from hatred to pity, so it increases friendship in friends who are sufficiently honourable persons to love generosity and to excuse faults that result from a virtue so remarkable.

This illustrious unfortunate shut herself up at first in a convent, where she remained some time. Then she left it and lived in great retirement, seeing only her nearest friends. Some years later she married very highly and became a duchess and maréchale of France, having wedded M. de Schomberg, a man sufficiently honourable to prefer merit to favour. I dared no longer go to see her, because when I spoke of her to the queen and asked, as a favour, that she would not think it ill if I went, she answered coldly that I was free, and could do as I wished. I told her, kissing her hand, that I should never wish to do anything that displeased her; and owing all to her and nothing to Madame

de Hautefort but civility and esteem, I pledged myself not
to see her again.   The Commander de Jars, who was much
more her friend than I was, and never failed in heart to
his friends, did as I did, and saw her no more until after
her marriage.

IV.

1644 — 1645.

AT the beginning of the regency the queen had established a council of conscience, at which were decided all matters concerning benefices, the choice of bishops and abbés, and the distribution of pensions that she wished to give to the glory of God and the advantage of religion. This council existed as long as the minister, seeing his authority thwarted, remained under some restraint; but as soon as he had acquired complete dominion over the queen's mind, the council of conscience went off in smoke; he wished to dispose as he pleased, without any contradiction, of the benefices as of everything else, in order that those to whom the queen gave them should be friends of his, without caring much whether they were true servants of God, saying that he supposed all priests were that.

This council consequently served only to exclude those he did not wish to favour; and a few years later it was abolished altogether because Père Vincent [Saint-Vincent de Paul] who was at its head, being a man of single mind, very devout and pious, who had never dreamed of winning the good graces of the Court people, whose manners and ways he knew not, was easily made, in spite of the queen's esteem for him, the ridicule of the Court; for it is almost impossible that humility, penitence, and gospel simplicity should accord with the ambition, vanity, and self-interest that reign there. She who had placed him in that position would gladly have maintained him. This is why she still had several long conversations with him on the scruples which continued in her mind; but she lacked firmness on this occasion, and finally let things go as it pleased her minister, not thinking herself as able as he, or as much so as she really was in many matters; which made it easy for him to persuade her to do what he chose, and to bring her round, after some resistance, to things he had resolved upon.

I know nevertheless that, in the choice of bishops especially, she had great pain in yielding, and much more when she recognized that she had followed his advice too easily in these important matters, which she did not always do, and never without privately consulting Père Vincent, as long as he lived, or others whom she thought men of worth. But she was sometimes cruelly deceived by the false virtue of those who sought the prelacy, for whom the pious persons on whom she relied to examine them answered perhaps too lightly. However, in spite of the indifference her minister seemed to show on this subject, God so favoured this princess that the greater number of those who were raised to that dignity during her regency did their duty and fulfilled their functions with exemplary sanctity.

The queen had appointed to the finances the president de Bailleul, a good man and a judge of great integrity, but too tame and gentle for that office, where justice is not the chief necessary quality. It was important for Cardinal Mazarin to change him for some one less precise but much harsher than he. He did not wish to turn him out at once, but he put d'Emery under him as controller-general with power attached to that office, so that little by little he could install as superintendent of finances a man who was his own creature and over whom he had absolute control, — which happened not long after.

At the same time the queen, who desired to remove Chavigny from the council, where the cardinal was not over pleased to have him exercise the office of secretary of state for foreign affairs (for which he was very capable and through which, having the management of the great matters that came before it, he became necessarily a part of the ministry), ordered him to resign and sell his office to the Comte de Brienne, who would then sell the one he held in the king's household to Duplessis-Guénégaud.   As the queen respected de Brienne not only for his integrity but also on account of her friendship for his wife, she gave him two hundred thousand francs towards paying for the office, which was sold to him for five hundred thousand.

The cardinal having no longer any one in the council to cause him jealousy, the Comte de Brienne making no difficulty in signing all the despatches they sent to him, nothing remained but the office of secretary of state for war, then held by des Noyers who had been dismissed by the late king.   This the minister made him give in commission to Le Tellier,[1] whom he had known in Italy, and who soon had the full title by the death of des Noyers.   He has since never lacked offices, having been very important throughout our period, much liked by the queen, and well regarded by the minister; and we shall see him play his part in very extraordinary matters.   In this way the cardinal had the gratification of filling for himself the offices of the four secretaries of state, the titular secretaries being merely his clerks.

After relating thus the state of the Court I think it is right to say something personal of the queen.   She waked usually between ten and eleven o'clock, on days of devotion at nine, and she always made a long prayer before calling

---

[1] Michel Le Tellier, father of the Marquis de Louvois.

those who slept near her. As soon as her waking was announced her principal officers came to pay their court to her, and often other persons entered, especially certain ladies who came to tell her of alms and charities to be done in Paris, in all France, and even in foreign parts. Her liberalities at all times were great, extended usually to whatever concerned piety, and her attention to all claims on her protection and justice never relaxed.

Men were not excluded from her audiences. During these early hours she gave them to several, entering into the business they brought before her according as she deemed it necessary. The king never missed, nor did Monsieur, coming to see her in the morning; not leaving her again till they went to bed, except for their meals and their games, — their youth not permitting them to eat with her, as they did later.

After half an hour's conversation, and those who desired to speak with her having had their audience, she rose, put on a dressing-gown, and, after making a second prayer, ate her breakfast with great appetite. Her breakfast was always good, for her health was admirable. After her bouillon she was served with cutlets, sausages, and boiled bread. Usually she ate a little of all, and dined on no less. Then she took her chemise, which the king gave her, kissing her tenderly ; and this custom lasted a long time. After putting on her petticoat, she took a wrapper and a black *hongreline*, and in that state she heard mass very devoutly ; and that sacred action ended, she returned to her toilet. At this there was unparalleled pleasure in seeing her do her hair and dress herself. She was skilful, and her beautiful hands thus employed were the admiration of those who saw them. She had the handsomest hair in the world, of a light chestnut, very long and in great quantity, which she

preserved for a long time, years having no power to destroy
its beauty. She dressed with care and the choiceness per-
missible to those who desire to look well without luxury,
without gold or silver or paint or any extravagant fashion.
It was nevertheless easy to see, in spite of the modesty of
her clothes, that she could be influenced by a little vanity.

After the death of the late king she ceased to wear rouge,
which increased the whiteness and nicety of her skin.
Instead of diminishing her beauty, this made it the more
esteemed, and public approbation soon obliged all ladies to
follow her example. She took at this time a habit of keeping her room now and then for a day or two to rest, and see
only such persons as were most familiar with her and least
likely to importune her. On other days she readily gave
audience to all who asked for it, whether on general business or on private matters. As she had good sense and good
judgment she satisfied all by her answers, given with kindness; and those who loved her could have wished that she
had always acted by her own ideas — as she at first intended,
to avoid the blame she saw given to the late king for abandoning his authority to Cardinal Richelieu, often saying at
that time to her servants that she should never do likewise.
But, unhappily for those who were about her, her resolutions
were weakened by a desire for repose, and by the trouble she
found in the multiplicity of business affairs inseparable from
the government of a great kingdom. In course of time, as
she became more lazy, she learned by experience that God
has not placed kings on thrones to do nothing, but to endure some at least of the miseries which are attached to all
sorts and conditions of life.

The queen did not often dine in public served by her
officers, but nearly always in her little cabinet served by
her women. The king and Monsieur kept her company

and were seldom absent. After her dinner she retired to her own room to be a short time alone; often giving an hour to God in devout reading, which she did in her oratory. After which she held her "circle," or else she went out, either to see nuns or pay her devotions; and on returning she gave some time to the princesses and ladies of quality who came to pay their court to her.

After the Duc d'Orléans returned to Court he came daily to see her. The Prince de Condé and the Duc d'Enghien also came occasionally. But as, at the beginning of the regency, they were not yet in the little secret council, as they were later, they retired early. The Duc d'Orléans stayed late, and Cardinal Mazarin never missed this fine evening hour, during which the conversation went on publicly between the queen, the princes, and the minister. At this period, therefore, the Court was a very large one. After this the queen retired to her private rooms. The Duc d'Orléans then had a private interview and returned to the Luxembourg, leaving Cardinal Mazarin alone with the queen. The minister stayed sometimes an hour, sometimes more. The doors of the rooms remained open after the departure of the Duc d'Orléans, and the Court people, assembled in the little chamber of the Palais-Royal adjoining the cabinet, remained there talking until the "little council" was over. When it ended the queen, shortly after, bade good-night to all who composed what is called the great world. The crowd of great seigneurs and courtiers remained in the grand cabinet, and it was there that took place, no doubt, all that gallantry and passionate intrigues can produce. A few men, with four or five persons of our sex, had the honour of remaining with the queen at all hours when she was in private.

When she had bid good-night, and Cardinal Mazarin had

left her, she entered her oratory and remained a full hour in prayer; after which she came out to supper at eleven o'clock. Her supper finished, we ate the rest of it, without order or ceremony, using, for all convenience, her napkin and the remains of her bread; and although this meal was ill-arranged, it was not disagreeable, through the quality of the persons present, and because of the jests and the conversation of the queen, who told us good things and laughed much because the women who served her, and who were not the most polite in the world, tried to rob us of all they could to keep it for the morrow. After this feast we followed her into her cabinet, where a gay and lively conversation continued till midnight or one o'clock; and then, after she was undressed, and often when she was in bed and ready to go to sleep, we left her to do likewise.

We followed this life punctually for several years, even during the little journeys to Fontainebleau and Saint-Germain, until the civil war and the siege of Paris, when the troubles became so great as to interrupt its system — I mean as regards our attendance, but not as regards the queen, for she was the most regular person in the world in all her habits of life. She held a council Mondays and Thursdays, and on those days she was beset by crowds of people. She fasted on all appointed days and, in spite of her appetite, all through Lent. When in Paris, she went every Saturday to mass at Notre-Dame, and usually spent the remainder of that day in resting; taking the greatest pleasure in getting away from the crowd that surrounded her, but which, towards the last, grew accustomed not to importune her as much then as on other days. She took the communion regularly on Sundays and feast-days. On the evening before the great feasts she went to sleep at the Val-de-Grâce, where she resolved to build a new monastery, finer than the one already there, and to add to it a church worthy of a queen, mother of a great king. She gave this in charge of Tubœuf. There she frequently remained several days, retired from the world, taking pleasure in conversations with the nuns. She sought the most saintly, accommodating herself to those who had but medium merit; but whenever they reached her esteem she honoured them with friendship. Good sermons from the sternest preachers were those that pleased her most. She went sometimes, but rarely, to visit the prisons disguised as a servant, and, to my knowledge, she one day followed the Princesse de Condé for that purpose. She had a waiting-maid, a pious and devout woman, who in the first years of her regency was shut up with her every evening in her oratory. The whole duty of that person was to inform the queen of the daily needs, public and private, of the poor, and to receive from her the money to relieve them. She was always touched by things she thought her duty. I have seen her during the war which happened later, when she had no money, sell her diamond ear-rings (which she had had very curiously made) to give money to those who were suffering by it.

The queen had not yet renounced all the pleasures she had formerly liked and which she thought innocent. Her amusements were all moderate; she loved nothing ardently. She once liked balls, but had lost the liking with her youth, and her long residence at Saint-Germain had accustomed her to do without such things. But she went to the theatre half-hidden behind one of us, whom she made to sit forward in the box, not willing, during her mourning, to appear publicly in the place she would have occupied in other days. This amusement was not disagreeable to her. Corneille, the illustrious poet of our epoch, had enriched the stage with noble plays, the moral of which could serve as a lesson

to correct the unruliness of human passions, and among the
vain and dangerous occupations of the Court this at least
was not among the worst.

The queen was grave and discreet in all her ways of acting and speaking; she was judicious and very secret as to
the confidences her familiar servants ventured to make to
her. She was liberal by her own impulse; and what she
gave she gave with a good grace; but she often failed to
give for want of reflection, and it was necessary to employ
too much help to obtain her benefits. This defect, which
was not in her heart nor in her will, came from her permitting insensibly her resolutions to be formed by the will
of others whose advice she respected, and her attendants
suffered in consequence. She gave in profusion to certain
persons who had the power to persuade her in their favour;
persons who by constant application to their own fortune
found means to make it.

She did not like to read, and knew very little; but she
had intelligence, and an easy, accommodating, and agreeable mind. Her conversation was serious and free both;
those she esteemed found great charms in her because she
was secret, and always glad to enter into the feelings and
interests of those who opened their hearts to her; and this
good treatment made a great impression on the souls of
those who loved her. I have spoken elsewhere of her
beauty; I shall only say here that, being agreeable in person, gentle and polite in her actions, and familiar with
those who had the honour to approach her, she had only to
follow her natural inclinations and show herself as she
really was, to please every one. But, in spite of her virtuous
inclinations, it was easy for the cardinal, making use of
"reasons of State," to change her feelings and make her
capable of doing harsh things to those she was accustomed

to treat well. In the beginning of her regency she was much praised for her kindness, and great hopes were founded on its effects. But when she was seen to dismiss those she had formerly relied on she was loudly condemned. Many publications were issued to decry a goodness which the people had believed in, and with reason. But this belief was held for some time in the rank of things doubtful by those who were now not prosperous enough to be content.

At the end of the year from the king's death [May, 1644], she quitted her deep mourning, which had made her seem beautiful, and the age of forty, so dreadful to our sex, did not prevent her from being still agreeable. She had a freshness and plumpness which placed her in the ranks of the handsomest women of her kingdom, and we saw her, as time went on, increase in years without losing these advantages.

At the beginning of this year [1644] preparations were made for war. The Duc d'Orléans went to command the army of Flanders, and the Duc d'Enghien [the great Condé], that of Germany. We shall see the first conquer several fortresses, and the second defeat the enemy with glory and renown.

President Barillon and several others of the principal parliament leaders were not satisfied because they were less considered than they hoped to be. On the first occasion that offered for a mutiny they took it; they began by complaining that the chancellor quashed in the council all the decrees of the parliament, and they loudly complained of their president, who seemed to consent with too much compliance. They assembled and made speeches against the royal authority, censured all things, and made the Court apprehensive of coming disorders and quarrels.

The day after this assembly [May 22, 1644], a command was sent to President Barillon, President Gayant, and others

of the cabal to retire.   President Barillon was a worthy man
and much respected; he had served the queen in the parliament, where he had much influence and reputation.   The
" Importants " were his friends; he and they had been servitors of the queen, and were so no longer.   He was sent to
Pignerol, to the great displeasure of many worthy persons,
and he died there a year later regretted by every one.   I
have heard the queen say that during the life of the late
king she had had no servant more faithful than this president, but that as soon as she was regent he abandoned her
and disapproved of all her actions.

Sometime after this dismissal, others of the parliament,
rebelling at the rigour they declared had been shown to
their company, held several assemblies.   They determined
to see the queen and complain of the wrong she had done
them, and they resolved to go to her without asking for an
audience.   At this time, though Monsieur had not yet
started for the army, he was at one of his country-houses,
and Cardinal Mazarin had gone to make a little journey and
meet Cardinal de Valençay, who was coming from Rome
but was forbidden to enter Paris.

The queen was in bed, alone in the Palais-Royal; I had
the honour of being with her.   They came to tell her that
the parliament was coming in a body, on foot, to make remonstrances about the affair of President Barillon.   It was
easy to see that the object of this assembly was to stir up
the people; and the persons who first gave notice of their
coming seemed to me frightened.   The queen, who had a
firm soul and was not easily startled, showed no uneasiness.
She sent for President de Bailleul, superintendent of
finances, rather liked in his corps; and, not willing to close
the doors as some advised, she ordered the parliament to be
received under the arcade which separated the two arches.

There she sent them word by the captain of her guards and the superintendent that she did not think it right they should come to her without her permission and without asking for an audience; that they must now return whence they started, for, having taken medicine, she could not see them.

To their shame they had to do as she commanded; and the queen laughed at me because these old dotards had frightened me so much that I advised her to send for the Maréchal de Gramont, major of her regiment of guards, so as to have some defenders if the populace should take part in the affair. A few days later an audience was granted on their demand; and their harangues, which demanded the release of President Barillon, were not listened to as regarded him, but other points of no great weight were granted. After this first commotion, the parliament remained for some time rather peaceable, ruminating their designs to infringe on the royal authority, which appeared a few years later.

When summer weather invited the princes to leave the pleasures of the Court for the toils of wars, the queen thought it time to seek cool airs out of Paris. She wished to pass the great heat at Ruel with the Duchesse d'Aiguillon. That house is very convenient through its vicinity to Paris, and very agreeable from the beauty of its gardens and the number of its streams, which are very natural. The queen took pleasure in the place, where her enemy Cardinal Richelieu had so long received the adoration of all France. It was not from that motive, however, that she chose it; she had too noble a soul to wish to trouble the repose of the dead by so petty a triumph. It was, on the contrary, to oblige his niece, the Duchesse d'Aiguillon, and give her marks of royal protection against the Prince de Condé, with whom she had great differences to settle. It is to be supposed, however, that the queen, acting from generosity, had a certain joy in finding herself able to do good by her mere presence to those whom she believed had done her much evil. She took great pleasure in her evening walks during the time she was in this delightful place, and in all the innocent pleasures that its beauty and convenience afforded. But it pleased the people of Paris to rise against certain taxes which were about to be placed on houses, so that the king and herself departed at the end of six weeks in great haste to pacify them, and the whole Court followed them very willingly to Paris.

One day during the queen's stay at Ruel, as she was driving in a calèche through the gardens she noticed Voiture, walking along in a revery. That man had wit, and by the charm of his conversation he was the amusement of the *ruelles* of those ladies who make it their boast to receive the best company. The queen, to please the Princesse de Condé who was seated beside her, asked him what he was thinking of. Voiture, without much reflection, made some burlesque verses in answer to the queen, which were amusing and bold. She was not offended by the jest; in fact, she thought the verses pretty, and kept them for a long time in her room. She did me the honour to give them to me afterwards, and, from the things I have already told about her life, it is easy to understand them. They were as follows: —

> " I 'm thinking how that destiny
> After so many unjust ills,
> Has justly come to crown you
> With splendour, honours, glory,
> But that you were *plus heureuse*
> As you were in other days,
> When — I 'll not say *amoureuse*
> Though my rhyme demands it.

"I 'm thinking, too, how this poor Love,
 Who always lent you arms,
 Is banished from your Court
 With arrows, bow, and charms;
 And what then will it profit me
 To spend my life beside you,
 If you can choose to treat so ill
 Those who have so well served you.

"I 'm thinking (for we poets
 Do think extravagantly)
 Of what, in your present mood,
 You would do if here before you,
 In this place and at this moment,
 Came the Duke of Buckingham;
 Which would be the worst dismissed,
 The duke or Father Vincent."

I must end this trip to Ruel with this trifle, and return to Paris to resume the gravity and seriousness required for that great city. One of our kings [Henri III.] has said that the head of this kingdom was always too big; that it was full of humours injurious to the rest of its members, and that a bleeding now and then was necessary. This time, however, the presence of the king and queen pacified everything; it was only a little blaze of straw, which did not in any way prevent the Court from enjoying in peace the comforts and pleasures that are ever to be found in that agreeable region.

Pope Urban VIII. died in July, 1644. He had held the Holy See for many years with the reputation of an able man and a great politician. The Cardinals Barberini, his nephews, who were protectors of France, were left masters of the election of his successor. Several partisans of Spain who sought to be raised to that dignity were opposed, particularly the Cardinal Pamphilo, who seemed to have more claim to it than any other; but finally, the king did not prevail; the Barberinis served France very ill on this occasion.

In this same month, the Queen of England, whom her rebellious people had driven into a little corner of her kingdom to give birth to her last child, was forced, only seventeen days later, to escape to France to avoid what she had to fear from the hatred of her subjects, who were at open war with their king, and wished to take her prisoner, perhaps to begin on her the lack of respect they owed to royalty. This princess, after being the most fortunate and most opulent of all the queens of Europe, with three crowns upon her head, was reduced to such a state that in order to lie-in it was necessary that our queen should send her Madame Peronne, her own midwife, and even the slightest articles that were necessary to her condition.

She had been taken to Oxford by the king her husband, who left her there; but having reason to fear that his enemies would besiege her, she started hastily for Exeter, where she gave birth to her child in the poverty I have just represented. She was ill with a serious malady which preceded her pregnancy, and in no state to help her husband. In this extremity she was forced to take shelter from the dangers with which her person and health were threatened. She wished to come to her native country, to drink the waters at Bourbon and find safety for her life which was in danger.

In France she was received with joy. The populace, regarding her as the sister, daughter, and aunt of their kings, respected her; the queen was delighted to help her in her troubles and to soften them as much as she could; although she had never been well-treated by her, who had, on the contrary, caused her many griefs while still in France. For the princess, being supported by the queen-mother [Marie

Van Dyck

Henrietta Maria
Queen of England

de' Medici] who did not like the queen, did her those little malicious things which are great ills to those who receive them at certain times, but are not capable of altering friendship as soon as they are things of the past. The King of England had contributed much to soften these dislikes; for after his marriage he took pleasure in all opportunities of obliging our queen, particularly in the person of Madame de Chevreuse during her first exile. So that when the Queen of England arrived in France, the queen had a fine occasion to return in person to that afflicted princess all that she owed to the King of England; and the two princesses having changed in feeling, the one was truly glad to oblige the other, and she who was thus well received and well treated showed the greatest gratitude.

The Queen of England remained at Bourbon three months endeavouring to recover her health, and our queen offered all that depended on the king and herself. I had the honour of approaching this unhappy princess familiarly, and I heard from her the beginning and end of their misfortunes, for she did me the honour to relate them to me in that solitary place, where peace and rest reigned without disturbance. I left her at Bourbon, where the queen, not contenting herself with the offers she had made to her, which were only compliments, sent her all the money necessary for her subsistence, also great sums which she conveyed to the king her husband. But as that unhappy prince, who was only too good, was destined to serve as a formidable warning to all kings of the weakness of their power, and of the pleasure Fortune sometimes takes in playing with crowns and overthrowing the best-established thrones, taking them and returning them at her caprice, all was useless to him.

As the memory of King Henri IV. is dear to Frenchmen, the Queen of England, his granddaughter, was constantly fol-

lowed by a great crowd of people running to see her. She
was very ill and much changed; her misfortunes had given
her such sadness, and her mind was so filled with her sorrows, that she wept continually, which shows what the sufferings of soul and body can do, for by nature this princess was
gay and talked pleasantly. But now, in the grievous state
to which she was reduced, she said one day to the great
physician Mayerne, who attended her, that she felt her mind
weakening, and feared that she might become crazy. To which,
as she told me, he answered brusquely, " You need not fear
it, madame, for you are that already." She certainly found
some remedy for her bodily ills in France, her native country, the air and the baths of which were beneficial to her,
but it needed much time to soften her other woes. I shall
tell elsewhere how she seemed to us when we saw her at
Court.

The campaign of the Duc d' Enghien increased his reputation to a dazzling glory, and he fought a battle at Fribourg
which will surely hold a great place in history; but as
chance willed that I did not remark its particulars, and
do not find them in my notes, I shall say no more about it.

Élisabeth of France, Queen of Spain, died at the beginning of this winter, a worthy daughter of Henri le Grand,
and most deserving of the esteem that Europe felt for her.
She was regretted throughout its whole extent, and her
people, who felt a great admiration for her, were afflicted.
The king, her husband, had not always loved her as she
deserved, because he was too gallant, not to say worse. But
before she died he was beginning to recognize her noble
qualities and her capacity. He left her for a time to govern
his kingdom, which she did with much glory, so that he regretted her greatly. I have heard my late mother (who had
the honour to know her on her return from Spain and before

the princess left France) say that she was beautiful and agreeable, and glad of the prospect of being queen of so grand a kingdom. She lived there some years pleasantly. The Prince of Spain was handsome and well-made, and they loved each other. It is even said that the king her father-in-law, finding her beautiful, put off joining them, with a notion of taking her for himself. I have since been told that this was only true in that he loved her as his daughter, and very tenderly. But the prince her husband, after he became king [Philip IV.] had so many mistresses of all kinds that, from the jealousy she had reason to feel, her whole life became a torture as keen as it was long and sorrowful. She had reason to complain, but her complaints were always useless, and though she was as chaste as he was voluptuous, the customs of Spain were rigorous against her.[1]

The queen, wishing to render to the memory of this illustrious queen, doubly her sister-in-law, all that was due to her as a daughter of France, ordered, according to custom, a service to be performed with the magnificence that was due to so great a princess. On such occasions it often happens that precedence, which is not well-regulated in France, produces bitter quarrels. Mademoiselle [daughter of Gaston, Duc d'Orléans] as the granddaughter of Henri IV., claimed that there was much distinction to be made between herself and the Princesse de Condé. On the other hand, the Duc d'Enghien, wishing to sustain his rank and the grandeur his birth and glory gave him, demanded of the queen that the duchess, his wife, should follow Mademoiselle on all occasions, declaring that the latter was only first princess of the blood. The queen,

---

[1] Her beautiful portrait by Rubens will be found in Brantôme's "Book of the Ladies," belonging to these " Historical Memoirs." — Tr.

paying at that time little attention to the interests of
Mademoiselle, without considering that she was then in possession of certain prerogatives which created a difference between her family and that of Condé, granted what he asked.
Madame de Longueville [the Duc d'Enghien's sister] who
had lost her rank by marrying the Duc de Longueville and
had taken a patent from the king under which she preserved
it, also wished to use this occasion to re-establish herself
openly in the rights her Bourbon blood gave her; she therefore claimed to follow the Duchesse d'Enghien and do as she
did.

Mademoiselle, being warned of the designs against her,
resolved not to go to the service of her aunt, the Queen
of Spain. When the time came to start, she said she
was ill and could not leave her room. The queen, as
soon as she knew what the difficulty was, felt displeased;
she sent her orders to go, and complained to the Duc
d'Orléans. That prince blamed his daughter, and disapproved
of her proceedings, so that Mademoiselle found herself deserted, not only by the queen but by her father, whose
grandeur she was sustaining by maintaining her own rank.
But not being able to hold out against such rough attack,
she yielded, against her will, to force, went to Notre-Dame,
and exposed herself to the pretensions of those who, having
the honour to be her relations, wished to equal her. On starting, she had ordered that two persons should bear her train,
but as soon as the Duc d'Enghien saw this, he signed to one
of his suite to join the person who was already bearing the
train of his wife, whom he led by the hand. Madame de
Longueville, seeing that Mademoiselle, by seating herself in
the canon's chairs in the choir, intended to put an empty
place between them, pushed the Duchesse d'Enghien, her
sister-in-law, and they both took the seats next to her

Mademoiselle was keenly affronted by this treatment. She wept, and made much talk about it; representing that she possessed many marks of distinction between herself and the Princesse de Condé, who was bound on all occasions to give way to her, — such, for instance, as having a dais in the king's house, a mailed coach [*carrosse cloué*], footmen with their hose turned over, and the privilege of giving the princesses of the blood chairs without backs in her own house, while she was in an armchair. Her anger was, however, crushed down by that of the queen against her. It was proposed to put her in a convent for a few days' punishment, but instead of bearing her trifling disgrace with noble indifference, she had recourse to the Princesse de Condé, or rather, she accepted the offer the princess made her to heal matters with the queen, who blamed her extremely. The Duc d'Enghien gave as his reasons that she ought to be satisfied with the prerogatives she had, without always pretending to fresh ones, and that the advantages she enjoyed were all she ought to have. Monsieur bethought himself later that his daughter was right. He then grew angry, complained to the queen, and went and sulked for three days at Chambord. The queen, who had allowed the Duc d'Enghien to do what he did, felt obliged, for the sake of peace, to relieve him of all fault and take the blame on herself, so that finally, with a few excuses on her part, and a few compliments from the Duc d'Enghien, the matter was pacified.

The Queen of England came to Paris soon after this affair, having been three or four months at Bourbon. The queen went out of the city to receive her, with the king and the Duc d'Anjou (the actual Monsieur). These two great princesses embraced with much tenderness and friendship, and paid each other compliments which were not mere compliments. They took the English queen to lodge in the

Louvre, which was then unoccupied ; and for a country-house they gave her Saint-Germain.   As the king's affairs were in good condition and the wars had not yet ruined the royal finances, they gave her a pension of ten or twelve thousand crowns a month, so that in all things she had great reason to praise the queen.

The Queen of England was much disfigured by the severity of her illness and her misfortunes, no trace remaining of her past beauty.   Her eyes were fine, her complexion admirable, and her nose well-shaped.   There was something so agreeable in her face that it made her beloved by every one, but she was thin and short ; her figure was even deformed, and her mouth, never handsome naturally, was now, from the thinness of her face, too large.   I have seen her portraits, done in the days of her beauty, which show that she was very pleasing ; but as that beauty lasted but the space of a morning and left her before her midday, she was accustomed to declare that no woman could be handsome after twenty-two years of age.

To complete the presentation of her such as I saw her, I must add that she had infinite wit, and a brilliant mind which pleased all spectators.   She was agreeable in society, honourable, gentle, and easy ; living with those who had the honour to approach her without ceremony.   Her temperament inclined her to gaiety ; and even amid her tears, if it occurred to her to say something amusing, she would stop them to divert the company.   The almost continual suffering she endured gave her much gravity and contempt for life, which, to my thinking, made her more solid, more serious, more estimable than she might have been had she always been happy.   She was naturally liberal ; and those who knew her in prosperity assured us she had exhausted her wealth in doing good to those she loved.

Her favourite, who, so the public said, had a share in the misfortunes of England, was a rather worthy man, of a gentle mind which seemed very narrow and more fitted for petty things than great ones. He had the fidelity towards her which ministers usually have; he wanted money, before all else, to meet his expenses, which were large. The princess no doubt had too much confidence in him, but it is true that he did not govern her absolutely; she often had a will quite contrary to his, which she maintained as the absolute mistress. She supported her opinions with strong reasons; but they were always accompanied with a charm, a raillery that pleased and corrected the signs of haughtiness and courage which she had shown in the principal actions of her life. She lacked the great and noble knowledge which is acquired by reading. Her misfortunes had repaired that defect, for grievous experience had given her capacity. We saw her in France lose the tottering crown she still wore, lose the king her husband by a dreadful death, and suffer with constancy the adversities it pleased God to send her.

The cabinets of kings are stages on which are performed continually the plays that occupy the minds of the whole world. Some are simply comic, others are tragic, and their greatest events are caused by trifles. After speaking of the horrible effects of Fortune, and the indifference with which she scoffs at crowned heads, we should consider those produced by that mad passion of ambition, which is not content with intrigues of pleasure, but, mingling in affairs more serious, never fails to create the greatest disorders when it masters the hearts of men.

V.

1645 — 1646.

THE spring of this year having prompted the princes to go to the army, they started, giving every public sign of the impatience they felt to toil in war for the glory of France and the good of the State. The Duc d'Orléans took command of the army of Flanders, the Duc d'Enghien that of Germany, while the queen spent a good part of the summer of this year in Paris. The Duc d'Enghien, after having, as usual, carried alarm and terror into Germany, fought a battle at Nordlingen [August 3, 1645] which was one of his finest actions. I lost there two relations of my own: Lanquetot and Grémonville, both honourable gentlemen. Their loss was sore to me, for, besides the relationship, they were friends to me, which has to be considered. The day that the news of the winning of this battle came, I was surprised as I returned from a walk in the Palais-Royal to see a great number of persons talking together in separate groups. The emotion that the love of country inspires in all hearts makes itself felt on such occasions. Some of my acquaintance came up to me to tell me that a battle was won, but also that a great many men were killed. The first feeling in all was joy, then followed fear, and each for himself seemed already regretting a friend or relative dead.

This consternation in others imparted itself to me, and though my affection for the queen was sufficiently strong not to fail in sharing the satisfaction that such great news would surely give her, the sorrow of families touched me, and my feelings were much divided. With these thoughts I went upstairs. Victories are the delight of sovereigns, all the more because they taste their pleasures without deeply sharing the pain of private persons. It was not that the queen on such occasions did not seem to have much humanity and to regret men of merit, but — in short she was queen.

The cardinal came at once to tell her the particulars of this great battle. When she saw him she went to meet him with a smiling, satisfied face. He received her by saying in a grave tone: "Madame, so many are dead that your Majesty can scarcely rejoice at this victory." Perhaps he spoke in this way to win the good graces of those present and to gain the reputation of being tender to his friends; but whether the sentiment was natural to him or whether he took pains to affect it from policy, he deserves praise for it. A man who exercises virtue, whether it be by his will or from his inclination, does not fail in being estimable; for motives are impenetrable, and it belongs to Him only who formed the human heart to know it and judge it. The cardinal began with the name of the Maréchal de Gramont, taken prisoner, at which he showed much regret; and then he read to the queen the list of deaths; it was by that reading that I learned I had lost my two relatives and several of my friends whom I regretted much.

While the princes of the blood were gaining almost continual victories over the enemy [September, 1645] and France through its good fortune was making itself revered in all Europe, the queen was meditating how to find money to continue the war with the same glory as heretofore. She resolved to go before parliament to get certain edicts passed, considering that course the quickest remedy to apply to the wants of the State. This remedy, however, is violent and injurious to the State itself; the people always fear it; and the parliaments usually seek by humble entreaties to moderate the excessive terms proposed to them. But it sometimes happens that they use this pretext to increase the authority of their office and to carry resistance far beyond the public good; that is to say, they endeavour to take part in the ministry, when times and occasions give them the audacity to aim for it.

The parliament of Paris believed that it could find, during the regency, opportunity to make itself felt; and those of this assembly who called themselves guardians of the king desired to make known their power by opposing that of the regent. During the late reign their authority had been humbled; they sought impatiently for means to raise it, and at last their conduct revealed their intention. It was veiled, however, by zeal for the public good; and in this first encounter they declared that the sole rule of their sentiments was the desire to do right. As soon as the queen proposed to go before parliament, they said that she had not the right to do so. She laughed at this and said her right was founded on precedent, for the late queen, Marie de' Medici, had gone there. She resolved, however, to wait the return of the Duc d'Orléans; for though she did not need his presence as a necessary thing, the prince was then living with her on such good terms that she thought, with reason, that she could not show him too much consideration; and moreover, she was convinced that the presence of the king's uncle would always be advantageous to her son's affairs.

The Duc d'Orléans having arrived, and the day being fixed to go to parliament, the captain of the Guards, as was customary, visited all the prisons and took the keys of the Palais de Justice. The queen rose very early, and dressed with more care than usual. She wore earrings of large diamonds mingled with very large and pear-shaped pearls. On her bosom she had a cross of the same sort, of great value. This adornment, with her black veil, made her seem beautiful and of fine presence, and as such she pleased the whole assembly. Many gazed at her with admiration; and all acknowledged that in the gravity and sweetness of her eyes they recognized the grandeur of her birth and the beauty of her life and morals.

The companies of the Guards and the Suisses were ordered to make a hedge, as was customary, along the way to the Palais de Justice; and the queen with the king, whose beauty was then perfect, walked between them with all the grandeur that accompanies a king of France when he marches in ceremony; on which occasion he is followed by his guards, his Suisses, his light-horse cavalry, his musketeers, and many gentlemen and nobles. Four presidents came to receive the king and queen at the Sainte-Chapelle, where their Majesties heard mass. The king, who was still in tunics, was carried to his *lit de justice* by his chief equerry. Mademoiselle de Beaumont, my sister, and I had gone before to see the arrival of the king and queen, and to be present at the function, in which we took much interest because the queen was the chief actress.

When the king was placed, she stationed herself at his right hand. The Duc d'Orléans (still called Monsieur) was below the queen, and the Prince de Condé beside him. Then came the dukes and peers and the marshals of France, according to the rank of their duchies. On the other side were Cardinal Mazarin and several ecclesiastical peers. At the feet of the king was the Duc de Joyeuse, his grand chamberlain, reclining on a hassock. Below was the chancellor of France, and beside him on the floor, were the judges of the courts. On the other side of the chancellor was a bench, on which were seated the Princesse de Condé, and the Princesse de Carignan, and farther down were the queen's maids-of-honour.   The four secretaries of State were below on another bench, opposite to the judges.   Madame de Senecé, the king's governess, stood beside the king; she seemed to me to be the nearest to the *lit de justice.*[1]   After this order was fully established, the king saluted the whole assembly; and after casting his eyes at the queen as if to ask her approval, he said aloud: "Messieurs, I have come here to talk to you of my affairs; my chancellor will tell you my will."

He pronounced those few words with a grace that gave joy to the whole assembly; and the joy was followed by public acclamation that lasted a long time.   When the noise ceased, the chancellor, in an eloquent discourse, represented the necessities of the State, the splendid and celebrated victories we had won over the enemy, the desire the queen had for peace, and the need of continuing the war vigorously in order to force the Spaniards to make peace by the continuation of our conquests; and for these results, he concluded, money was required, for in that lay the whole secret. The first president [Matthieu Molé, son of the great president under Henri IV.] praised the queen strongly, exaggerated the good fortune of France, the wise conduct of the minister, and the valour of the princes of the blood.   In the same manner he represented with much vigour the necessities of the people, and made an harangue that was calculated to please both king and subjects.   The advocate-general Talon [Omer Talon] spoke in a bolder manner; he represented to the queen the oppressed people, ruined by past and present wars, asked mercy for them on his knees in a pathetic and

---

[1] This description tallies very closely with Saint-Simon's famous scene and diagram of Louis XV.'s first *lit de justice* under the regency. — Tr.

touching manner, and said things much opposed to the supreme authority of favourites. The parliament thought that he had spoken well; but I think that the minister was not well pleased, for I heard the speaker blamed by the Court adulators.[1]

The queen went to bed immediately on her return, to rest from this fatigue. After her dinner I found her in bed, and the cardinal with her. On opening the door of her room I made a noise; whereupon she asked one of her women, standing out of respect at a little distance, who it was. She heard, from myself, that it was I who entered, and she did me the honour to call me to her and wished me to give my opinion as to what had taken place that morning in parliament. She asked me if the king had not pleased me infinitely when he spoke with such grace, and whether I had noticed his tender action in turning towards her; and she specially ordered me to tell her what I thought of the harangues. As she saw by my answer that I was pretty well satisfied with the freedom of the advocate-general and spoke of it with respect, she replied in these noble words, worthy of a great queen: "You do right to praise him; I strongly approve the firmness of his speech, and the warmth with which he defended the poor people. I esteem him, for we are always too much flattered; and yet I think he said a little too much for a person as well-intentioned as I am, who desire with all my heart to relieve the people."

The queen and her minister then talked of peace, and she showed an extreme desire for it; but according to what the minister then told her, and I think he spoke the truth, it was necessary to continue the war to constrain the enemy to

---

[1] In Omer Talon's "Mémoires" he gives an account of this, and shows how his intervention only added to the bad state of the financial affairs. —Fr. Ed.

make peace. In all this conversation, which was long, I saw nothing in the queen but upright intentions for the good of the State and the relief of the people; even the cardinal seemed to me touched by it.

Other persons came in whose presence changed the topic. They spoke of Mademoiselle de Rohan, who, to satisfy the then reigning star, was about to marry Chabot, a gentleman of good and illustrious family, well-made, and a very worthy man, but, as I have said elsewhere, very inferior to the princes whom she might have married. She had great beauty, much intelligence, and was herself of illustrious birth; with it all she was very rich, as the heiress of the house of Rohan allied to that of our kings, and daughter of that great Duc de Rohan so renowned in the history of the wars of the Huguenots. He had been their leader; and by his "Memoirs" we learn from himself the events of his life.

Mademoiselle de Rohan married therefore from inclination, after having passed her first youth with the reputation of so great a pride and a virtue so extraordinary that it was thought she could never be touched by any passion; but the love that captured her heart forced her to be more gentle and less ambitious. Chabot was descended from the admiral of that name; but he was only a simple gentleman, without property or any establishment, whose sole advantage was that he had the good fortune to please a girl whom the Comte de Soissons thought to marry, and who could have married the Duke of Weimar, as rich in glory as the Cæsars and Alexanders, whom she slighted with many others, among them the Duc de Nemours, the eldest of the princes of the house of Savoie, who, as I have been told, was handsome and well-made. This was her last triumph, and the beginning of Chabot was that he profited by the failure of that marriage, seeing that the object of the desires of so many princes appeared to care for no one.

She continued several years in this state; during which Chabot, under the name of relative and friend, often entered her room, and, by means of a sister of his who was with her, acquired her confidence. This familiarity gave him an opportunity of insinuating himself into her heart; and when she perceived it she could no longer drive him out. I do not doubt that her reason and her pride gave her strange disquietudes, and often ill-treated the new-comer who wished to overthrow their empire. That soul so haughty had doubtless felt all that pride can make a person with so much ambition suffer. Honour, a powerful phantom which gives and takes away the reputation of honest men more in accordance with the clamour of the many than in obedience to true justice, often prompted her to renounce the friendship that so touched her.

Nevertheless, I do not know if the sternness of her reflections was not too great; for it seems as if that which is in conformity with God's demands might always be excusable, and that her greatest fault in the matter was her failure of respect towards her mother. But that which calls itself the great world decides in another manner; and though every one knows how difficult it is to please that world, we all submit to its tyranny. We run incessantly after its approbation, our lives are spent in that servitude, and never do we taste either sweetness or liberty because we have not the boldness to rise above vulgar opinions. At last, however, in spite of her combats, the pride of this illustrious heiress was lowered, and her reason driven off as importunate.

The Duchesse de Rohan, her mother, was strongly opposed to the marriage, and the relatives of the house of Rohan were in despair. The friends of the heiress, who had revered her as a divinity, either from jealousy of Chabot, whom they regarded as their own equal, or from zeal to her interests, became her most cruel enemies. They banded together against her in order to persecute her; which they did with an ardour in which there was far more outrage than love. This harshness which she encountered in the souls of her false friends, took away from her all the sweetness of her marriage, and made her know by experience that we are not to seek for true satisfaction in this life, and that whatever side the spirit of man turns to, it finds nothing but thorns.

The fine autumn season (October, 1645), so suitable for a stay at Fontainebleau, induced the queen to go there, where (not to change our topic) we were to see a marriage far more dazzling than that of Mademoiselle de Rohan, because of the rank of the personages, whose birth was royal and sovereign, who had done nothing that was not strictly in order, but about whom nevertheless there was something extraordinary. The King of Poland, king by election and legitimate heir to the crown of Sweden, wishing to marry, had inquired, *sub rosa*, if Mademoiselle wished to be a queen. She received the proposal with great contempt; the age of the king, his gout, and the barbarism of his country made her refuse him in a manner that showed she did not think him worthy of her. He then had some thoughts of Mademoiselle de Guise; but that princess was in no favour at Court, because she had friends who were not friends of the cardinal; and although she had virtue, merit, and some remains of her great beauty, the marriage could not take place, for the queen had no inclination for it, and Mademoiselle de Guise took no pains to bring it about.

The old king then selected the Princesse Marie [de Gonzague], who had been proposed to him with others. This princess, daughter of the Duke of Mantua, had been beautiful and agreeable; and was still so, although she had passed the first years of that youth which has the privilege of embellishing every woman. Monsieur, the king's brother, had been in love with her when he was presumptive heir to the crown. The queen his mother, Marie de' Medici, who had other designs for him, feared this passion, and sent the Princesse Marie to Vincennes, where she was for some time the innocent victim of a laudable affection. But the usual inconstancy of men and the downfall of Queen Marie de' Medici, in which the prince was involved, put an end to this little romance. When a hero gives up his love at the first unpropitious event it is to be supposed that the heroine will not be pleased and that the story is no longer charming. This love, which at first made a great noise and doubtless an impression on the heart of the Princesse Marie, had short duration in that of Monsieur. But the remembrance of it was bitter to her who was forgotten, and I have heard some friends of the princess say that from the time of her imprisonment she hated the Duc d'Orléans with irreconcilable hatred.

After this they talked of marrying her to the King of Poland; but as such propositions do not always succeed he married instead of her a German princess, who did not live long, and left him with one daughter. The Duke of Mantua having died, the Princesse Marie remained in Paris, leading an easy and pleasant life among her friends. She thought only of amusing herself and enjoying the pleasure which the society of honourable people gives. In this agreeable condition, however, she was not exempt from vexations, for she had but little means and few husbands at her command. Her affairs grew at last so bad that, the grand equerry Cinq-Mars having, during his favour, loved her, she listened favourably to him. His passion pleased her; and through this sentiment it was that he entered upon the great designs that ruined him, trusting to the hope that he might become *connétable*, and that with that rank and the splendour of his favour he would be worthy of marrying the daughter of a sovereign. His ruin, which she felt keenly, was in no way honourable to her; it made her friendship for him public and caused her much confusion.

After this unfortunate affair, which discredited her and seemed to have lowered that noble pride which never wholly abandons persons of her birth, she had reason to believe she could no longer find happiness in life and that all things would go against her. But the Princesse de Condé had a regard for her; she took up her interests warmly, and applied herself with care to bring about her marriage to the King of Poland. She spoke of it to the queen and to Cardinal Mazarin, and made her son the Duc d'Enghien and all his cabal act in favour of it. She increased a desire in the queen's mind to choose her in preference to Mademoiselle de Guise; and the cardinal, on his part, believed that the Princesse Marie, who had no interests contrary to his, and who was poor and crushed by ill-fortune, would feel much gratitude. All these things together made him send Bregi as ambassador to Poland to negotiate the marriage. The latter succeeded so well that he made the king resolve to send ambassadors to ask for her. The Duc d'Orléans, who had seen her troubles without pity, now saw her luck without envy; if he had any feeling left for her, hatred had more share in it than love.

The Polish ambassadors were received at Fontainebleau in the great salon of the queen, whose apartments are very beautiful. When they entered, the Princesse Marie was in the circle. She rose, so as not to be present at their harangue, and retired to a corner of the room to see them from a distance. She made use of me to screen herself from their sight, and by putting me before her prevented the men who were to be her subjects from perceiving her. After the ceremony, which only lasted the length of a compliment, these persons, who were all dressed in the French fashion and did not seem like foreigners, asked where she was. Some among them, who had already been in France, knew her, and pointed her out to the ambassadors. We saw them turn towards her to salute her, and as I did not hide her much, in spite of her efforts, one of them, as he withdrew, made her a profound bow and all the others in his suite did likewise. At the audience which he had with her the next day he treated her as Majesty and with the same respect as if she had already been his queen.

During the winter we beheld the second Polish embassy, which was fine and worthy of curiosity. It represented to our minds that ancient magnificence which passed from the Medes to the Persians, the luxury of which has been so well depicted by ancient authors. Though the Scythians have never had the reputation of being given to sensual habits, their descendants, who, at present, are neighbours to the Turks, seem to wish in a way to imitate the grandeur and majesty of the Seraglio. It appears that there still remain among them certain vestiges of their former barbarism; nevertheless, our Frenchmen, instead of scoffing at them as they proposed to do, were constrained to praise them and acknowledge frankly, to the advantage of their nation, that their entry into Paris deserved our admiration. I saw them pass in the Place Royale, from the house of Madame de Vellesavin, who gave us a great collation, where we found very good company to eat it.

The Palatine of Posnania and the Bishop of Warmy were

those whom the King of Poland selected to come and marry
the Princesse Marie and bring her to him. They chose to
appear dressed in the fashion of their country, the better to
show their magnificence and the splendour of their stuffs.
The Duc d'Elbeuf was appointed by the queen, with a dozen
other persons of quality, to receive them, and the carriages of
the king, the Duc d'Orléans, and the cardinal were sent for
them. But, to tell the truth, all this seemed wretched in
comparison with what these foreigners brought with them;
and yet they had traversed all Germany! They made their
entry into Paris by the Porte Saint-Antoine, with much gravity and the best order in the world.

First we saw pass a company of foot-guards, dressed in red
and yellow, with great jewelled buttons on their coats. They
were commanded by two or three officers, richly clothed and
very well mounted. Their coats were Turkish jackets of
great beauty. Over them they wore a wide mantle with
long sleeves which they allowed to hang negligently down
the sides of their horses. Their jackets were enriched with
buttons of diamonds, rubies, and pearls, and the mantles the
same, which were lined like the jackets.

After this company came another of the same kind commanded by officers more richly dressed. Their jackets and
mantles were the same colour as that of their heiduques,
green and gray. We then saw two other companies on
horseback, who wore the same uniform as those on foot, one
being red and yellow, the other green and gray, except that
these were of richer material, and the caparison of the horses
finer; also they wore more jewels. After them came our
académistes,[1] who, to do honour to the foreign embassy and
dishonour to their own land, had gone to meet it; they

---

[1] Meaning persons from the riding-schools, which were then called
academies; these were nearly all young seigneurs. — FR. ED.

seemed poor, and their horses also, though they were loaded with ribbons and feathers of all colours. On this occasion the French fashion of wearing no adornment but ribbons appeared mean and ridiculous.

After these companies came many Polish seigneurs, each with their suite and their liveries, dressed in heavy brocades of silver and gold. Their stuffs were so rich, so beautiful, and the colours so vivid, that nothing in the world could be more pleasing. Diamonds glittered on their jackets; and yet, amid these riches, it must be owned that their magnificence had much that was barbaric. They wore no linen; they never slept in sheets like Europeans, but in skins of fur with which they wrapped themselves. Under their fur caps their heads were shaved, all but one little lock at the top of their heads which they allowed to hang down behind. As a general thing, they are so fat that they are sickening to look at; and in all that concerns their persons they are dirty. Each Pole had a Frenchman at his side. These were men of the Court, all well-made, who had gone to meet them.

This procession covered a long space of ground; consequently its entry was very fine. There was one chief officer, who, as a mark of his dignity, wore three cock's-feathers in his cap, and the decoration of his horse was composed of the same kind of feathers. Some of their horses were painted red, and this fashion, though fantastic, was not thought unpleasing. The Palatine and the Bishop of Warmy came last; behind them were the Duc d'Elbeuf and his son the Prince d'Harcourt. The Palatine was handsome in face; he had a fine complexion and black eyes, with a good expression, and he wore his beard rather long and rather thick. The bishop also had a good expression, and was in no way different from the others, not even in the shaved head. After them came their coaches, covered with massive silver where ours have only iron.   The horses that drew them were handsome and fat and did not seem tired with their journey.   In short, all that we saw was worthy of being shown on parade. They crossed the whole city in this state; the populace were in the streets, the people of quality at their windows.   The king and queen were on a balcony which overlooked the open space, intending to see them; but they did not have that pleasure, because it was too late when the procession passed. They were taken to lodge at the Vendôme mansion, which was empty on account of its master's exile; and there the king provided for them every day, magnificently.

These foreigners had audience in the grand gallery of the Palais-Royal, which was shortened to one half of its length by a platform on which the queen stood.   The princesses and duchesses who formed the circle, with the other ladies, were behind her.   It was intended to celebrate the marriage with all the ceremonies required on such occasions, in order to show the grandeur of France to this barbaric nation; but as precedence was not established, and each prince wished to go before the others, the plan was stopped by this difficulty. Great murmuring had arisen on all sides, and so many old disputes were revived that the queen thought best to smother the whole thing by having the ceremony in private.   They began with Mademoiselle, in order to exclude all the rest, so that never was a wedding as solitary when done beneath the purple and a sceptre.

The day being chosen, the Princesse Marie came very early in the morning from the hôtel de Nevers to the room of Madame de Bregi, wife of the ambassador of France, who lodged in the Palais-Royal. This room was near enough to the chapel for her to go down easily when all was ready. I went to see her as she was dressing for this celebrated day. I found her looking handsome, and whiter, I thought, than usual, though she was naturally very much so; but ladies on great occasions are never satisfied with what nature gives them. She had a fine figure, and was then of a reasonable plumpness. She was thirty-three years old. Her eyes were black and handsome, hair of the same colour, complexion and teeth beautiful, and the other features of her face neither handsome nor ugly; but altogether she had beauty, with the grand air in her person that befits a queen. She seemed to deserve all she had expected to have in marrying the Duc d'Orléans, and all she was really to have in marrying a king.

Her wedding dress was a body and petticoat of cloth of silver with silver embroideries. Above this she had intended to wear her Polish royal mantle, which is white, strewn with great flashes of gold; but as the marriage was performed without ceremony the queen was of opinion that she ought not to wear it. She was left therefore with only the body and white petticoat, which latter, being intended to be worn underneath, was too short and had not the dignity required by the occasion. She was decked with the pearls and diamonds of the crown, which the queen had put together with her own hands. This adornment accompanied a closed crown made of large diamonds and very large pearls of great price. When she was ready to put the crown on her head, she doubted if she ought to do so before the ceremony, and she ordered me to go to the queen and ask her opinion; the queen did me the honour to tell me that as yet she had no right to wear it. When she was dressed she wished to show herself to the queen, who was in her own apartment, and she crossed the terrace which joins the two buildings, with two of her friends, my sister and myself.

The Poles, who were in the courtyard below awaiting the hour for the mass, seeing her, sent up shouts of joy and gave her many benedictions. She found the queen in her room, and, after thanking her for the kindness she had shown her, she addressed the cardinal, who had worthily served her, and told him she came to show him whether the crown he had placed upon her head became her. The queen, who was wearing her great pearls and her mourning mantle, then led the princess to the chapel through the great gallery. There was no one present but the king, the queen, the queen that was to be, the little Monsieur and the Duc d'Orléans. The princess knelt upon the foot-cloth laid in the centre of the chapel, the king on her right side, the queen on her left. Monsieur the king's brother, and the Duc d'Orléans, the king's uncle, were behind on their knees upon the foot-cloth; consequently the latter was for this day her inferior. This moment, when she saw herself raised above that faithless prince, above even the queen whose subject she had been before her father became sovereign, was no doubt most agreeable and glorious to her.

The Bishop of Warmy celebrated the mass and the marriage of his king and queen, whom the Palatine married in the name of his master. After mass was said they placed the crown upon her head. It was Madame de Senecé and Champagne, the hair-dresser, who performed that office for her. Besides the Poles, there was no one in the chapel but the royal personages and those of the blood royal whom I have just named, except the Maréchale d'Estrées, Madame de Montausier, and Madame de Choisy. The last three were the intimate friends of the Queen of Poland, and she had entreated the queen to allow them to be present. Madame de Bregi, my sister, and I were also present.

As good is usually mingled with evil, all the grandeur of

the Queen of Poland lost much of its splendour when she arrived at her capital, and her joy was evaporated by the presence of the king she had come so far to seek. In Warsaw she was received with little acclamation, for the king was old, oppressed with gout and fat, and so ill and gloomy that he would allow no ceremonies on her arrival. He did not think her as handsome as her portraits, and showed no esteem for her person. I heard from the Maréchale de Guébriant, who accompanied her by order of the queen, that this old husband received her in church seated on a chair from which he did not rise, or even pretend to do so.

When she came beside him she knelt and kissed his hand. He received her salute without the slightest sign of gentleness or benignity. He looked at her gravely and let her kiss his hand without saying a word. Then he turned towards Bregi, the ambassador, who stood beside him, and said aloud: " Is that the great beauty about which you told me wonders?" The Maréchale de Guébriant told me that the princess, who saw nothing in him but rudeness and perceived the disgust he showed for her, was amazed; and this bad reception, added to the fatigue of the journey, made her so ugly that the king had reason to be disgusted. The red of vexation and shame is not a good rouge for ladies, and grief takes the fire from their eyes.

The king, ill and gouty, rose from his chair after this cruelty, and went to the altar, where, without ceasing his rudeness, he married the queen again; after which they sat down to assist in singing psalms to the praise of God, and in thanks to Him for their marriage. The queen was then taken to the king's palace, where their Polish Majesties were served at supper with a meat which seemed horrible to the eyes of the queen and the Maréchale de Guébriant, but worse a thousand times to their taste. In short, all that they saw frightened them, and at night the queen, terrified at the position in which she found herself, said in a low voice to the maréchale that she had better return to France. The rest of the day was passed in the same way. The king did not speak to her, and far from showing her any tenderness, she was obliged, after waiting for him, to go into another apartment and pass the night alone.

Madame de Guébriant made complaints, and told certain of the nation whom she knew among those who had accompanied the queen to Poland, that France would be very ill-pleased if contempt were shown to what she had sent them. She said she could not return satisfied if she did not see the king less indifferent to the queen. Her complaints did lessen to some extent the contempt of the king; they forced him to treat the princess rather better, and live with her as his wife. When Madame de Guébriant left her, she was growing more contented, and consoling herself with the magnificent gifts that were sent to her from all parts; for in that country when the kings marry, their subjects are accustomed to make the new queen presents of great value. The hope of growing rich comforted this queen. She became rich, and the treasure she amassed served her soon after in the great trials God sent her, which have made her illustrious through the proofs she then gave to all Europe of her firmness and courage.[1]

This winter was spent by the Court in perfect tranquillity. A few little jealousies between Mademoiselle and the Princesse de Condé occupied the queen's cabinet, but without disturbing it, and if the queen had only followed her own

---

[1] On the death of the king, Ladislas III., she married his brother and successor, Jean Casimir. Her sister, Anne de Gonzague, was the celebrated Princess Palatine.

sentiments, and confined the exercise of her will exclusively to herself, we could have boasted that our Court was the most agreeable in the world, and so have enjoyed the pleasantest life ever tasted by those who have the honour of approaching great personages.

VI.

1646 — 1647.

THE queen was personally amiable; she treated her servants as friends, though she never took enough pains to do good to those she esteemed and to whom she felt kindly. Persons of right feeling, though deprived of benefits from her through the avarice of her minister, had at least this consolation, that she distinguished them by her esteem, and, though she did not do them many favours, it was not because she thought they were unworthy of them. We were obliged, therefore, to content ourselves with the queen's kind treatment; and this pleasure, which contained in itself enough glory to satisfy a faithful heart, was accompanied by great peacefulness. Self-interests did not light the consuming fires of jealousy among us, and our hopes were always so dead, our ambition so crushed, that we could say we had seen a Court only in picture, because we saw it without venturing to form desires about the great interests that usually charm men.

The queen, who, during the lifetime of the late king and after God had given her children, had talked only of the desire she felt to have them instructed in all knowledge, was much embarrassed when it became a question of how it should be done. There is no one into whose mind it does not come that princes ought to know more than one thing, and we must agree that Latin is not the most necessary knowledge. Politics is the true grammar which they ought to study; and history, good in all languages, will show them examples, and give them views by which to govern great kingdoms, to control by the same laws peoples of different natures, to maintain them in peace with their neighbours, and make them feared by their enemies. The evil is that this is not a science that can be taught to children; it is only through the experience of some years that these things can be learned.

For this reason the queen, convinced that Cardinal Mazarin was the ablest man in Europe, resolved at last to yield up to him the care of educating the king her son. She left to him even the choice of the king's governor, and it was the cardinal who appointed the Marquis de Villeroy to a post so important. He was the wisest man at Court; he had commanded the armies; but his great qualification was knowing better than any one else the interior affairs of the kingdom, and having both capacity and ideas for matters of State. The tutor appointed under him was the Abbé de Beaumont, a doctor of theology, brought up under Cardinal Richelieu. He had integrity, but never having devoted himself to belles-lettres was little capable of embellishing the mind of a young prince and of occupying it with the great and interesting things which ought not to be unknown to sovereigns. The Marquis de Villeroy and the abbé both replied to those who made them suggestions, that their conduct was ruled by the *superior,* to whom was given superintendence of the royal education, this being a title newly invented to make all employments and all offices dependent on the cardinal. I ought to render one testimony to the truth, namely: that the Marquis de Villeroy (soon after Duc and Maréchal de France) told me at the time, speaking of the king, whose natural intelligence he admired, that he was not master of the way in which he was being brought up; and that if he were listened to, he would not leave so good

a soil without cultivating it at the time it was most important to do so. For that reason he wished his friends to do
him justice and not blame him for doing his duty ill.

It is true that he took pains to present to the king those
who excelled in any science or art; and he never lost an
occasion to relate to him things that had happened in his
time, and good sayings that he had heard from persons of the
old Court; about which he made reflections that might be
useful to him. The tutor, on the other hand, jealous of his
office, took no pleasure in making the king talk with men
of intellect, for which he might perhaps have acquired a taste
together with a curiosity to learn a thousand things of which
he was ignorant; for the king had a natural desire to be
told things he did not know, and would himself talk only
of things he knew.

He was made to translate the Commentaries of Cæsar; he
learned to dance, to draw, and to ride on horseback; and he
was very skilful in all exercises of the body, as much so
as a prince who is not to make a profession of it ought to
be. But the queen, who had reserved the supervision she
would naturally have in the education of her son over and
above that she had yielded to her minister, took great care
to maintain in the soul of the young king those sentiments
of virtue, honour, and piety, which she had instilled into
him from infancy; caring more to prevent a young mind
like his from losing the innocence of its morals than to
see him better instructed in those things that are apt to
take from youth a certain timidity which precedes good
judgment and is lost but too soon.

At the beginning of the summer [May, 1646], the queen
made a journey to Compiègne, whence she went to Amiens
to accompany the Duc d'Orléans on his way to command
the army in Flanders, to which, soon after, the Duc d'En-

ghien was added. I stayed in Paris, because, not having certain advantages in servants, journeys were fatiguing to me and very costly. Monsieur delayed a few days later than the queen in order to prepare himself for war, and I remember that many of my friends came to bid me adieu who were killed in that murderous campaign. Valour, so vaunted by all nations and practised by ours, noble as it is, has its drawbacks; and the bravest who rush with such joy to its opportunities, have even more if they return with their legs and arms. It desolates families and robs the Court of its best, and, to tell the whole truth, though nothing in the world is finer than valour, nothing is worse than war.

The queen was away on her journey six weeks. Nothing extraordinary happened, and her return brought us joy, for not only was her intimacy with us gentle, agreeable, and glorious, but we were so accustomed to the honour of seeing her that Paris, during her absence, seemed to us another city, and our life another life. In these first years of the regency the Court was so tranquil and our life so delightful that it was impossible not to love it. Mademoiselle de Beaumont, however, noticed an alteration in the queen's face after her return which threatened her with a little storm. Though the queen on arriving in Paris told the Princesse de Condé, who was with her, that she was glad to see us again, it is certain that this young lady in particular had had the misfortune to displease the minister. Her conduct was rather imprudent. She was a daring girl, whose spirit was high, rough, and ill-regulated. She blamed the government with so little caution that she often found spies where she thought she was safe; and though these qualities were mingled with noble sentiments, as the vessel was without a pilot it was easily wrecked on that sea, although at the time it was perfectly calm.

During the queen's absence she had gone to make a trip with M. and Mme. de Chavigny, who continued to stand ill at Court. This intimacy displeased the cardinal, though it had nothing in itself but what was praiseworthy; but this displeasure induced the cardinal to request the queen to dismiss her. It is not difficult to make great personages dislike those who talk much and who may therefore be suspected of rashness. On this pretext her dismissal was asked and granted. Though Mademoiselle de Beaumont and I were of different temperaments, and her manner of acting was the opposite of mine, chance had made us friends; I loved in her — without approving her proceedings — her frankness, her spirit, which was natural, and her sentiments, which seemed to me to have a certain stoical virtue. But I made her continual harangues as to her conduct which I did not like, and as to the vehemence of her decisions. She always wanted to reform the State, from that false glory that people give themselves by despising others, and not at all from any true source of honour and integrity. She was the only one who knew of the blame I gave her, and as we were often together Cardinal Mazarin for this reason desired that I also should be sent away from Court.

He judged of my thoughts by the friendship I had for her and by the approval I appeared to give to her words. The queen, who had known me from my childhood, and knew that my intentions were upright, could not doubt my fidelity. She was good enough to answer for me to her minister, and to assure him of the propriety of my conduct without inquiring of me; so true is it that on all occasions it is best to do right and not boast of it. This was the cause of my good fortune that the queen never had any ill-opinion of me; and as Cardinal Mazarin was not strongly determined on my ruin, he let himself be persuaded by her; and thus I saved myself from a punishment I did not deserve, and a peril I did not perceive until it had passed.

Commands were sent to Mademoiselle de Beaumont not to see the queen again. I was astonished when, on the evening of the same day, I heard this news. It was thought that I should be included and made to feel on this occasion the consequences of the word "cabal." My friends were anxious about me, and when I entered the queen's room, though I myself was far from having any fear, I noticed a change on their faces; indifferent persons looked at me from a distance; and all, whispering to their neighbours, thought me lost. One of my friends had the boldness to approach me and pay me a compliment. I asked him, laughing, the reason of such serious discourse, and from him I heard of the dismissal of Mademoiselle de Beaumont. From this, I comprehended easily all the rest. I was sorry for the misfortune of my friend, but I did not feel, I think, any trouble in my soul that could shame me. As I was sure of my own innocence, I went abruptly into the cabinet where the queen was; and in that instant, despite the charms of her presence and the honour I had in being admitted to it, it crossed my mind that the benefits we possess at a Court, and even the favour I had had there, are not true benefits worthy of esteem; and that perhaps my dismissal, casting me against my will into solitude, might be to me a veritable happiness; for it is not one to live in a place where it is almost impossible to keep one's self from weaknesses which give as much pain as they do vexation to those who are intelligent enough to recognize them.

I was not long in this effort to strengthen myself by reason against my dismissal. The queen, who was afraid that the affair of Mlle. de Beaumont would cause me uneasiness, took care to remove it. As soon as she saw me

she assumed a kindly face and spoke to me amiably; and
this care, at this moment, showed me the generosity of her
soul, which was quite independent of the sentiments of
others.   She was undressing to enter her bath, for it was
very hot weather.   As soon as she was in it, I knelt beside
the bathtub to speak with her, and I asked her the reason of
my friend's dismissal.   She did me the honour to reply
as follows: that she had sent her away because she had
blamed her conduct in a displeasing manner; that she was
one of those persons who cry out against everything, more
from bad taste than from any good reason they have to
do so; who disapprove of all they see, and who discern the
actions they pretend to judge solely through their self-
conceit.   She added that she wondered how I, who had not
the same sentiments or the same heart, could have friendship with her and be social up to that time with a person so
far from my own nature.

It was time to say no more, and I merely tried to soften
the queen's resentment.   I excused my friend on the hasti-
ness of her mind and her impetuous temperament; and, trying to justify her good intentions, I assured the queen that
the foundation was good, and that in all essential things I
believed she would never fail in fidelity to her service or in
zeal for her interests.   At that moment the queen drew her
hand from the water and laid it all wet upon mine, which
she pressed, saying, in tones to be remembered: "You are
too good, Madame de Motteville; I assure you she would
not do as much for you, and I know what I say."   Those
words impressed themselves deeply on my soul, and although
they did not make me wholly suspect my friend, because it
would not be just to doubt for so slight a cause, they at least
made me more easily enlightened in the future, so that in
course of time I became altogether undeceived.   The hard

experience I have had of the fictitious friendship of human beings has forced me to believe that there is nothing so rare in this world as probity, or a good heart capable of gratitude to those who act uprightly.

Cardinal Mazarin also spoke to me on the subjects of complaint he thought he had against me; he told me that my friends did me harm, meaning this exiled one and Commander de Jars. He let me know that Mlle. de Beaumont made me offensive in her way, and that the queen had been told that when she wanted to point some specially sharp satire against her she always said, "Madame de Motteville and I think, or say, or judge thus and so," and to strengthen herself she brought me into the game about whatever she alleged.

I easily understood the cardinal's mind when he spoke to me in this manner. I knew very well that no regard for me led him to make me that confidence; and that his only object was to part and disunite us, by letting me know I must follow that course if I wished to please him. But, as for truth, I think he did not deceive me, and that Mlle. de Beaumont, who, in spite of her free-thinking mind, was shrewd and politic, wished to have confederates. I had often, also, surprised her in ways of acting to insure that I was not more agreeable to the queen than herself. I contented myself, however, by replying to the minister as I had to the queen. I excused her of whom he complained as best I could; and, separating my conduct from that of others, I tried to persuade him in my favour. I did not acquire his good graces in this way; because he never esteemed those who made it a principle to act honestly and without treachery; but as he had softness and benignity and had seen the queen show an inclination to protect me, I found it easy to cure his mind of its dislike. My words had enough force to induce him to leave me in peace, but not enough to produce any good effects on my fortunes. I own that I did not apply myself to succeed in that. Moreover, I always had friends whom he hated, perhaps justly, whose proceedings I was never willing to blame; and through this fidelity which we owe to one another, I have preferred the pleasure of serving them to that of promoting my own affairs.

The queen had entirely settled down into following the advice of this minister; he knew that we were not necessary to her, and he no longer feared that any one could injure him with her. For this reason he continued with us on the same terms. As for me, he let me live on without doing me either good or evil; as for those who displeased him, he found means to dismiss them when they had given enough cause by their conduct to obtain the consent of the queen. But the truth must be told that he used his power with laudable moderation; he loved the State, and served the king with a fidelity that deserved the confidence the queen placed in him.

Directly after the death of the Duc de Brézé [killed at the naval battle of Orbitello] the Prince de Condé attacked the Duchesse d'Aiguillon, who claimed that the Duchesse d'Enghien could not inherit from her brother the Duc de Brézé, because she had renounced her inheritance on marrying. At the same time the prince asked of the queen the vacant admiralty, the government of Brouage, and all its offices. The admiralty was not granted to him, because the control of the sea would have made a first prince of the blood too powerful in France; and the government of Brouage remained in the hands of one of the Duc de Brézé's favourites, named the Comte de Daugnon, who had quietly taken possession of it against the will of the queen and minister.

On this refusal, the Prince de Condé left the Court, pre- tending to grumble, and went to his own estates. The Duc d'Enghien, who was with the army commanded by Monsieur, wrote to the queen and loudly asserted his claims. He declared them legitimate, and that he hoped to obtain this justice from her. I saw the letters that he wrote her. From their style, it was easy to judge that he did not mean the blood of France to be useless to him, and that he had a pride of heart which might one day be trouble- some to the king. It was said of him that his courage and his genius led him more to combats than to politics. On this occasion, however, he observed all the rules of policy, and, quitting the audacious manner in which he was wont to wrangle with Monsieur about everything, he began by humbling himself wholly to him. As they were in the same army he affected to show him the greatest assiduity, and even sought with care to win over the Abbé de la Rivière. Their intimacy advanced so much that Monsieur wrote to the queen and to the cardinal in favour of the Duc d'Enghien, which caused great uneasiness to the min- ister. The enmity of those two important personages pleased him much more than their union.

The Prince de Condé was a great politician. He was timid and afraid of quarrelling with the Court. He loved the State, and it was said of him now that his counsels were always for order and justice. He gave them with much intelligence, and it was often remarked that he would have made a great king. The baseness he had shown under his brother Louis XIII. had been to his shame, but.he was now held to be wise and prudent. As he was beginning to grow old and knew the evils a prince of the blood must endure if he revolts against the king, he readily allowed himself to be persuaded that he must not grumble too long. A few

days later he sent to Le Tellier, secretary of State, to lodge
his complaint.   Some negotiation took place, the conclusion
of which was that the decision on his claims should be put
off till the end of the campaign, and that meantime they
would all be good friends.   Thus the prince's wrath passed
easily away.   He returned to Court, was treated well, and
his grievances were apparently calmed — after the manner
of great personages, who nearly always hate each other, and
make pretence to the contrary as a matter of parade.

The Princesse de Condé, who was then with the queen,
although she was ambitious and would have liked to see
all the crowns of Europe on the head of her son the Duc
d'Enghien, never ceased to protest to the queen that she
had no interests separate from hers, and that her friendship
for her was stronger than her desires for the grandeur of
her son ; so that the queen was apparently half convinced,
and continued to live with her in her usual manner.   If,
without being a dupe, she chose to believe what the princess
told her, I make bold to be certain that though the latter
did not feel the friendship she testified to the queen, she
was at least touched by her caresses and the pleasures of
favour.   From the Princesse de Condé's nature, I feel sure
she would have been in despair to have her family quarrel
with the Court, as much from fear of losing its delights, as
for the sake of her greater interests.

The queen spent nearly the whole summer at Fontainebleau, and the one spot in the world where the heat is
greatest served as her retreat for the hottest season.   The
amusements· of the ladies were entirely confined within
the limits of the river Seine.   Every day they spent many
hours in the water, or in the forest which they had to pass
through in order to reach it ; the dust of the one being
washed off by the other.

The king, who was still a child, bathed also, and his governor, the Maréchal de Villeroy, who never left him, did the same. The queen, and all those who had the honour to accompany her, usually wore long chemises of gray linen which trailed on the ground. The king's governor wore the same, and modesty was in no wise wounded. All the men under sixty were at the army; none remained with the queen but her officers and a small number of courtiers attached to the service or the fortunes of the minister; otherwise the Court was deserted. I found, nevertheless, that we were a good company, for, to my thinking, a Court is never more agreeable than when the crowd is not there.

In Flanders, our army, though large and fine, did not do great exploits. They besieged Courtray with thirty thousand men, and the Duc de Lorraine with equal numbers camped in front of us. The two armies were a long time looking at each other without doing themselves any harm. We offered battle to the enemy, but they did not accept it. Only a few little fights took place; but at last they ventured to attack our lines, and we took the place [June 30] in their presence and to their shame.

After this conquest the army went straight to attack Mardick, which the Duc d'Orléans had taken the previous year and which, this year, had been surprised and retaken by the enemy in three hours. Clanleu, whom the Duc d'Orléans had placed there in command, being absent when the enemy attacked, was blamed for this loss. Though he was known to be valiant, there was guilt enough in being imprudent or careless. He was doubly so because this siege, by which Monsieur undertook to repair his fault, cost much blood to France, and much treasure. The duke was blamed for undertaking it; he had no naval force, and the enemy, having a free exit towards Dunkerque, could enter as they pleased, so that this paltry little place was able to defend itself. He excused himself on the score of the Dutch, who still made a show of being on our side. They had promised him to be before the place at a certain time with a number of vessels capable of preventing all communication by the enemy. As they meant in the end to desert us, they failed to keep this promise in time, and the duke failed in his project. This was the reason why those who were in Mardick defended themselves so easily against our attacks and made the affair so disadvantageous for us.

The enemy made a sortie on the side of the Duc d'Enghien; and that prince, rushing to the support of his men, was wounded in the face [August 15] by a pot which was flung from the town, and came near killing him or putting out his sight. The Comte de Flex, son-in-law of the Marquise de Senecé, lady-of-honour to the queen, was killed, — a good man who, with many fine qualities, deserved much. The young Comte de Roche-Guyon had the same misfortune; he was son of the Duc de Liancourt, and sole heir of his father's great wealth, and that of his uncle the Maréchal de Schomberg. He had married the heiress of the house of Lannoi, who was left pregnant of a daughter to whom she gave birth soon after her husband's death. This young seigneur was extremely regretted, — as much out of considerations for his father and mother, who were respected by all good people, as for the charm of his person; every one pitied his fate.

The Duc de Nemours was wounded in the thigh. He was an amiable prince and worthy of all esteem. His wound caused great anxiety to his friends, and many ladies, so it was secretly told, made vows for his recovery. The Chevalier de Fiesque, who, his friends declared, had intelligence and virtue, was killed; he was mourned by the daughter of a great house, who honoured him with a tender and virtuous love. I know none of the particulars, but, according to general opinion, it was founded on piety and virtue, and consequently very remarkable. Soon after his death, this virtuous young woman, wishing to despise utterly the grandeurs of the world, left them all, as unworthy to occupy a place in her soul; she gave herself to God, and shut herself up in the great convent of the Carmelites, where she now serves as an example through the life she leads. The Marquis de Thémines, sole heir of his house, had the same unfortunate fate as the others. He was son of the Maréchale d'Estrées by her first husband. He showed much promise and was a great loss to his family.

The day the courier who brought the sad news arrived, all the rooms at Fontainebleau resounded with cries. These illustrious dead and wounded were personages of the Court and among the most distinguished; their relatives and friends wept for them before the eyes of the queen. She went to see Madame de Senecé to console her for the loss of her son-in-law, who left a young widow of extreme virtue, and little children who lost much in losing him. The queen endeavoured to soften the bitter sorrow of others by the compassion she felt for it, and by the feelings she showed to them. The Princesse de Condé was for several days in great anxiety; her fears led her to believe that they were concealing from her the danger of her son's wound. To the condolences of those whom she did not think in her interests, she answered, being sour and proud, by telling them they were sad because he was not wounded badly enough.

The queen might have consoled herself, for the Duc d'Enghien was dreaded in the matter of the government of Brouage, and for his claim to the admiralship, which she did

not choose to give him.   One evening, lying on a little bed
in her cabinet, and talking of him to me with the esteem
which he deserved that she should feel for him, after
expressing a wish for his recovery, she said a thing which
came from the confidence she always had in God : " I believe
that God, to whose providence I confide myself wholly, inasmuch as He has saved him, knows that he will not do me
harm ; and if he should do me any, it will be according to
His orders, and for my good and my salvation." Her
prophecy has been accomplished ; the prince, after doing
great services to the king and to her, did her harm. She was
compelled to do the same to him ; but I do not doubt that
she profited by the good use I saw her make of all the
troubles that afterwards come upon her from this source.

The Duc d'Orléans, at the queen's request, returned to
Fontainebleau, September 1, 1646, where she awaited him to
end their summer together in that agreeable place with the
amusements to be found there. She wished to leave the
Duc d'Enghien to his amusements of cannon and sword,
the accompaniments of a warrior who finds his pleasure in
battle and the conquest of cities. The king and queen,
wishing to welcome Monsieur, intended to go out and meet
him, but as their Majesties did not encounter him soon, their
plan ended in only a drive. The cardinal continued on until
he met him, and returned with him a few hours later. This
arrival filled the Court with the Ducs de Guise, d'Elbœuf, de
Candale, and a fine troop of men of quality, who were not
sorry to rest from the fatigues of the siege of Mardick in the
loveliest spot in the world.

As soon as the Duc d'Enghien found himself in a position
to act alone, he besieged Furnes, September 9, a little town
near Dunkerque, which he took in a few days. This plan,
the precursor of a greater, pleased the minister. He had

counselled attacking that place before they went to Mardick, but the Duc d'Orléans would not consent, considering the enterprise too difficult. The friendship which had seemingly existed between the two princes during the campaign was not strong enough to keep their hearts from being filled by jealousy and self-love. The Duc d'Orléans did not see without vexation the project the Duc d'Enghien had of taking Dunkerque, which he had kept secret from him; and the Duc d'Enghien did not find himself sole master of that great design without feeling the utmost joy. I have heard Comminges, who was with him for some time, say that he was not as much wounded when he found himself alone as he was when his superior was with him; and Comminges suspected him of having feigned a greater wound than he had, in order to let Monsieur go away in the belief that he was not in a state to undertake anything.

The queen received, September 13, 1646, an ambassador extraordinary from the Queen of Sweden, who apparently came only to bring about the alliance of the two crowns. The person chosen by the Swedish queen for that purpose was the Comte de La Gardie. He was son of the Connétable of Sweden; his grandfather was French, of, it was said, rather ordinary birth. He was well-made, with a haughty manner and the air of a favourite. He spoke of his queen in terms both passionate and respectful, so that he was readily suspected of greater tenderness than that which he owed her as a subject. He was betrothed to a cousin-german of the queen, whom she herself made him marry. Some said that if she had followed her inclinations she would have taken him herself, but she conquered them by her reason and the grandeur of her soul, which could not endure that lowering. Others said that she was born free-thinking, and that being able to put herself above custom, she either did not love him, or no longer loved him, when she gave him to another. However that may be, the man seemed worthy of his luck, but more fitted to please than to govern.

From the manner in which he spoke of the queen his mistress, it seemed that she needed no minister, for although very young she managed all her affairs herself. Besides the hours she gave to study, she employed many, he told us, in the care of her kingdom. Judging by the description he gave of her, she had neither the face, nor the beauty, nor the inclinations of a lady. Instead of making men die of love, she made them die of shame and vexation, and was the cause of the great philosopher Descartes losing his life in that way because she did not approve of his philosophy.[1] She wrote to the queen, to Monsieur the king's uncle, to the Duc d'Enghien, and to Cardinal Mazarin, letters which I saw and which were much admired for the gallantry of the thoughts, the beauty of the style, and the facility with which she expressed herself in our language, which was familiar to her, as were many others. At that time all the heroic virtues were attributed to her; she was placed on a par with the most illustrious women of antiquity; every pen was employed in praising her, and it was said that the highest sciences were to her what the needle and distaff are to the rest of our sex. Fame is a great talker; it often likes to pass the bounds of truth; but truth has strength; it does not long leave a credulous world abandoned to deception. Some time later it was known that the virtues of this Gothic queen were only middling; she had no respect for Christianity, and if she practised its precepts it was more from fancy

[1] Christina, Queen of Sweden, daughter of Gustavus Adolphus; born 1626; ascended the throne 1632; abdicated in favour of her cousin, Charles Gustavus, 1654; and died in Rome 1689. It was the severe climate of Sweden that killed Descartes, and not her ill reception of his philosophy. — TR.

Christina Queen of Sweden

than feeling. But she was learned to the level of the most learned man; and up to this time she had a great reputation at her Court, among her peoples, and throughout all Europe.

To welcome her ambassador, balls, comedies, great repasts, and all ordinary amusements were given to him. He adorned the drive by the canal of Fontainebleau with a coach of gold and silver embroidery which was made expressly for his queen. It was drawn by six horses, richly harnessed, followed by a dozen pages in the Queen of Sweden's livery, which was yellow and black with silver lace. This image of another Court, uniting with the reality and beauty of ours, made the drive by the canal most agreeable.

Shortly after our return from Fontainebleau, the news arrived of the taking of Dunkerque, which gave great glory to the Duc d'Enghien and much joy to the minister, who felt that it contributed to his own glory. He believed, with much reason, that the prosperity of the State was the foundation of his own good fortune, rather than the magnifying of the crown. The Maréchal de La Meilleraye took at the same time Porto-Longone in Italy; and this victory, though little fruitful for France, was an agreeable success to the cardinal, who liked to triumph and make himself feared in his own country.

About this time died the illustrious Bassompierre, much lauded in the last century for his gallantry. He had gone to Pons to see d'Émery, the neighbour of Bouthillier, father of Chavigny, to whom the beautiful mansion of Pons belonged. There he fell ill of a continued fever, of which he was cured in a few days; but on his way back to Court, his servants found him dead in his bed in the morning, at an inn where he passed the night, although he had shown no sign of more illness.

This seigneur, who was valued by Henri IV., favoured

by Marie de' Medici, and so lauded and admired in the days of his youth, was no longer regretted in ours. He still preserved a few remains of his past beauty; he was civil, obliging, and liberal; but the young people could not endure him; and I have seen some of them unjust enough to turn him into ridicule because he liked to invite them to good cheer when he had not enough dinner for himself alone. They said he was no longer in the fashion, that he told too many little stories, and talked too much of himself and his times. Other defects they put upon him, some of which I agree to. They accused him, as if it were a great crime, of liking to please and of being grandiloquent, and also that, coming from a Court where civility and respect were the rule towards ladies, he continued to live by the same principles in one where men thought it shamed them to pay any civility, and where unbridled ambition and cupidity are the noblest virtues of the great seigneurs and the most honest men of our century.

The cold severity during the reign of the late king, and the temperament of Cardinal Mazarin were among the causes of the present rudeness; for the latter, besides his avarice, despised honest women, belles-lettres, and all that contributes to the politeness of men. The sterility of favours, the desire to obtain them, and the impossibility of doing so by deserving them, have rendered courtiers incapable of seeking distinction in noble ways; but as their ambition becomes stronger and more ill-regulated, it triumphs over their hearts; and the result is that they cannot endure a man who has preserved the old customs; in which they certainly are, to my mind, wrong. The relics of old Maréchal de Bassompierre were worth more than the youth of some of the most polished men of our day.

The Duc d'Enghien, soon after, arrived from the army

victorious, and demanded, with apparent humility and real boldness, the reward of the admiralship. The queen had already taken that dignity in her own name to keep it for the king, and Cardinal Mazarin therefore possessed it, without appearing to do so, for several years. The prince made many propositions which were not received, such as that of giving him an army for Franche-Comté, which he would afterwards have erected into a sovereignty. This proposal was evaded, for it recalled the evils which the Ducs de Bourgogne, princes of the blood and sovereigns, had formerly done to the kingdom. Other proposals were then made to him, which he rejected. The Duc d'Orléans, with his good intentions and kindliness, showed great interest in maintaining the peace of the Court; so that during these secret negotiations matters did not cease to appear in a good state. The Duc d'Enghien was not strong enough, even if his intentions were worse than they were, to form a party for himself with the hope of good success. Many persons were disposed to quarrel, but the queen was still too well supported, and the victories strengthened her power. The Duc d'Orléans was content, and the cardinal not yet enough hated; she had therefore nothing to fear.

While they were thus striving to satisfy the Duc d'Enghien, who wanted much, and to whom they wished to give little, the Prince de Condé, his father, fell ill and died in three days. His offices and his governments, which were very considerable, served to pay to his son the debts he thought were due to him. He was sorry, no doubt, that he had not pressed for a decision sooner, having boldness enough to take both advantages; but not having done so, he had not enough boldness to insist on the two inheritances, which would have made him master of France. The offers that had been made to him about that of the

Duc de Brézé, his brother-in-law, were of no small importance. He could then have had Stenay, Jametz, and Clermont; but he refused them, to claim more. In the end he obtained them because the minister had not the strength to refuse him when, in the quarrels that afterwards arose, his power lessened and that of the princes increased.

The Prince de Condé, first prince of the blood and full of merit, died about midnight on the day after Christmas, 1646; he ended his life as a Christian, and his last hours must have effaced before God the passions of his youth. Though his forefathers had been Huguenots, he was always the inveterate enemy of that religion, and he ever remained firmly in the true one. Henri IV. had caused him to be declared presumptive heir to the crown; he was then so poor that his property was reckoned at ten thousand francs a year. At his death it was said that he left a million a year, besides his office as grand-master of the king's household, and his various governments. His defects equalled his virtues; both were considerable. Besides the bad reputation he acquired in his youth, he was avaricious, and also unlucky in war. That is the mildest term one can use about a prince who was said not to be valiant. Those who saw him when young said that he was then handsome; but in his last years he was dirty and slovenly, and had few remains of his good looks. His eyes, which were very large, were red; his beard was neglected, and his hair, as a usual thing, very greasy. He always wore it tucked behind his ears; in short, he was in no wise agreeable to look upon.

But, beyond what I have said of him, it should be added that he always wanted the laws of the State observed, and that in the councils he invariably protected justice. He was the scourge of partisans, and had shown on many occa-

sions that he had no greater passion than that for equity
and honest reasoning. This same spirit led to order in
his household; he took care himself to send his servants
to mass on Sundays and fête-days, and at Easter he was
accustomed, in order to oblige his people to do their duty
on that sacred day, to give them each a quarter of a crown.
I have heard it said, but I do not know if it is true, that
he sometimes went to the public markets to inquire himself
into the price of provisions, and to know the details of
everything, that he might look after the police, and famil-
iarize himself with the populace; not, perhaps, without
design to please them and attach them to his person.

He was preparing to oppose Cardinal Mazarin, whose
conduct he did not approve. It is to be believed that he
expected that revolts would arise during a long regency,
which would give him an opportunity to attack him. The
queen could not endure that in the councils he should offer
the slightest opposition to the matters there treated; and
therefore he was nearly always an obstacle to the minister's
plans; which often proceeded from the rectitude and zeal
that prompted him for the good of the State. When dying,
he asked pardon of the minister, and assured him he had
never had any design against him, other than that of doing
his own duty and satisfying his conscience. He gave his
blessing to his children on condition that they lived as
good Catholics. He advised them never to fail in what they
owed to the king, and assured them that the greatest misfortune that could happen to a prince of the blood was
to take sides against his sovereign, because that was losing
a noble station to become the slave of those who served
him. He behaved to the Princesse de Condé as if he had
loved her all his life; but the truth is, he never considered
her until he found she could serve his interests at Court,

where she was better liked than he.   She was not in despair at his death; and the illustrious Madame de Rambouillet was much lauded for saying on this occasion that Madame la princesse had never had but two happy days with her husband: the day he married her, on account of the high rank he gave her, and the day he died, through the liberty he returned to her and the great property he left her.   Besides being well-treated in his will, she had, as heiress of the great house of the Montmorencys, large claims upon the estate of her late husband.

On that same Christmas day the Duchesse d'Orléans gave birth to a daughter,—a cause of great grief to her husband, who passionately desired a son; and as he was kind and much-loved, Frenchmen desired it for him; for naturally we like the race of our kings and desire to see it preserved. What afflicted Monsieur was joy to the Duc d'Enghien, who thus found himself first prince of the blood, not only by the death of the prince his father, but because this daughter did not prevent him from assuming that rank at once, and enjoying its prerogatives for the rest of his life.   The advantages are great, and can never be lost when once they are possessed.

The new Prince de Condé was more fortunate than Monsieur, for he already had a son, who, child as he was, had borne the holy-water from the king to his grandfather. The body of the late prince lay in state for three days, and as he had been very miserly in life, the Court people made amusing jests on the pain his soul must be feeling in the other world at such great and useless expense about his body.   The wit of man is always ready to laugh at things serious.   Such examples ought nevertheless to make him enter more deeply into a sense of the nothingness of the vanities and grandeurs of this world.

The queen went to see the Princesse de Condé, more to rejoice than condole with her; and she also visited the whole family, except Madame de Longueville who had been for some time absent, having gone to Munster to join the Duc de Longueville, whom the queen had sent there at the beginning of her regency to work for peace.

VII.

1647.

THE chief affairs of the Court, those of which it seemed to think the most, were amusement and pleasure. I have already said that the queen loved the theatre, and went there in secret during the year of her great mourning; but she now went publicly. Comedies were played every two days, sometimes Italian, sometimes French; and quite often there were assemblies. The preceding year the rector of Saint-Germain, a severe and pious man, wrote to the queen that she ought not, in conscience, to permit such amusements. He condemned the theatre; particularly Italian comedies, as freer and less modest. This letter had troubled the soul of the queen, who did not wish to permit anything against what she owed to God. Being still uneasy on the subject, she consulted many persons. Several bishops told her that plays which represented, as a usual thing, serious histories could not do harm; they assured her that the courtiers needed such occupations to keep them from worse things; they said that the piety of kings ought to be different from that of private persons, for being public personages they should authorize public amusements when they were of the class of harmless things. Accordingly the theatre was approved, and the gayety of Italian comedy saved itself under the wing of serious plays.

The Court assembled in the evenings in the little *salle des comédies* at the Palais-Royal. The queen sat in a box to hear more conveniently, and went there by a little staircase which was not very far from her chamber. She took the king, the cardinal, and sometimes persons to whom she wished to pay attentions, either for their rank or as a favour. We received such favours with pleasure, because those who have the honour to approach kings familiarly can never prevent themselves from regarding these trifles as very important things; all the more because they are counted as such in public estimation.

When the rector of Saint-Germain saw that the theatre was fully established, he woke up in good earnest and spoke against it like a man who wished to do what he thought his duty. He came to see the queen and maintained to her that this amusement was a mortal sin and ought not to be permitted. He brought his opinion signed by seven doctors of the Sorbonne who held the same sentiments. This second pastoral reprimand caused fresh uneasiness to the queen, who resolved to send the Abbé de Beaumont, the king's tutor, to consult in the Sorbonne itself a contrary opinion. It was declared by ten or twelve doctors that, provided nothing was said on the stage that could bring scandal or was contrary to virtuous morals, the theatre was in itself harmless and could be attended without scruple; and this was founded on the fact that the usage of the Church had greatly lessened the apostolic severity which the early Christians observed in the first centuries. By this means the queen's conscience was set at rest; but sorrow to us who have degenerated from the virtue of our fathers, sorrow to us for thus becoming infirm in zeal and faithfulness! The courtiers cried out against the rector and treated him openly with ridicule. They tried to persuade the queen that Père Vincent, a worthy man and one of great piety, had taken part in this affair in order to work the ruin of her minister, by condemning things that he had authorized. But on several occasions she replied to this that she did not believe a word of it.

Though I only mention great affairs in passing, as a woman who cannot know them thoroughly and has often neglected to notice them at all, it has happened, nevertheless, that many have been discussed in the cabinet and that I have applied myself to listen to the actors in them when they spoke. Those that were of consequence, coming thus to my knowledge, I shall write down as they may happen to occur to me, — without being careful to know them all, or any of them to their full extent, because I have no intention of writing a regular history. But I have taken care to tell only the truth; which has always come to me solely from those who had the chief part in such affairs. The peace which the Dutch made with Spain, which I shall mention here, is a proof of what I say; it is a fragment which I let fall as I go my way; it will find its place with others of the same nature, and as it will not be treated with more order or connection than those, it will not have more worth or value.

This people, rebellious against its king, which had caused such trouble to Philip the Second, which had sated the cruelty of the Duke of Alba under his yoke, given employment to the valour of the Duke of Parma, and put to such proof the virtue of Marguerite and that of the Infanta Clara-Eugenia — this republic, in short, so celebrated for its power, for the boldness of its enterprise, for its establishment and the glorious actions done by the Prince of Orange in governing it, had sustained its rebellion by the assistance of France; but this assistance it now resolved to abandon, and to put itself completely in possession of legitimate liberty.

Liberty had already been offered to the people of Holland, but the ministers of France, Cardinals Richelieu and Mazarin, had always hindered it. The depressed condition of their real master, whose affairs were in a bad state, now gave them the means of making peace with him and preserving their usurped States, their conquests, and their supremacy. Accordingly they made a treaty with him (which was not concluded until some time later) and became peaceably lords of their country, of which they remained sovereigns, with the shame of being as bad Christians as they were bad subjects. To keep some terms with France they delayed signing this treaty, saying that they wished to bring about a general peace before they separated entirely from us. Orders were given to the Comte de Servien, who was at Munster, to go to Holland and endeavour to break off this particular treaty; but he did not succeed; these people, following the example of all others, thought only of their own interests and the strengthening of their own grandeur.

D'Estrades, who was envoy to the Prince of Orange from the king when this arrangement was concluded, told me that the cupidity of the Princess of Orange was the cause of it; and that the Spaniards had won her over during the last days of her husband's life. He declared that that prince, who resembled his forefathers in valour and capacity, would never have consented to the peace had he been in a state to follow his feelings of glory and ambition. He was convinced that the end of the war would be the end of the power of his house, and that when he no longer made himself feared by arms his people would despise him. But his maladies, by diminishing the strength of his body, diminished also his strength of mind, so that he did not oppose the negotiation as he would have done had he been in better health. If the greed of a woman began the work, the avarice of the minister, in spite of his desire to prevent the peace, concluded it. D'Estrades, relating to me all the particulars, said that the princess only allied herself with Spain out of vexation that Cardinal Mazarin failed to send her some diamond earrings which he had led her to expect.

But not to leave so long the Court of our regent let us return to the princes, who were the only cause of uneasiness that the queen now had [January, 1647]. The Prince de Condé, having become rich and powerful, was regarded by the whole Court as the one whose friendship or hatred was to make or mar the fortunes of men.

That victorious air which the battles of Rocroy and Fribourg and the taking of Furnes, Mardick, and Dunkerque had given him, made him so considered by his masters that most persons sought his protection rather than that of the Duc d'Orléans. That is why his court was so very large; those who, through their great establishments, were in a position to do harm or good having offered him their services and attached themselves to his interests; whenever he came to visit the queen he filled her room with the most distinguished personages of the kingdom. His favourites, who were the greater part of the young seigneurs who had followed him in the army and now shared his grandeur as they did his glory, were called the *petits-maîtres*, because they belonged to one who seemed to be the master of them all; and this new title effaced that of the *importants*.

At the end of the Shrovetide [March 2, 1647] Cardinal Mazarin gave a great fête to the Court, which was very fine and much praised by adulators, who are to be met with at all times. It consisted of a comedy, with stage scenery and music in the Italian fashion, which seemed to us most beautiful, although we had seen others that were wonderful and regal. He had brought the musicians from Rome with great trouble, also the machinist, who was a man of much reputation for such scenery. The dresses were magnificent, and the whole preparation of the same kind. Worldlings were delighted, the devout murmured; and those ill-regulated minds who blame everything that takes place did not fail, as usual, to poison pleasure, because such persons cannot breathe its atmosphere without vexation and wrath.

This comedy could not be ready till the last days of the carnival, which caused the cardinal and the Duc d'Orléans to urge the queen to let it be played in Lent; but she, who kept her will in all that related to her conscience, refused consent. She even showed some annoyance that the comedy, which was played on a Saturday for the first time, was arranged to begin late, because she wished to make her devotions on the Sunday; and the evening of the days on which she took the communion she was accustomed to retire early in order to rise earlier than usual the next morning. She did not wish to lose the pleasure altogether, for the sake of him who gave it; but in order not to fail in what she thought her duty, she left the play in the middle to pray to God and sup and go to bed at the suitable time, so that nothing might upset the regularity of her life. Cardinal Mazarin showed some annoyance at this; and though the matter was a mere trifle, with only enough serious foundation to oblige the queen to do as she did, she was nevertheless considered to have acted against the feelings of her minister. And as he showed he was vexed, this little bitterness was a sweet morsel to a large number of persons. Idle tongues and ears were busy with it for days; and even the gravest persons felt moments of joy which were to them delectable.

The Maréchal de Gramont, eloquent, witty, Gascon, and bold in flattery, set this comedy among the wonders of the world; the Duc de Mortemart, great amateur of music and great courtier, seemed enchanted with the mere name of the lowest actors; and the pair, in order to please the minister, made such exaggerations when they talked of it that they became wearisome at last to persons who were moderate in speech.

The next evening the celebrated comedy was played again, and the queen saw the whole of it. On Monday there was a ball, given on the stage of a hall arranged with scenery, which could be moved in a moment; it was really the finest thing ever seen. The hall was gilded and lined with great frames in which were pictures painted in perspective; a most agreeable sight to those who occupied the amphitheatre. This hall was also furnished with seats and hassocks placed in niches around it, and did not look as if the hand of man had anything to do with it. At one end was a throne raised about four or five steps, on which were cushions, chairs with arms, and a dais overhead of silver and gold cloth, with fringes worthy of such furniture. Four great crystal chandeliers lighted this hall, which seemed a veritable fairyland, representing in our day the era of Urganda and Armida.

The king, to show civility to the Prince of Wales, would not take his own seat, but gave it to Mademoiselle, who was decked that evening by the queen's own hands with the crown jewels, pearls and diamonds, fastened with little cherry-coloured and black and white ribbons. This adornment was beautiful and pleasing, particularly the bouquet she wore upon her head. It seemed as if those great diamonds and pearls were strewn among the flowers, and that all the beauty and wealth of nature were gathered there expressly to deck her. From this bouquet issued three feathers, of the three colours of the ribbons, which drooped to her throat, and she made us see on this occasion that a handsome person becomes handsomer for being decorated. The king wore a suit of black satin embroidered with silver and gold, through which the black appeared only enough to set off the embroidery. Cherry-coloured plumes and ribbons completed his adornment, but the beautiful features of his face, the sweetness of his eyes joined to their gravity, the whiteness and brilliancy of his complexion, together with his hair, which was then very blond, adorned him more than his clothes. He danced perfectly; and though he was then only eight years old, it could be said of him that he was the one of the whole company who had the most distinguished air and assuredly the most beauty.

The Prince of Wales received much praise and pleased everybody. But the one whose suit obtained the most approbation was the Vidame d'Amiens, son-in-law of the Maréchal de Villeroy. He wore an embroidery of gold and pearls, the workmanship of which was so delicate that there was nothing of the common order in it; it seemed to disdain jewels as if they were something too vulgar.

The Duchesse de Montbazon came decked with pearls, and cherry-coloured feathers on her head, and though she was then more than forty years of age, she was still in dazzling beauty, showing that a fine autumn is always beautiful. Mademoiselle de Guise was present, no longer young, though much more so than the Duchesse de Montbazon. Her beauty, her kind manner and her modesty, with pearls and a black gown, made her admired by all who saw her. All the other persons of an age to adorn a ball did their best to please the spectators. The queen's maids-of-honour, Pons, Querchy, and Saint-Mégrin, tried to make a few natural conquests by the care they took to embellish themselves in all sorts of ways. Happy they if, among so many lovers, they had been able to catch husbands according to their ambition, and the unruliness of their desires.

The comedy was again represented on the following day, the Mardi gras. It ended very late and we had had no supper. The cardinal offered us his, and we went to eat it with him, — Madame de Bregi, Mademoiselle de Beaumont, my sister, and I (for Mlle. de Beaumont was now restored to the

good graces of the queen).   This was the only meal he ever
gave us in his life, and it was not much.   He treated us with
great indifference and coldness.   He despised women and
did not think them worthy of esteem, unless, by intrigues or
malice, they found means to obtain his confidence.   We left
him very ill-pleased at not being better received, particularly
Madame de Bregi, who being a handsome woman made a
profession of being so, and even had the audacity to pretend
that the great minister had a certain feeling of tenderness
for her.   For this reason she felt his coldness more than the
rest of us, who were quite resolved to put up with it and
well accustomed to his disdainful manners.

The Prince de Condé, seeing the month of March advancing, began to think of his journey to Catalonia.   Before he
started [March 20, 1647] he had a short emotion which
troubled the peace of his heart.   He had let himself be overcome by the beauty of Mademoiselle de Toussy, and this
weakness slipped into his heart at a time when, in spite of
his youth, he was beginning to profess loudly a contempt for
the mad passion of love, and a resolve to give himself
entirely to that of glory.   He played the braggart against
gallantry, often declaring that he renounced it, and even did
so at this ball, though it was a place where his presence
appeared to advantage.   He was not handsome ; his face was
ugly in shape ; his eyes were blue and keen, and there was
much pride in his glance.   His nose was aquiline, his mouth
extremely disagreeable, because it was large and his teeth
projected too much ; but in his whole countenance there was
something grand and haughty, with a certain resemblance to
an eagle.   He was not very tall, but his figure in itself was
perfect.   He danced well and had an agreeable air ; his
bearing was lofty and his head fine, — its arrangement with
curls and powder being required to make it appear so.   But

even at this time he neglected his person much; and in the deep mourning which he wore for his late father he was not pleasing, for, his face being long and thin, this negligence was the more disadvantageous to him.

The Prince of Orange died about this time. His death, for the reasons I have given, was a loss to France, and his merits having made him respected throughout Europe, he was much regretted. The unfortunate King of England, who had honoured him with his alliance, was now finding himself on the verge of his fatal destiny. He was betrayed by the Scotch, to whom he had gone in search of fidelity and troops to avenge him on the parliamentarians; but that barbarous people delivered him to his enemies. I heard it said that they asked him if he was not content to go back to England, and he answered that it was more just he should go to those who had bought him than stay with those who had sold him. He went, only to be kept a prisoner in the Isle of Wight, where he stayed till his death. Many proposals were made to him by the parliament and his subjects. But, whether he found them contrary to his conscience, or lacked ability to choose those that were suitable (as was said by persons capable of judging), he did not accept any, and was reserved by God's decree for the most cruel and amazing end a king can come to.

In France we no longer have, thank God, religious wars; there are now only contests frequently arising among our learned men on questions of theology. There was one on Grace which seemed to have been ended by a decision of Pope Urban VIII., against which none of the doctors declaimed; but in their hearts both sides were still of the same sentiments made public by their writings. Père Des Mares, of the congregation of the priests of the Oratory, who preached the Lent of this year with much zeal and wholly

according to the Gospel as to morals, was admired by people
of the highest quality, the finest minds, and even those who
were most retired from the world.   But, as to doctrine, he
was thought to be of the opinion of Jansenius, Bishop of
Ypres in Flanders, who had written a book in the spirit of
Saint Augustin on this great mystery.   And, as it was difficult for him, as for other preachers, to treat this matter so
delicately that no word could be found to cavil at, nothing was
talked of in Paris but "the Jansenists" and "the Molinists."

. This question, as to which there was no one who did not
take an interest for the satisfaction of his conscience, not
only divided the schools, but social life [*les ruelles*], and the
city as well as the Court.   Those who were called Molinists
(from Molina, a learned Spanish priest) had on their side the
censure of five propositions in the book of Jansenius; and
those called Jansenists maintained that the five condemned
propositions were not in that book.   This defence, their
wholly exemplary lives, the austerity of which they made
profession, drew to them the esteem of a great number of
persons of solid piety; and they would have been esteemed
by every one if they had avoided the blame that may justly
be cast upon them of having taught women (in French so
beautiful that it made the sex quit their novels) those great
difficulties on which it is forbidden to write, together with
questions of conscience about which none but confessors
should be instructed.   It has cost us so much to have learned
the knowledge of good and evil that we ought to agree that
it is better to be ignorant of such matters than to learn
them; especially for us women who are accused of being the
cause of all evil.   We see such great men, with all their intellect and all their learning, ruin themselves in heresies
which they think they draw from Holy Scripture!   I cannot
withhold myself from saying that no Christian should decide

for himself that which is environed by so much obscurity; nor should he enter into the details of mysteries which the councils themselves cannot elucidate, and which they command us to believe surrounded by all their darkness. God himself having chosen, no doubt, to hide from us this knowledge and enclose it in its own immensity, we must hope that in heaven souls, separated from their earthly natures, will learn its wonders and see the causes for which it has pleased Him to leave them ignorant of the deep abysses of Grace, and the manner in which it operates in the soul for our salvation.

The great Saint Augustin, whose ideas are revered in the Church, and whose writings seem to have produced the opinions of those who are called Jansenists, has never clearly explained these wonderful secrets. The saint himself could not comprehend them; he speaks of their Author with admiration, and confesses humbly that the judgments of God are inscrutable, and His ways past discovering. The most learned know nothing when it is a question of understanding them; and I believe that this great teacher of grace, teacher of all Christians, and of the Jansenists in particular, would have willingly said, when in this world, with the Italian poet, —

> " Ampi volumi immensi
> De le tue glorie eterne
> Son le sfere superne;
> E con dorata, e lucida favella
> Di te parla ogni stella.
> Io lo so, Signor, mà non penetro i sensi,
> Ch' a la lingua del mondo avvezzo essendo
> La favella del ciel non ben comprendo." [1]

[1] The celestial spheres are ample and vast volumes of Thy eternal glories; and each star speaks of Thee in golden words. I know it, Lord; but their meaning I cannot penetrate, because, being used to the language of earth, I cannot comprehend the language of heaven.

Whenever I hear men speaking of God in relation to the hidden mysteries, I am delighted not to be obliged to know more than my *Pater*, my *Credo*, and the Commandments of God. As to the matter of which I have been speaking, I know that it suffices me to believe we have nothing but that which we have received; that I can do no good without the grace of God; and that he has given me my free will.

The queen at once took the side of the Jesuits [Molinists], who had the advantage of governing the king's conscience. She thought herself obliged to oppose opinions which were considered novelties and might disturb the Church. On the other hand, one had reason to be surprised in seeing those who appeared to maintain the orthodox opinions allowing the publication, under their name, of maxims quite contrary to the Gospel touching morality, without sufficiently rebuking the authors. The queen, zealous for good, was often led to say with pain, not intending to lay it on any special person, that she knew no perfect virtue, nor any piety without much weakness.

Early in the year the Duc d'Orléans started for Bourbon to take the waters, and Madame followed him. They went there for health in order to give a prince to France, a grandson of Henri IV., which Monsieur passionately desired. The princess never made long journeys, whether from crotchets or real illness; she seldom went out, declaring that the least agitation made her faint. I have sometimes heard Monsieur laughing about her, and telling the queen how she took the communion in her bed rather than go to the chapel which was close by, without her having, apparently, any real illness. When she came to see the queen, once in two years or so, she had herself carried in a chair, but with such fuss and affectation that her arrival at the Palais-Royal was celebrated as if it were a little miracle. Often she would get only three steps from the Luxembourg, when she had to be taken back, being attacked by some of the many ills she said she felt, but which never appeared. She ate bread which she carried in a provision pocket; and Russia leather boots were her mortal enemies. She was sister to the Duc de Lorraine, and Monsieur had married her during his exile from France, without the consent of the late king. When Nancy was taken she had to fly, disguised as a page, in the bottom of a cart; and was forced to pay with great distresses for the honour she had gained in marrying Monsieur.

That prince, on his side, being then heir presumptive to the crown, though obliged to leave her in Flanders when he returned to France, remained inviolably faithful to her. As he showed no firmness for others who had attached themselves to him, King Louis XIII., his brother, urged him, on his return to France, to consent to the rupture of the marriage; but this he would never do, and he brought his wife to France as soon as the death of the king and that of Cardinal Richelieu enabled him to do so.

I have heard it said that on arriving at that beautiful palace of the Luxembourg in Paris some one asked if she did not feel great joy at finding herself in that superb place; to which she coldly answered that after the joy of again seeing Monsieur, all the rest seemed nothing to her. She had a good mind, and reasoned well on all subjects about which she chose to talk. She seemed, by what she said, to have heart and ambition. She loved Monsieur ardently; and hated in the same way any one who could injure her with him. She was handsome in the features of her face, which were beautiful and well-formed; but she was not agreeable; her whole person lacked I know not what that was pleasing; but as for actual ugliness, she had it only in her teeth, which were already decayed. It was said of this princess that she was beautiful without being so, and had intellect but seemed to have none because she made no use of it. She was fat and thin both; her face was full and her bosom handsome, so her women said, but her hands and arms were very thin. It must also be said that she had not a fine figure, but neither was she deformed. In short, all contrasts were collected in her in a surprising manner; and it was impossible to speak of her except with an ambiguity to be used about no one else.

It was also true that Monsieur loved her and did not love her. He lived with her and treated her well; he never deliberately annoyed her; and when he thought her dissatisfied or grieved he did all he could to cure her little thoughts. He never left her, and when he was at home he spent nearly all his time in her room, showing sometimes that he esteemed her virtue and her intelligence. But he had a favourite [the Abbé de la Rivière] whom she did not like; he had raised him to extreme grandeur and had confidence in him, and she was never able to do him an injury. Monsieur often laughed at her delicacies and whims with the ladies who served her, and even with the queen, to whom he used to say that she was visionary, that her piety was ridiculous, that she never talked except to her confessor, whom she consulted about the merest trifles. Neither did he spare her favourites, who were among the silliest creatures in Paris. He said, speaking of them, that persons of merit, lacking discernment, ought to be ashamed to be on good terms with them; that her court was decried because those who were obliged to see her, on account of her rank, found there none but persons unworthy of her favour and approbation. So it may be said he loved her, but did not love her often; and the respect he had for her was varied in the same degree.

Those who knew her intimately told me she was naturally insensible to friendship; and that, if she loved Monsieur, that feeling had no other operation in her than to incite her to scold him continually and cause him much vexation; so that their union was as inexplicable as all the rest. As the princess was both healthy and ill at the same time, and as she belonged to those virtuous women who like to follow their husbands, her physician obliged her much by ordering her to the baths of Bourbon because Monsieur was to take them. She ceased to complain in order to make the journey, because she always wanted to be with him; and not only did she make it, but she did not go in a chair, as she first intended. She never left the coach in which Monsieur was, and seemed to bear the fatigues of the journey more easily than the most robust women.

The Duchesse d'Orléans might justly have a passion for Monsieur. He was agreeable in person. His complexion and the features of his face were handsome, the expression of his countenance pleasing; his eyes were blue, his hair black. He looked like the son of a king, but badly trained. In spite of his natural restlessness and his grimaces, it was easy to see both birth and grandeur in his person. He was kind and easy of access. He had intelligence, spoke well, and jested pleasantly. He had read much and knew history thoroughly, with much other studious knowledge. Nothing was wanting in this prince for society, except that he was rather vainglorious, with that coarse pride which made him hold his rank too stiffly, though it did not prevent his treating kindly those who approached him. I have seen women of quality standing in the room where he was, to show the respect they owed him, without his having the civility to ask them to sit down; and men complained that in the roughest weather he never told them to put on their hats, which the king, his brother, always did.

He was accused of being timid and lazy. But I have heard it said that he sometimes went into very dangerous places, as far in the advance as the common soldiers. But there is one stain on his life which dishonours him. It was when, in his youth, he formed a party in France for the interests of the queen his mother, and the Duc de Mont-morency, fighting for him, was made prisoner before his very eyes; he could have saved him, but he did not, and was the cause that that great seigneur, the most amiable, as I was told, of men, was beheaded. His favourite, the Abbé de la Rivière, whose interest it was to preserve him, kept him as much as he could from going into danger; and Maréchal de Gassion, one day when the prince had done personally well and had bravely risked musket shots, said, after praising him, that he had been lively that time because his suckfish [remora] was not there. It was for this reason that the Court desired this year that the Duc d'Orléans should not command the army; and the doctors who sent him to the Baths gave no little pleasure to the ministers; for not only did his expenses as commander increase immensely the royal budget, but the finest plans were rendered useless by cares for his preservation. The maxim of conquerors is to risk; but it was impossible to propose schemes of that nature to a general of such consequence, who, after the king, the queen, and the little real Monsieur, held the first place in the kingdom, and whose life was therefore precious to France, which naturally loves the children of her kings.

The Comte d'Harcourt, that unfortunate general, returning from Catalonia, arrived in Holy-Week [April 20, 1647]. The queen, by advice of the cardinal, received him coldly. It was the minister's habit to do harsh things through her, and to reserve favours, benefits, and pardons for his own bestowal; for the queen was convinced that the more friends the cardinal made, the more the peace of her regency was secured. With this idea, she told Comte d'Harcourt that she thought him wrong for having undertaken the siege of Lerida against the orders of the king. He replied like an able man, though he was not suspected of being one, that he entreated her very humbly to believe him incapable of failing in respect or fidelity to whatever concerned his duty and the obedience that he owed to her wishes; and (in order not to importune her with his reasons for so acting) he begged her to let him inform the cardinal, who, he hoped, would have sufficient equity to justify him to her. His scheme succeeded; for as the minister only wanted to mortify him, he took him back into his good graces after a great explanation, and, as the count himself had foreseen, he received good treatment from the queen when he next presented himself before her.

The festivals passed as usual. The queen, after having taken the Lord's supper at home on Holy Thursday, went to shut herself up at the Val-de-Grâce to spend the rest of Holy-Week in retreat and prayer. We went there, my sister and I, very early on Good Friday morning, in order to profit by her example. She had risen and dressed by five o'clock, and was already employed in meditating on the wonders which God on that day had worked in our favour. She heard the Passion preached at seven o'clock by a Jesuit, who did not make himself admired; and after the service was over, she went to adore the Cross with the saintly nuns who live in continual penitence and show by all their actions that the Cross is ever in their thoughts and before their eyes. She did these things with a devoutness fit to edify the most hardened to the laws of God.

After returning to her chamber she spoke to us, to my sister and me, of the instability of the things of earth, of the importance of our salvation, the danger in which we continually are of failing in what we have to do for the accomplishment of that great work, which we agreed at that moment was the first and chief of all. After his dinner the king came to see her, bringing the cardinal with him, and about a dozen of the Court who were necessary about his person. The queen took great pleasure in showing them the whole house, and the designs she had for a beautiful new convent which should preserve to posterity eternal signs of the honour it had received in being the place where she went to enjoy solitude.

The king and Cardinal Mazarin were present at the *tenebræ*. The former was admired by his people, who saw him, through the nun's grating, running hither and thither, blowing out the candles and behaving like a child that loves to play. The minister, who accompanied all his actions with great modesty, played the pious and devout personage, though perhaps he was not so at all. He took care to seem regular in his external actions, and it was impossible to reproach him for a vice, or for any irregularity which might go by that name.

When the king had departed and the queen found herself alone in her desert, she went into the infirmary to visit a nun who was dying of a cancer in her breast, which had rotted away the side of it. The smell from the wound was not only such as to be offensive to the queen, who liked sweet odours, but to men the most used to infection and the misery of hospitals. She stayed a long time and chose to see the wound dressed; which was a pitiable sight. The disease had so eaten away the part on which it had fastened that we could see into her body. After this act of charity we

Mon cousin vous avez signalé par de si belles preuves
le zèle que vous avez pour le service du roy —
monsieur mon fils, et je suis tellement persuadée
de l'affection que vous avez pour moy que quand
quelque entreprise ne réussira pas entre vos mains
je croiray tousjours fort facilement qu'il a esté
impossible de faire mieux. aussy quelques —
remerciemens que contienne vostre lettre de la
façon dont j'ay pris le succès de Lérida, comme
d'une grace que je vous ay faicte, je cognois
fort bien que je ne vous ay rendu que —
justice. Mon cousin le card.. Mazarin m'a
rendu compte de l'ample despesche que vous
luy avez faicte, et je luy charge de vous faire
sçavoir mes intentions sur ce qu'elle contient
et particulierement sur v[ost]re retour par deça

de sorte qu'il ne me reste qu'à vous
asseurer que je suis avec plus de
tendresse que je ne puis vous dire.

V[ost]re affectionnée cousine
ANNE

De Dieppe le ...
2.e d'Aoust 647.

(FAC-SIMILE LETTER.)

ANNE OF AUSTRIA TO THE PRINCE DE CONDÉ
(THE GREAT CONDÉ).

left the queen to enjoy the rest that is found at the foot
of altars.   The next day she returned to the Palais-Royal
to be present on Easter-day in its parish church and perform
her devotions.

The fêtes over, nothing was talked of but war and journeys.   The Court had planned to go to the frontier and even
beyond Amiens and Compiègne, but in spite of this excitement which seemed to foreshadow battles, the peace that
reigned in the Court itself and made it pleasurable induced
the queen to have that fine comedy, with scenery, of which I
have already spoken played three or four times before her;
she was always present and never wearied of it.   The last
time was to entertain Madame de Longueville, who had
lately returned from Munster.

This princess, who, though absent, reigned in her family,
and whose approbation every one desired as a sovereign good,
returned to Paris in May, 1647, and did not fail to appear
there with even more lustre than she had when she left it.
The friendship that the Prince de Condé, her brother, felt for
her gave authority to her actions and manners, and the grandeur of her beauty and of her mind so increased the cabal
of her family that she had not been long at Court before she
occupied it wholly.   She became the object of all desires;
her reception [ruelle] was the centre of all intrigues, and those
whom she liked were considered at once as the darlings of
fortune.   Her courtiers were revered by the minister; and
before long we shall see her the cause of our revolutions
and of all the quarrels that came so near destroying France.

The Prince de Marsillac had formed an intimacy with M.
le Prince [the Court title given to the Prince de Condé] ever
since the queen, changing to many, had changed to him,
and after promising much had thought it her duty not to
give him what he asked.   In attaching himself to M. le

Prince through policy, he gave himself to Madame de Longueville in a rather more tender manner, joining feelings of the heart to regard for her grandeur and fortune. This gift of himself was apparent to the eyes of the public; and it seemed to the whole Court that the princess received it with welcome. In all that she did later, it was clearly seen that ambition was not the only emotion that filled her soul, for the interests of the Prince de Marsillac held a large place in it. She became ambitious for him; for his sake she ceased to love repose, and in becoming sensible to that affection she became insensible to her own fame.

Her ideas, her intellect, and the opinion formed of her discernment made her the admired of all men; they were convinced that her esteem alone was enough to give them reputation. Though she ruled all souls by this means, that of her beauty was no less potent; for although she had had the small-pox since the regency began and had slightly lost the purity of her complexion, the glow of her charms always attracted the inclination of those who saw her; above all, she possessed in a sovereign degree that which the Spanish language expresses by the words: *donayre, brio, y bizaría.* Her figure was admirable; the very air of her person had a charm, the spell of which extended even to her own sex. It was impossible to see her without liking her, and wishing to please her. Her beauty, nevertheless, consisted more in the colouring of her face than in the perfection of its features. Her eyes were not large, but beautiful, soft and brilliant, and the blue was wonderful, like that of the turquoise. Poets could only compare to lilies and roses the tones of her face; and the silvery fair hair that accompanied such marvels made her resemble an angel — such as the weakness of our nature makes us imagine them — much more than a woman.

It may be said that at this time all grandeur, all glory, all gallantry were held in this Bourbon family, of which M. le Prince was the head, and success was no longer thought a good unless it came through their hands. The Prince de Conti,[1] younger brother of this brother and sister, had just left college and was beginning to appear in society. He was handsome in face, but as his figure was deformed he was destined for the Church. He possessed many benefices, and several persons attached themselves to him in the hope of making their fortune on this line. The young prince, finding that his sister, Mme. de Longueville, had so great a reputation, desired to follow her advice and sentiments, and allowed himself to be tempted to win respect through her. He sought to please her, more even as an honourable man than as her brother; he had intelligence and he succeeded.

The queen, who was by nature neither jealous nor ambitious, nevertheless showed some coldness towards Mme. de Longueville. She did not like this manner of publicly professing to be a *bel esprit;* she disliked all the ways of it. She herself had reason and good sense; all that was in her was natural and without art; and these two personages, according to the measure of their age, both being infinitely amiable, were so different in character that it was impossible that the inferior, who lived as a queen and did not render great duty to her sovereign, could please the latter.

The occupation given by the plaudits of the great world, which usually regards with too much admiration the fine qualities of people of high birth, had deprived Mme. de Longueville of the leisure to read and to give to her mind a knowledge sufficiently extended to call her learned. She was by nature too much concerned about sentiments; which

---

[1] Armand de Bourbon, brother of the great Condé, abbé and prior of Cluny. He left the Church and married Anne Martinozzi, niece of Cardinal Mazarin; their son Louis-Armand married the daughter of Louis XIV. and Mme. de la Vallière. — TR.

passed with her for infallible rules, and were not so always;
and there was too much affectation in her manner of speaking and acting, the greatest beauty of which consisted in the
delicacy of her thoughts and a very just reasoning. She
seemed constrained; and the refined satire, of which she
and her courtiers made profession, often fell upon those
who, wishing to pay her their duty, could not help feeling
that the honest sincerity which should be observed in polite
society was apparently banished from hers. The virtues
and laudable qualities of the most excellent beings are
mingled with things that are their opposite; all men share
the clay from which they get their origin, and God alone is
perfect.

May 9, 1647, the queen took the road to Compiègne, intending to go as far as Amiens. The cardinal stayed three
or four days behind her in Paris to conclude some business,
and started to join her on the 15th of the same month. As
he was indefatigable in working, and did the duties of all
the secretaries of State, wishing to know everything, he was
so continually busy that it was almost impossible to see him.
Italians are usually haters of a crowd and bustle; for this
reason the minister disliked to show himself — so much so
that persons of quality murmured at being forced to wait at
his door until he would see them. They were not repulsed,
however, by the contempt shown to them, which, apparently,
produced no other effect upon their souls than to make them
more humble and grovelling; but as the French allow themselves to be easily governed by favourites, so are they also
as easily led into talking against them. The cardinal, knowing this, was accustomed to say, in speaking of these people,
that he was willing to let them talk provided that they would
let him do. The murmuring began from ear to ear in the
antechamber of the man who sneered at their attentions,

and was uttered in a loud voice as soon as the mutterers were out of it. Sometimes I grew weary of hearing him so abused; for, besides the fact that it was often unjust, what in itself is useless always seems to me disagreeable.

The cardinal had as many lights as a man who was the artisan of his own grandeur could have. He had great capacity, above all, industry, and marvellous shrewdness in leading and amusing men by countless deceptive hopes. He never did harm unless from necessity to those who displeased him. Usually, he was content to complain of them, and these complaints produced explanations which readily restored to him the friendship of those who had been unfaithful to him, or who thought they had cause to be vexed with him. He had the gift of pleasing, and it was impossible to keep one's self from being charmed by his sweetness; but this same sweetness was the cause, when not accompanied by the benefits it seemed to promise, that those who were weary of expecting fell into disgust and vexation. Until now, the complaints of private persons had made no great impression upon the public mind, and they were founded more on the loss of his favour than on hatred to his person.

The respect that the halo of royal power, which surrounded him gloriously, impressed upon the hearts of the king's subjects arrested much that human malice tried to blame in him; and the tranquillity of the Court, joined to fortunate successes in war, had given him, up to this time, more reputation than the worst of the courtiers could give him shame. But, little by little, they went on discovering defects in him; some of which could be attributed to all favourites, others of which were essentially his. They said that he ignored our customs, and did not trouble himself sufficiently to have them observed; that he did not take pains, as he should have done, to govern the State by its long-established laws;

that he did not protect justice and law as he was bound by
his position as prime minister to do; and that he thus failed
in the care he owed to the public weal.   These sins of omis-
sion, though great, could not rightly dishonour him, because
he may have had good intentions which, if known, would
have justified him to the public.

It may be said, nevertheless, that, with the temperament
he had, these accusations were not far wrong, for it was his
nature to neglect too much to do good.   He seemed to
respect no virtue, and to hate no vice.   He appeared to have
neither; he passed for a man habituated to the custom of
Christian virtues, but showing no desire for their practice.
He made no profession of piety, and gave no signs to the
contrary by any of his actions, unless it were that satirical
remarks occasionally escaped him which were at variance
with the respect that a Christian ought to have for whatever
concerns religion.   In spite of his greed he had not yet
seemed miserly; and the finances were more wasted at this
period of his administration by partisans than at any previous
time.

He also, as I have said elsewhere speaking of the queen,
granted the dignities of the Church to many persons who
claimed them from profane motives; and he did not always
appoint to the bishoprics men who could honour his choice
by their virtue and piety.   Religion was too much neglected
by him; he was always too indifferent to that sacred trust
which God had committed to him.   By nature he was distrustful; and one of his greatest cares was to study men in
order to know them and guard himself from attacks and
from the intrigues that were formed against him.   He professed to fear nothing, and to despise even the cautions that
were given him about his person, though in reality the principle of his greatest care was his personal preservation.

The few days that the minister remained behind in Paris served only to still further foment the jealousies that were beginning to appear; because many of those who wished to see him could not succeed in doing so.   When he got into his coach to go away the whole courtyard of the Palais-Royal was filled with *cordons-bleus*, great seigneurs, and persons of rank, who by their eagerness seemed to be only too happy to look at him from a distance.   All men are naturally slaves to fortune; I can truly say that I never saw any one at Court who was not a flatterer, some more, others less.   Self-interest, which blinds us, takes us unawares and betrays us on occasions which concern us; it makes us act with more feeling than intelligence; and it happens often enough that we become ashamed of our weakness; which, however, we do not perceive except through sage reflection, and after the occasion for doing better has passed.

VIII.

1647.

THOUGH peace could not, at this time have been so glorious for France, it would not have failed to be convenient and advantageous to her. The long wars had exhausted her in men, forces, and money.[1] It was doubted in those days whether the minister really wished for peace. At any rate, the fortunate moment passed, and this period, propitious for good fortune, was not destined to soon return. God puts, when it pleases Him, limits to our ambition; He knows how to humiliate those who trust in their own wisdom, and shows to kings and ministers that they are not the masters of their own fate. The cardinal may, perhaps, have had good motives for delaying the peace, which seemed to all Europe to depend on him only; but, as it is easy to suspect a minister

---

[1] Laporte relates in his memoirs dreadful details of this misery, which kept on increasing: "The king saw quantities of sick and maimed soldiers following him everywhere, and begging for help to relieve their misery, without his having a single penny to give them; which amazed people much.

"Besides the misery of the soldiers, that of the people was awful; and wherever the Court went the poor peasants flung themselves around it, thinking to be in greater safety, because the army devastated the country. They brought their cattle, which immediately died from hunger, for they dared not lead them to pasture. When the cattle were dead they died themselves incontinently, for they had nothing to live on but the Court charities, which were middling; each one considering his own interests first. They had no shelter from the great heat of the day and the chilliness of night, except that of awnings, carts, and vans which were in the streets. When the mothers were dead the children soon died; and I saw on the bridge of Melun three children lying on their dead mother and still sucking her." This went on from 1646 to 1652. — FR. ED.

of having more regard for his private benefit than for the public weal, and as the common opinion was that peace would have been the ruin of that benefit because all the strength of the cabinet could have gathered more easily against him, Cardinal Mazarin was judged as a man who apprehended this very danger.

The queen, who desired peace, always assured me in those days that she knew for a certainty that her minister did his best to give it to France and to all Europe. She said that what others had reason to apprehend would not happen to one in his position, for he was well assured that she would never permit intrigues against him, and that the same confidence she had had in him during the war she would have during peace. But he may have deceived the queen, who was certainly unable to convince the public. Nevertheless, it is possible that he wished for peace at that time, and had reason to do so; for besides appearing always to aim at the good of the State, he was avaricious and master of the finances. It may be believed, therefore, that peace would have brought him the means to amass much treasure, which to him would possess a considerable charm.

In Paris the murmuring was great about our losses in the war. The honour of the taking of La Bassée [Flanders] was granted to Maréchal de Gassion, but the blame for the victories won by our enemies was put upon Cardinal Mazarin. They were adduced as signs of his bad conduct of the war, and his adversaries presented them to the public as evident proofs of all that they preached against him.

This murmuring caused several banishments. The Comte de Fiesque was the most important of the exiles. He had been well-treated by the cardinal, but on the downfall of the Duc de Beaufort, whose friend he said he was, he declaimed against him loudly, telling him, in justification, that between

two equal friends one should always follow the unfortunate,
and quit the dominant one.   He therefore shared the misfortune of the one by exile, and showed that he hated the power
of the other by his speeches.   The cardinal, however, urged
by the friends of the Comte de Fiesque, wishing to forget
the affronts he thought he had received, brought him back
from this first exile with every sign of true reconciliation.
He followed, in thus forgiving, his natural inclination which
inclined him to gentleness and peace.   That of his pardoned
enemy was different; he was never content and was always
finding fault with the actions of those who governed.   For
this reason his temperament kept him from profiting by the
truce between them; so that his conduct forced the minister
at last to send him away again.   The Abbé de Belebat was
also exiled, and Sarrazin [the poet], for having written satirical verses; together with others of small note who had said
in wine-shops and public places a few silly things.

An ordinance was issued, forbidding all persons to talk
about the affairs of the State; and the queen showed much
aversion to those who said more than they ought.   She remarked to the Maréchale d'Estrées, seeing the arrival in the
streets of Amiens of Madame de Choisy, who came to speak
to her on behalf of her brother, Belebat: "That poor woman
makes me pity her, for her journey is useless; I am resolved
to punish severely all those who talk against the government."   And the Maréchale d'Estrées, in relating to me
what I here write, added that the queen held firm against
the prayers of Madame de Choisy, and openly blamed Cardinal Mazarin for being too kind and too long-suffering.

The queen after seeing that order was restored on the frontier and the army of the king in a condition to defend itself,
left Amiens and went to spend some days at Abbeville.
From there she came to Dieppe, intending to go to Rouen;

but our province and particularly the town of Rouen was so
insensible to the honour the king did it that it carefully
evaded the visit. The queen, on her side, pretended to dread
the fuss and annoyance of the visit and of all the harangues
they would have to listen to. She resolved to return by
Gournay, Gisors, and Pontoise, and stayed but three days at
Dieppe, though the place was agreeable to her. She liked
the view of the ocean which she saw from the windows of
her chamber, where also she could see the fireships burning at
sea for her amusement. The king went to see the large fine
ship the Queen of Sweden had sent him, and a naval combat
took place on the occasion. To crown the joy of the inhabi-
tants they were allowed the honour of guarding the person
of the king, which was partly necessary because he had few
of his guards with him.

The people of Dieppe, who had always been faithful to
Henri IV., the king's grandfather, deserved to receive this
mark of the confidence reposed in them; and as they took it
in that spirit they went about the streets shouting that it
was right to confide the king to their care, for there were
no Ravaillacs among them. Women ran after their Majesties, and all the villagers of that region followed them,
crying out endless benedictions, which, in spite of their
horrible Norman accent, pleased their Majesties. I heard
the queen herself say that the affection she recognized in
this people had been agreeable enough to relieve her of
the annoyance she usually felt at such importunities.

Though the queen desired to evade harangues, she could
not entirely exempt herself from them. The parliament of
Normandy came to welcome her, also the "Chambre des
Comptes" and the "Cours des Aides." On this occasion we
saw what is not extraordinary to see, but what, in itself, is
ever terrible to the mind of man. The chief judge of Rys,

about sixty years of age but in vigorous health, died suddenly at the head of the staircase as he left the queen's presence, and so quickly that there was no interval between his life and his death. The king and queen ran to him, to make him open his mouth and take remedies, but they found him lifeless and their kindness was of no use. I had joined the queen at Dieppe to be with her as long as she was in our province; I therefore saw this sight, with the feeling of horror one has when it is seen near-by. The queen took the road to Paris with satisfaction, whither I followed her soon after.

I reached Paris August 28, very wearied with my journey, because I had been travelling all the time. The country is beautiful with repose and solitude only when we can enjoy the innocent pleasures that Nature gives in woods and streams. I found the queen in the chamber of the Duc d'Anjou, who was ill with a disease sufficiently important to cause uneasiness to so good a mother as herself.

He was beginning to get better, and his room was filled with the most important personages of the Court. This annoyance, which is inseparable from illness, was such that the little prince was inconvenienced by the fine company and entreated the queen to send them all away and stay with him alone. The queen told him that she dared not do so, because the Princesse de Condé and many persons of rank were there. To which he answered: "*Eh! bon Dieu*, madame, pray laugh at that. Are not you the mistress? What is the good of your crown if not to do what you will? You send me away when it pleases you, though I am your son; is it not fair that each should have his turn?" I was with the queen, and as she thought he was right, she did me the honour to say to me: "I must satisfy him; but not in his way; I shall go myself, and that will draw away those who annoy him." She led away the princess, and the rest whom she could not dismiss.

This young prince [1] had intelligence from the time he could talk. The clearness of his thoughts was accompanied by two fine inclinations, which were beginning to appear in him and are necessary to persons of his birth, namely; liberality and humanity. It is to be wished that he had been deprived of the idle amusements allowed him in his youth. He liked to be with women and girls, and to dress them and arrange their hair. He knew what became them better than any woman; and his greatest delight, as he grew older, was to deck and adorn them, and buy jewels to lend or give to those who were his favourites. He was well-made; the features of his face seemed perfect. His black eyes were admirably fine and brilliant; they had sweetness and gravity combined. His mouth was in some respects like that of the queen, his mother. His black hair, in heavy natural curls, suited his complexion; and his nose, which promised to be aquiline, was at that time quite well-formed. It might be expected that, if years did not diminish his beauty, he would dispute the prize with that of the handsomest women; but, as for his figure, it seemed as though he would never be tall.

That same day, in the evening, the king's lawyers came before the queen at her command. She sent for them to complain of the parliament, which opposed a certain tax laid upon provisions, which up to this time had not been levied because the president, de Mesmes, holding the sessions of 1646, had forbidden its being put in force. But in spite of this prohibition, the affair was again brought up for discussion in the Council, where, on account of the need of

---

[1] Philippe d'Orléans, husband of Henrietta of England, and secondly of Élisabeth-Charlotte, Princess Palatine, the mother of the Regent. — TR.

having money, it was proposed to maintain the royal authority in this matter.

The parliament, which assumed to have the right of examining the edicts that laid burdens on the people, having maintained what President de Mesmes had done, and ordered that very humble remonstrances should be sent to the queen on this affair, their resistance made the Court resolve to offer them other edicts less difficult to pass. A conference was held on this subject at the Palais-Royal, when the counsel for the king and that for the parliament were present. The queen was not present, because it is a rule that subjects shall not confer with masters. They all sat down at a large table; the Duc d'Orléans at the head, Cardinal Mazarin opposite to him; next below Monsieur was the chancellor, and next below the cardinal was President de Mesmes; the rest according to rank. D'Émery, at that time superintendent of finance, was at a corner of the table, but had no seat there; and the four secretaries of State were in their usual place. It was expected that the chancellor would make a speech; but the cardinal had sent him a memorandum, made by Lyonne, his secretary, on which were written, by his order, the principal points of the speech. The chancellor felt that he could not maintain the credit he had acquired whenever he spoke in public if he submitted to this dictation; he therefore preferred to say nothing, and excused himself as being indisposed.

At this conference it was finally determined to pass the original tariff, because the parliament considered that by the new propositions made to them the advantage to the people would be no greater. They resolved merely to modify it, and they decreed that it should be levied for two years only, at the end of which time they forbade that it be levied any longer; and at the same time the Cour des

Aides was forbidden to interfere. In getting the money, Cardinal Mazarin was satisfied; so was the queen, because she was saved by this agreement the fatigue of going to parliament in person to get the new edicts passed; which she would have been forced to do had the affair not ended amicably.

On the 11th of September, 1647, we saw, arriving from Italy, three nieces of Cardinal Mazarin, and a nephew.[1] Two Mancini sisters and the nephew were the children of the youngest sister of his Eminence; the third niece was a Martinozzi, daughter of the minister's eldest sister.

The eldest of the little Mancinis was a pleasing brunette with a handsome face, about twelve or thirteen years of age. The second, also a brunette, had a long face and pointed chin. Her eyes were small but lively, and it might be expected that when fifteen years old she would have some charm. According to the rules of beauty it was impossible at this time to grant her any, except that of having dimples in her cheeks. Mademoiselle de Martinozzi was blonde; her features were beautiful, and she had much sweetness in her eyes. She gave promise of becoming very handsome, and had we been astrologers enough to divine in her face the prospects of her fortune as we did those of her beauty, we should have known even then that she was destined to high rank. The last two were of the same age, we were told about nine or ten years old.

Madame de Nogent went to Fontainebleau, by the cardi-

[1] Cardinal Mazarin had two sisters living in Rome; the eldest married to Comte Martinozzi, had two daughters; the other, married to Signor Mancini, had three sons and five daughters. The eldest Mancini became Madame de Mercœur and died young. The second was Olympe, Comtesse de Soissons; the third was Marie, Louis XIV.'s love, finally married to Prince Colonna; the fourth was Hortense, Duchesse de Mazarin; the fifth was Marie-Anne, Duchesse de Bouillon. Anne Martinozzi, daughter of the cardinal's eldest sister, married the Prince de Conti. — Tʀ.

nal's order, to meet them. The minister would never incur great obligations to any of the more important persons of the Court, for fear of being forced into inconvenient gratitude. He treated this affair like a man whose chief care is to seem uninterested; and the opinion his familiar courtiers formed was that he abandoned these children to the Comte de Nogent, a great flatterer and capable of carrying flattery to extremities, expecting him to do them the honours of the great world, while he himself could always say, "It is the humour of that man," and turn him into ridicule with the queen if he thought it useful; in fact, he often treated him in that manner about his conceited speeches and buffooneries.

This man [Nogent] had all his life imitated wit; he affected to make people laugh, talking incessantly, though no one could accuse him of saying anything. In this way he attained to the luck of making a great fortune. There was no person of rank at Court who received greater benefits from it than he, whether by private privileges, by prerogatives and preferences to favours of distinction, or through the great property he had begun to amass under Cardinal Richelieu, who contributed more than any one to make him rich. This great sayer of nothings found means through silliness to rise and to obtain that which his birth denied to him, and which virtue and great merit would not have given him so easily. He had intelligence after his fashion; he was not malicious, and I never heard him say harm of any one, no matter who. Perhaps on great occasions the desire to please made him commit great faults in the sight of God, but as for what appeared externally, if he did not protect the unfortunate, neither did he contribute to ruin them. He gave pleasure when he could, in his own way, which was to turn all things into jest. Though it was difficult to respect him, it was still more difficult to hate him, for he never gave any real grounds for doing so.

This illustrious chatterer was the man who, by means of his wife, presented to the queen the nephew and nieces of her minister. She wished to see them the evening of their arrival, and saw them with pleasure. She thought them pretty, and the time the children spent in her presence was employed in remarks on their appearance. Madame de Senecé proposed to the queen to go and see them the next day and pay them her compliments; but she was made to understand that the cardinal did not wish them to be visited, on the plea that being lodged in his house where he liked to be in peace, visitors would disturb him much if he allowed them to come there.

When this revered uncle, so fortunate and so powerful, saw the arrival of his nieces, he left the queen the moment that they entered her room, and went off to bed in his own house. After the queen had seen them they were taken to the cardinal; but he seemed not to care for them much; on the contrary, he jested about those who were silly enough to show them attentions. But, despite this scorn, he certainly had great designs based on these little girls. His indifference about them was all pure comedy; and by that we may judge that it is not only on the stage that comic actors play good parts.

The next day the nieces were again brought to the queen, who kept them some moments near her to examine them better. Cardinal Mazarin was there also; but seemed no more touched by them than he was on the first day. After this, they were shown in public. Every one hastened to see them, and the spectators made a point of extolling them, sometimes as very agreeable, and sometimes as very beautiful; they even gave them intellect on sight, and all the

praises that could be thought of were amply bestowed by
their liberality.

While the courtiers were hastening to talk in this way, the
Duc d'Orléans came up to the Abbé de La Rivière and me, who
were talking together near a window, and said in a low voice:
" So many persons are round these little girls that I doubt if
their lives are safe: they will be smothered by force of being
looked at." The Maréchal de Villeroy, who had the gravity
of a minister, came up at the same time and said: "See
those little girls who now are not rich; they will soon have
fine châteaus, good incomes, splendid jewels, beautiful silver
services, and perhaps great dignities; but as for the boy, it
needs time to make him great, and he may only see his fortune foreshadowed," — meaning that his uncle might fall
before he was old enough to be raised very high; in which,
without knowing it, the maréchal prophesied truly.

The girls became greater ladies than he thought, but the
boy never really enjoyed his luck, for death robbed him
of the favour of him who might have put him in the way to
be respected of all men. An Italian friend of mine told me,
some time later, that people in Rome were amazed when they
heard in what way these children had been received in
France; and especially that princes and great seigneurs
thought of marrying them. In their own land and according
to their birth, these nieces would have had few suitors, and
few people in Rome would have flocked to see them; but the
rank they had at our Court as soon as they came there is sufficient proof of the position of him who gave the lustre which
Italians could not approve. They laughed at our nation for
allowing itself to be governed by a man whom they did not
like because they knew him too well; it is natural to men
to admire only distant things: *Fugga il tetto nativo, chi gloria
brama.* — " Flee the native roof, you who to glory aspire."

The Princess Palestrina, Donna Anna Colonna, who returned to Italy soon after their arrival in Paris, assured me that the cardinal told her in confidence, speaking of his nieces, that already the highest men in the kingdom had asked him for them. And yet he had said to his friends some years earlier, pointing to certain statues he had brought from Rome, that those were the only relatives he meant to bring to France; but, like the sage, he changed his mind, and let himself be urged by the queen, to whom he would not refuse this favour, to allow his nieces come. He did nothing in this that was contrary to reason; it was just that he should let his own family share his grandeur, and use them to strengthen still further his own fortunes. If those who are masters do not attempt to limit a minister's ambition, he is excusable if, during their power, he desires more than the just reward of his services. It is natural to men to want more glory, more happiness, more wealth than they have, and often more than they deserve.

The next day, at the queen's *lever*, a little affair happened to a Court lady, vexatious and harsh enough to be put in the list of mortifications which persons often taste in the course of their lives. The Duchesse de Schomberg, on giving up the name, as I have told, of Madame de Hautefort, gave up also her claim to the office of lady-in-waiting (then still possessed by her grandmother, Madame de La Flotte) for a compensation of two hundred thousand francs. But, as the longing for favour is an invisible chain which attaches every one to the person of kings, some from inclination, others from self-interest, and as few ever willingly detach themselves, Madame de Schomberg did all she could to recover the good graces of the queen, and would have liked to resume with her the familiar intercourse of times past.

It is the rule that the lady of honour shall have the right

to serve the queen by handing her the chemise unless she cedes that honour to a princess of the blood; and when the lady-in-waiting is present she shares the service in certain things with the lady-of-honour. Madame de Schomberg, since her marriage, when alone with the queen had had the honour to serve her; and the queen had pleasantly received the service, to do her a favour and not rebuff her, but never as though she had a right to take the part of lady-in-waiting on such occasions.

She attempted one day to enjoy the same privilege when the Princesse de Condé and Madame de Senecé were present. The queen then said to her, and rather severely, for the old friendship was entirely passed: "Madame, do you not see that Madame de Senecé is here and you are taking her office?" The Duchesse de Schomberg answered rather brusquely that she saw her very well, but the service she was doing was her own. The queen, a little excited, said at once: "Your office, madame! Did you not resign it when you married, for two hundred thousand francs which I gave you in compensation?" "Yes, madame," replied Madame de Schomberg, "but I have not yet received the money. That is why I think I have the right to exercise the office."—"Oh! very well, madame; you will be paid," answered the queen; "there is enough money in France for that; but you must know that it is difficult to re-enter my heart when once a person has gone out of it." The lady, keenly touched and pained, answered only by tears, and followed the queen the whole day, unable to keep from weeping before her. She had done the thing against her will, so as not to displease her husband, who wished her to obtain a return of past favours.

The queen, moved to pity, spoke to her and made her several caresses to soften her pain, but, as this lady told me later, she returned home resolved never again to try to obtain the queen's good graces. She contented herself after that with seeing her like the other duchesses, who only go to the Louvre at the hour of the *cercle ;* and shortly after, without fuss or complaint, she and the Maréchal de Schomberg went to their own house and government to live the Christian life which alone gives peace of mind and tranquillity of soul.

This little tale made a great noise at Court; every one spoke of it as he or she personally felt. Some blamed Madame de Schomberg for imprudence in risking such displeasure; others accused the queen of harshness, which is a thing she never felt to any one.

Some hours later, having asked her what the affair was which was making so much stir, she told me what I have just written down; and she told it with the more kindness because, as she said, she was grieved that the lady had forced her, against her disposition, to cause her this vexation, for she did not like to give pain to any one whomsoever ; but that she could not let herself be taken for a dupe, and she saw plainly that Madame de Schomberg acted in that manner, not to regain her friendship (which motive would have been kindly), but to claim her former office for the purpose of keeping it for her sister, d'Escars, for whom she, the queen, had a great aversion; and it was not just that because she was a queen she should have to be served, against her will, by those she did not like. The Duchesse de Schomberg afterwards told me the same thing, and said that she had hoped to preserve the office for her sister.

The queen, who found pleasure in change, left Paris, September 15 [1647] to spend the autumn in that beautiful habitation of Fontainebleau, leaving in Paris the little Monsieur, who was not yet sufficiently recovered to bear the fatigue of a journey. The Maréchal de Villeroy, anxious to please the man who had made him the king's governor, put it into the heart of the young king to wish to take the youngest of the three Mancini girls on this trip; and he asked it so eagerly of the queen that she willingly requested the cardinal not to send his little niece to the Jesuits.

The evening before the queen's departure, I went up to the minister, to pay him the homage due to one who received the same from the greatest in the kingdom. He returned my compliments by making a sham quarrel, as he frequently did; for it was his way to give us often such alarms. He told me that he was informed that Sarrazin, the dismissed poet, had made satirical and malicious verses in my apartments, which attacked the person of the queen. My mind was so far from thinking anything of that nature that at first I did not sufficiently notice the horror of this insult. I merely answered, as if laughing, that the joke was hard on a person like me who took no pleasure in satirical verses against my greatest enemies; and that I thought I should do myself a wrong to answer such falsehood seriously, though it was four years since I had seen the man. This was the truth. From that I passed to other matters about which I had to speak to him, and said no more.

I am convinced I paid my court to him very ill; for, not wishing to do us real benefits, he took pleasure in causing us false anxieties; so that we might feel ourselves obliged to him for pardoning our imaginary wrong-doings and leaving us in peace. At other times he treated persons with such gentleness and apparent good-will that it was impossible to avoid being charmed by him; when he wished to please he deceived the most distrustful persons. But towards me such favours were rare. After I returned home, recalling this malicious act which the minister's policy or the baseness of some malignant mind had done me, I spent several hours of the night in murmuring against the world, against the ambitions which delude us and the weakness which retains us in it.

I complained to the queen, who thought I had good reason to be displeased; and in spite of the approbation she usually gave to all that came from the cardinal, her natural equity made her regret that he had listened to this tale and had spoken of it to me as a believable story. She assured me, moreover, that she would tell him what she thought of it, and I venture to believe that she made him see that the accusation he had made to me was wholly unreasonable.

This princess was full of kindness and justice; she was not suspicious, not easy to prejudice, and when they told her evil of any one of whom she had a good opinion she resisted strongly. We should always have had smooth seas with her, without tempests, if he in whom she had confidence had not too often had the power to change her own impressions by the pains he took to despise before her those she esteemed; but when he wanted to ruin any one it was necessary, in order to succeed, that he should arrange matters in a way to deceive her with the appearances of a real cause.

As my case could not convince her, I felt on this occasion as on the others I have mentioned, how upright her soul was when her natural instincts were not darkened. I can also say with truth that whatever she knew that might harm those to whom she wished well she never told to her minister; and among those whom he hated and wished to drive from Court there were some whom she supported against him solely because of their innocence, — either because it was better known to her than that of others, or because they really had more. The cardinal often said to

Le Tellier (as the latter told me himself) that the queen's piety hindered him, and that she yielded with difficulty on whatever she thought to be for the glory of God. She had insight enough to know the right; and if she had had the strength to always defend it, the pens of historians could not have praised her enough; but she was too distrustful of herself, and her humility easily convinced her of her incapacity to govern the State.

This feeling, in some respects unjust and unreasonable, did much to establish the power of her minister, who, without it, might have worthily filled the office in which the late king placed him and the queen maintained him. If he had thought himself less necessary to her he would have taken more pains to deserve the esteem of the people. If he had had reason to fear the ill offices that others might do him with her, he would have had more consideration for right-minded persons, who would always have had influence upon her because by nature she felt good-will to them. And also, if the queen had esteemed herself more and maintained her own sentiments (as she did sometimes when she thought her duty required it), her good intentions would have improved those of her minister, who really had fine qualities which, if well managed by a power above his own, would have made him a minister worthy of general respect.

The greatness of his genius placed him above other men, not only by luck but by the superiority of his knowledge. Never did any of those who were in his confidence and intimacy have power over him, unless some necessity in his affairs or his designs required it. He had great experience in foreign affairs, and was capable of the highest enterprises. He worked hard. His policy was shrewd; he was clever at intrigue; he attained his ends by circumlocutions and wiles that were well-nigh impenetrable. He was not malignant or cruel. At first he had not even an excessive ambition; for up to that time he had declined the great establishments that other favourites obtain. He had taken neither places, governments, dignities, nor offices. Nor did his avidity for money appear then such as it really was; and those who accused him of it were unjust. Many who courted him owed him great favours, and of those many were much richer than he. He was quite agreeable in person; and in spite of his defects he will always be spoken of as an extraordinary man. His prodigious power will amaze the whole world, and the marvellous events of his rise to fortune will lift him very high. He has had the destiny of great men, alike in his good and his evil fortunes; he may also have their reputation, for I doubt if all the centuries put together can produce a greater.

The Prince of Wales [Charles II.] came to Fontainebleau to see the king and the queen. They entertained him with balls, comedies, and excursions. He seemed to have increased in good looks. The unhappy state of his affairs made every one regard him with the tenderness that accompanies pity, and through that sentiment his good qualities received greater lustre. He even showed some beginning of inclination for Madame de Châtillon, which was thought a good augury. His mind, however, was never brilliant and he stuttered somewhat. In that he resembled his father, who, as I have heard, did so a little, and his grandfather, the late king [James I.] who did so much. The king and he behaved together like young princes who felt embarrassed by each other's presence; both were shy, and without that freedom of spirit which intercourse with the world gives to private individuals. The king, whose beauty had charms, though young was already tall. He was grave, and in his eyes could be seen a serious expression which marked his dignity. He was even prudent enough to say little, from fear of not speaking well. The Prince of Wales kept silence also; but they had at least the comfort of banishing the ceremonies of their rank, which softened the rest.

The Court having returned to Paris in October, the king, in the midst of the finest possible health, suddenly, November 10, left his games, wearied of the comedy, and then told the queen that he felt ill and had pains in his loins. At first it was thought to be nothing, but the next day his fever was high, which alarmed the queen very much, who now feared a continued fever. A courier was sent to the Duc d'Orléans, who was at one of his country-houses, telling him of the king's state.

Two days later the disease degenerated into small-pox, which at first consoled the queen, who had feared something worse. She left her apartment on the same day and slept in that of the patient. As the king's fever continued, her anxiety increased, and the doctors were unable to reassure her. All the young people who laid claims to beauty and those who had not had the small-pox left the Palais-Royal. I think I was the only one, who had not renounced youth, who would not leave the queen on this occasion. I own that I made an effort over myself to give her this proof of my zeal, for though I had had the disease, it is quite common to have it twice, and commoner still to think of one's own safety. My sister, moreover, had not had it, and I might have conveyed the infection to her. But God preserved us.

The king, up to the eleventh day of his illness, gave the queen no greater anxiety than she had felt before the small-pox appeared. She suffered from seeing him suffer; but as it is a disease which is common to children, she was quite resolved to be comforted for the loss of his beauty provided his life was saved. On the 21st of the month, at nine in the morning, while the queen had gone to Notre-Dame to make her devotions, the king grew worse; the fever increased; he fainted, and remained in that condition for three-quarters of an hour.

The queen, on her return, finding him in this state was struck to the heart with such grief that it needed but little more to kill her. All that day the king, according to the doctors' opinion, was in the greatest danger, and the queen never ceased to weep. The Duc d'Orléans was constantly beside her; and this increased her pain; she found no comfort or consolation in shedding tears before him. That evening, about midnight, the king grew better; but the next day his illness increased very much. On Sunday, the fourteenth day, he was so ill that the doctors thought him in danger of immediate death, because, since the eleventh day, on which he had fainted, the small-pox had gone in, and four bleedings which were taken did not diminish his fever. Its heat was so great that it entirely dried up whatever had issued from his body.

All that day the queen seemed to choke; for her nature was not to weep, and when she was in sorrow she usually shut it up within herself. This sorrow made her feel keenly all that love and fear can implant in a soul possessed by a violent passion. Though she followed no policy on this occasion, yet, having naturally a firm mind and much reserve in her outward actions, she did not choose to show her weakness, especially before those who would have profited by her misfortune. But, as nature cannot continue in such a state without some sign appearing, she fainted on that day by the king's bedside; and that night, very late, having retired, with no witnesses but the cardinal, a few of her women, and myself, she wept bitterly. Seeing her in that state, we begged her to go to bed; which she did; but could find no rest in any place. At last, about midnight, God gave her back the child so dear to her, and whose life was so necessary to France. The fever lessened and the small-pox came out once more. Monday and Tuesday the doctors purged him, and thenceforth the disease diminished until he was completely cured. The queen's alarm having passed, she told us that she felt in the midst of it that, had she lost the king, she could not have survived him, and that the submission she should have wished to show to the divine will would doubtless not have prevented her grief from strangling her.

During this illness the king seemed to those about him to be a prince wholly inclined to gentleness and kindness. He spoke humanely to all who served him, said obliging and intelligent things, and was docile to all that the doctors desired of him. The queen received marks of affection from him which touched her keenly; at all moments he called to her, and begged her to stay by him, assuring her that her presence lessened his illness. The queen told us afterwards that in all her sorrow she had feared losing him from tenderness only; and that she should have mourned for him because she loved him, and in his quality as son, not as king; which, she said, in no wise touched her.

Frenchmen had reason to hope that they would one day see this young king become as great through the qualities of his soul as he already was by his crown. They regarded him as a king given by God himself in answer to the public prayer, and as a child of benediction; his perfections filled the eyes of his subjects, partly by his person, partly by his inclinations, which all seemed good and tending towards virtue and glory. The impress of the power to which God destined him was already marked on his person and on all his actions. We never saw in him those headstrong sentiments which are natural to most children. The queen, through reason and the obedience he gave to her, led him always to do what she wished of him.

I often noticed with astonishment that in his plays and amusements the king never laughed. Those who had the honour to approach him told him too often, I thought, that he was the master; and when he had some little differences with Monsieur, occasions which happened of course in their childhood, the queen always insisted that he should be obeyed, and seemed to desire that his power should be respected as much as he was loved. All these anticipated grandeurs could not seem dangerous to her, in view of the natural innocence of the young monarch; which gave her reason to hope that God, the author of Nature, in sending him from on high, as He did to Solomon, a spirit of wisdom with the gift of persisting in virtuous ways, would render his life pleasing in His sight, and his reign accompanied by continual prosperity. " The principality of the virtuous shall be stable."

As the king grew better, the mind of the queen recovered its usual tranquillity ; and the Court, on the arrival of the Prince de Condé, was filled with additional grandeur and adorned with fresh beauty through the numbers of worthy persons whom he brought with him. He had known of the extreme danger of the king, but would not hasten his return, expressly not to show eagerness at a time when it might have seemed that he came only to share the power of the Duc d'Orléans, of which, apparently, he might have claimed the greater share. He maintained this moderation, though the queen had sent several couriers urging him to come.

A few days after the happy recovery of the king, the suffering the queen had endured from his illness, and the violence she had done herself in not wholly showing it, her wakeful nights and anxieties, gave her a fever which was very strong for two days. Cardinal Mazarin seemed alarmed; but when the doctors thought she was about to have a severe illness the fever suddenly left her, which caused much joy to those who loved her and had reason to be anxious at her illness. The evening of her amendment, as I approached her and wished to touch her pulse to see if her state was as good as we hoped, she did me the honour to put her hand in mine; and I having kissed it with joy at finding it so cool, she said she did not doubt that I was very glad of her improvement, adding these noble words: that death had never caused her fear; but in the state in which she left the king and the kingdom, France and her children caused her pity; that this made her offer some wishes for life; but that the greatest of them all was that God would give her grace to employ it well in His service.

The Christmas festivities stopped for awhile all public and private matters. The queen, being at the Val de Grâce, saw the little Monsieur, whom she had not yet dared to see for fear of giving him the infection. A few days later he returned to the Palais-Royal, and was allowed to see the king, whom he did not recognize, so changed was he. All the ladies returned to Court, and the king was shown to every one, though still in a bad state from the swelling and redness of his face. He scolded those who had abandoned him; which was taken as a good omen, and as a sign that he would not be so indifferent to friendship as princes usually are. Though I had not quitted the queen during his illness, I had not approached him. The queen, seeing that I made an effort to follow her into his room, where, in spite of the glory of a crown, there was danger, commanded me not to enter it. I had, therefore, my share in the king's little plaint, for which I consoled myself like the rest, who were not much afflicted by it, but felt honoured by his resentment.

Thus ended this year [1647], without much happiness, or yet real evils. Nevertheless, the ablest men at Court and the best-informed told me on that day that they feared the future of the State would be troubled by many evils, in view of the bad disposition that existed in all minds. The queen, on the contrary, on the evening of the same day, said to us, as she was seated at her toilet-table while undressing, that it gave her joy to enter upon a new year, because in the one just ending she had had nothing but trouble, little success in war, and much anxiety from the illness of her children, whom she had feared to lose. But she was deceived in her hopes, and had cause to regret the repose she had hitherto enjoyed. The troubles that came upon her later taught her that the human being knows neither his strength nor his weakness; that our desires mislead us, and that we ought to allow ourselves to be guided by that superior Power who rules us. Otherwise, we find that by our own choice we are oftener led to evil than to good.

IX.

1648.

On the Epiphany the queen, having made her devotions, passed the whole evening in great solitude. As she liked repose, and her own power was a matter of indifference to her, no one was urgent to enter her cabinets when she was alone. The Duc d'Orléans and the cardinal supped that evening with the Prince de Condé; and when such feasts occurred all the courtiers desired to be in the train of one of the three; so that the sovereign's apartment was left deserted. Far from objecting to this, she was delighted that her creatures should follow the minister, and, without enjoying the pleasures of solitude, which are books and revery, she remained very willingly alone, without either pleasure or trouble.

This evening, in order to amuse the king, she did us the honour to have a cake brought to Madame de Bregy, my sister, and me, which we divided with her; drinking her health in hippocras, which she ordered for us; and she admitted that on this occasion she should, in spite of her natural inclinations, have felt bored without our company; which was a great favour, for, truth to tell, her kindness had more share than her heart in the good treatment we received from her. God alone, the king and Monsieur, her minister and his affairs absorbed her wholly; and the cardinal was all the more agreeable to her because he took great care to keep her unoccupied, and was glad to relieve her of the greater part of the trouble her regency imposed upon her.

The next day the comedies began again by the wish of the king and the whole Court; and the ladies, much pleased at this revival, came in full dress, intending to drive away forever from the Palais-Royal all recollection of unpleasant things. The king appeared with his blotched and swelled face, and looked the uglier because he had so lately appeared in beauty; and as it was at the theatre on Martinmas-day that he was taken ill, Beautru [one of the first members of the Academy, and ambassador to England and to Spain] was fain to say that he came to return his disease to the stage.

January 7, eight hundred merchants of Paris assembled and rebelled against a tax imposed upon the proprietors of houses, or for other reasons of which I did not take particular notice. They deputed ten of their number to speak on their behalf to the Duc d'Orléans. These deputies went to the Luxembourg and entered the duke's room, demanding justice and letting him know they were resolved not to suffer these taxes; for, in spite of the universal poverty of the kingdom, Paris, at any rate, chose to be rich, and would not hear of giving money to the king. The Duc d'Orléans made them hope for some amelioration, promised to speak of it to the queen, showed them their duty and the obedience they owed to her will, and dismissed them with the usual saying of princes: " We will see about it."

The next day the same troop assembled again. It went to the Palais de Justice, and finding there the President de Thoré, son of d'Émery, superintendent of finances, they shouted against him, called him the son of the tyrant, and from threats they came within an ace of attacking him personally; but, thanks to some of his friends, he escaped from their hands. The next day they muttered loudly against him, and threatened to make him suffer for the wrongs that were being done them. This man, whose firmness will be seen on several occasions to equal that of the most illustrious Romans, told them, without emotion, that if they did not keep silence and obey the king's will, he would have gallows erected in the square on which to hang instantly the most refractory among them. To which these insolent people answered that they would use those gallows themselves for the wicked judges from whom no justice could be got and who were slaves to royal favour.

On that same day, January 9, so famous for its events, the masters of petitions [*maîtres de requêtes* — magistrates whose duty it was to present petitions and other written demands to the council of State] mutinied also in the council because it was proposed to increase their body by a dozen new officers. As they had bought their offices at a high price, and this increase in number would diminish their value, they declared that many families in Paris would thus become embarrassed, and so, resenting an evil they feared, they refused to report the cases of private persons, and swore among themselves on the Holy Gospels not to allow this increase, and to resist the persecution that might be made upon them from the Court side. They promised one another that if any of them lost his office by this opposition to the will of the king, they would all subscribe to repay him the value of the said office.

They went to see Cardinal Mazarin; and one of them named Gomin, spoke so strongly and with such boldness that the cardinal was startled. Council was held in the queen's room to decide on the remedies for these turmoils. D'Émery had the whole people on his shoulders shouting against him; and the chancellor had the masters of petitions to restrain and console. The latter really complained less of d'Émery than of him who governed all; but, not daring at present to fulminate against the cardinal, they attacked the superintendent strongly and cast their wrath in the meantime upon him. Therefore, in consequence of these matters, the council sat long on that day and opinions were much contested.

The chief president [*premier président*] and the king's lawyers were sent for, a resolution was taken to issue fulminating decrees against all parties; and then, it being now evening, the Prince de Condé and the cardinal went to sup with the Duc d'Orléans, to bury under good cheer and cards this beginning of troubles which did not cause as much uneasiness to the princes as it did to the minister. He now began to see that he was the object of public hatred, and that this hatred would fill the princes of the blood with the sweet delusions that please great personages, making them hope that through troubles and changes their authority would increase as that of the king and queen diminished; for, as the Spanish proverb says, *Rio turbio ganancia de pescadores;* "troubled waters are the fisher's gain."

On the night of the 10th the burghers vented their ill-humour by constant firing. The lieutenant of police having sent through all the quarters of the city to know the cause, they answered that they were trying their arms for the king's service, adding that if they were asked to pay money they would follow the example of the Neapolitans and revolt. I am even assured that men had gone from house to house during the night advising the burghers to lay in a stock of food. All this was caused by cabals against the Court by the parliament, by the masters of petitions, and by that spirit of rebellion which some demon, visible or invisible, was beginning to inspire in the soul of each individual. Since then this demon has produced all that we have seen of civil discord; it has caused great evils, and made our condition such that we can never in our old age resemble our fathers, whose custom it was to laud the days of their youth and prefer them to the present.

On the morning of the 11th, the queen, on going to mass at Notre-Dame (which she did regularly every Saturday), was followed by about two hundred women into the church itself. They tried to kneel before her to make her pity them; but the guards prevented their approach, and the queen passed on without listening to their clamours. She told us, on her return, that she had been tempted to speak to them. Surely the words of a queen so amiable would have been powerful over those minds; but she owned to us that she had feared the insolence of such *canaille*, and had therefore thought it wiser not to enter upon the subject with people who never listened to reason, who could not comprehend it, having in their heads only their petty interests and being consequently unable to appreciate the causes, however just they may be, that compel kings to ask them for money.

After midday a council was held on immediate affairs, before which the chief president appeared; and after long consultation on remedies for the evil, it was decided that the queen should order the king's lawyers (who had been summoned for the purpose) to take measures to maintain the authority of the king. That evening commands were issued to the regiment of the Gardes to remain under arms, and sentinels and guard-houses were posted in all quarters of the city. The Maréchal de Schomberg was commanded to do the same with the Swiss guards, and Paris on that night was like a military camp. The noise of fire-arms was incessant; and these small appearances of war foreshadowed a revolt of greater consequence, which, according to the behaviour of the people and the bad disposition of the public mind was likely to lead to some dangerous result.

On the morning after the 12th, the king went to Notre-Dame to hear mass, and to make his first outing after his illness an act of grace and gratitude to Him who had restored him to life. It was more than a week since the queen had expressed the desire that the king should make this little trip through Paris, therefore it was decided not to delay it, lest it should be said they showed fear of those who were so anxious to inspire it in the queen and in her minister. But instead of having his usual guard for such occasions, he went with every necessary precaution around him. All that could serve to magnify the royal majesty attended him, in order to excite by that means in the minds of the people the respect that such things usually produce in feeble souls. Many of the principal officers were on horseback, and nearly the whole Court accompanied him with the usual guards. While the king was at Notre-Dame, the queen held a council, at which it was resolved that their Majesties should go a second time before parliament to pass the edict creating the new masters of petitions, and the other decrees which were murmured against; and this was done in order not to show relaxation of the resolves already taken, and to make evident that the resistance of officials and people was counted as nothing.

According to this resolution, the king went to parliament, January 15; not with the beauty he had had on the former occasion, but with the same ceremonies. The chancellor made a long harangue; he represented the necessities of the State, the need the king had that his people should give him means to meet the costs of the war, in order that by war we might obtain a good peace. He spoke strongly on the power of kings, tried to establish as a fundamental law the obedience of subjects to their princes, and showed plainly the necessity of union between the head and the members, saying that without it no kingdom could enjoy true happiness.

The chief president, though an able man and usually very eloquent, wishing to please the Court, delivered a speech which seemed feeble to his colleagues and was not praised even in the cabinet. That of the attorney-general, Talon, was strong and vigorous. He represented the misery of the people, and implored the queen to remember it in her oratory; telling her that she ought to consider that she ruled a free people and not slaves; but, as things were, these very people found themselves so oppressed by subsidies and taxes that they might indeed say nothing was their own but their souls — for those could not be sold at auction; and the laurels and victories won from the enemy with which the necessities of the people were being met, were not meat to feed them nor clothes to cover them. He said, moreover, certain things which showed the universal dissatisfaction of all Frenchmen at the delay of peace. His boldness was not approved by the minister.

That evening the cardinal made war on the queen about her being sent to her oratory by Talon. In this he was seconded by her familiar servants, who thought she already remained there too long, and, in the interest of their own pleasure, continually reproached her for it. Thus the most serious lessons given to kings make no good impression on their minds; for a turn to ridicule is usually given them, which drives away the virtuous thoughts to which they might otherwise have given birth. Princes seldom meet with persons who speak to them strongly; and those who do so are the ones most frequently treated as ridiculous by the courtiers. This is why, their reason being weakened by the care taken to disguise from them the truth, sovereigns do not apply themselves to distinguish the true from the false; and,

letting their mind go to laziness and lightly passing over
good and over evil, they are nearly always carried whithersoever
ever their ministers are pleased to lead them.

The queen, by nature equitable, pious, and well-intentioned,
often fell for these very reasons into this misfortune; and,
not seeking to know fundamentally and studiously the cause
of the evils that she saw before her eyes, it was impossible
for her to remedy them; consequently they became excessive
and brought her in the end to the condition of fearing all
things. To maintain the royal power, of which she had a
lofty idea, it is much to be wished, for the sake of her own
happiness, that she had herself shown clearly that she did
not choose to have the king's subjects oppressed, nor yet to
allow them to be disobedient to her. In those two points
lies the justice of kings towards their subjects, and that of
subjects towards their sovereign.

The queen, as I have said already, had a soul sufficiently
enriched by the gifts of God to govern well; her ministers
said that her opinions on affairs of consequence, and her
first sentiments, were always those of reason and justice;
whereas those of her prime minister showed nothing that
seemed to proceed from a lofty soul. On this very day certain
counsellors of the parliament, who came to see me,
admitted that they had been much touched by the presence
of the queen. They agreed with me that she had the gift of
pleasing, and they said that France would have been happy
indeed had she chosen to govern it, or, at any rate, if she had
not abandoned it too much to her minister.

The decrees were fairly moderate; the visit to parliament
was made more to maintain the royal authority than to increase
crease its demands. The edict for creating the twelve new
masters of petitions was the principal object, because it was
felt that the revolt of the present officers must not be allowed.

But as this affair, in the order of destiny, was fated to be the cause and the beginning of many great events, this little remedy, far from curing the evil, greatly embittered it and had results which made us see that God, when it pleases Him, can give to the ant the strength of the elephant.

The people thought they had reason to cry out against those who were trying to rob them, and they declared that the more taxes were levied, the more the king's coffers were locked. It was heard on all sides that the salaries of the crown officers and those of the leaders at Court were cut down, that the lesser men were not paid at all, that favours had ceased, and that the queen had lost the beautiful quality of liberality which she held as her illustrious birthright; and this, though the revenues of France were still paying much.

The Court was indeed beginning to appear in a condition of mortifying want. The minister tried to convince every one by his speeches (and I think he spoke the truth) that the Duc d'Orléans and the Prince de Condé were squandering the king's money, and therefore it was out of his power to do favours. Tubeuf, at that time still in the public service, told me that the Treasury account for the last year had amounted to one hundred and forty-two millions. The cardinal was accused of having usurped a large portion of that sum for himself; but his modesty was still restrained within narrower limits. The two princes, by taking much money, prevented him from using it as he pleased; he was at that time only the corsair, the princes were the great robbers who resembled Alexander.

The outcry against the minister made the war its pretext. This sufficed to make him hated by the people, always easy to excite by plausible reasons of the public good, and ever charmed by the good words "peace" and "rest." I remember that one of my friends, arriving from Rome about this time, told me that, having been ordered to say to the pope how much peace was desired, and that, in order to obtain it, all our hopes of fortunate successes in the field would be sacrificed to the public good, his Holiness replied in sarcastic tones that he did not meddle in the affair of the peace, but he saw plainly that in order to obtain it *voi altri Francesi non volete donare che quel che non avete;* "to get peace, you Frenchmen will only give that which you have not."

The next day the queen summoned before her the masters of petitions. She received them in her great cabinet, accompanied by the Duc d'Orléans, the Prince de Condé, her minister, the king's council, and the whole Court. The chancellor gave them a severe reprimand, which the queen interrupted, of her own monition, to tell them they were strange people to wish to limit the king's authority; and that she would show them he had power to create what new offices he chose. The chancellor, continuing his harangue, dismissed them from their offices and ordered them to give to the queen the paper which it was said they had signed among themselves; or else to sign another paper stating that they had never written it.

When they heard this speech and this command, some of them, without considering the respect they owed to the queen, shook their heads boldly, and all gave signs that they were not inclined to obey. After making a profound bow, they went away, ill-pleased, and with the firm intention of defending themselves. They felt there were clouds in the sky, that the weather was bad for the Court, and that they themselves had a chance to resist; consequently this severity had no good result.

The next day, January 20, they presented themselves before parliament in a body in order to oppose the enregistering of the decree against them. Presenting themselves as parties in a case, they stood before the bar; and although the decree had been issued in the king's presence, the chief president did not abstain from receiving them in opposition to it. The Court was ill-pleased, and the minister made loud complaints; but the chief president was clever enough not to be shaken and to succeed in convincing the cardinal that it was all in order. He told him that the ordinances required him to receive them; that parliament had power to assemble and deliberate over matters that had even been decreed in presence of the king; and also that they possessed the right to remonstrate with him. This answer obliged the queen to summon the parliament in a body to tell them that at first she had thought their conduct blamable in listening as they had to the opposition of the masters of petitions; but that having subsequently learned they were entitled by their ordinances to do so, she excused them, and consented that they should have assembled, as they had done, to confer, and even to go so far as to remonstrate; but she ordered them not to go further, and not to assemble again.

The parliament replied with fine protestations of fidelity; and then, without the slightest regard to the queen's command, they assembled as many times as they thought necessary to satisfy their fancy. We shall see other such commands, often reiterated and often as little respected.

In the beginning of these disturbances in Paris the Duc d'Orléans kept himself one with the queen's interests and supported her authority· in every way that he could. He was not, perhaps, sorry at some disturbance, for that, of course, rendered him more necessary to her; but he laid no schemes to increase it, and his intentions seemed upright and altogether in the line of equity and justice. The Abbé de La Rivière, through his temperament, his interests, and his common-sense, turned his master ever towards peace; flattering himself with the hope of becoming some day a cardinal, he rendered to the queen and her minister such services as he thought most useful and agreeable to them. The mischief-makers and the malcontents were in despair because, desiring disturbances and change, they saw it was impossible to get much of them so long as the Duc d'Orléans, uncle of the king, continued attached to the interests of the queen. What might really be called kindness in the character of the duke was attributed by them to weakness; that which to men of honour seemed a virtue, they despised, saying that if the master lacked courage, his favourite de La Rivière was the cause of it; and that out of base self-interest he prevented him from acquiring glory and grandeur.

The Prince de Condé, on his side, acted in the same manner; his advantage being wholly in living at Court in the good graces of the queen. The Duc d'Orléans did not overshadow him enough to obscure his own grandeur; the reputation of the duke was not dazzling like his own; and the rank of lieutenant-general of the kingdom and of the armies of the king, and that of being son and uncle of kings, could not take from the prince the glory of having won two great battles. For these reasons he reigned in the cabinet almost as sovereignly as if he had been the sole prince of the blood; and, the Duc d'Orléans having no son, all the grandeur of the second branch of the family came to the prince, and made his court much larger than that of the duke, to whom, however, he paid great respect and homage in order to keep him satisfied with appearances, while he enjoyed in reality the solid advantages of power, and gave to his creatures and his friends all that he pleased.

The Shrovetide of this year went by without any unusual fêtes. There was a ballet at which the Duc de Joyeuse, Louis de Lorraine, danced (January 23), also the Ducs de

Candale, de Damoille, de Roannet, and several others, which was fine. The Court gaieties were moderate, and suited to the gravity and seriousness of the queen; she did not like them any more than she ought. In the evening, which is the hour for amusement, the crowd left her and she remained in her own apartments solitary, tranquil, and content. The courtiers all went to the cardinal; the queen wished it; desiring nothing in the world more than to make over to him her power, being persuaded that that of the minister strengthened her own. Moreover, I can say with truth that her natural indifference put her above the sentiments which self-love and ambition usually produce in the human heart. No doubt she despised too much the one advantage of kings — that of commanding, and of being able to contribute by their authority and their benefits to the happiness of mankind, thus sharing in a way the supreme power of God himself. But this defect in her proceeded in part from a fine cause which deserves more praise than blame. The effect, nevertheless, was so contrary to her interests that she would have done well to correct it; and for that very reason I scarcely dare to call attention to its merits.

I have remarked that the murmuring against the cardinal was great for not having brought about a peace. Every one, in these first disagreements, fearing to bring on civil war, blamed him for this one thing, and for having said, sometimes very publicly, that peace had been in his own hands. The populace cried out against him, and minds that were ready for revolt could not forgive him that fault.

The Dutch had requested the Duc de Longueville, when he was on the point of returning to France, to delay his departure from Münster for a short time; which gave rise to the hope that through their intervention Spain would make a treaty with us. But the King of Spain, who was beginning to see a change in the luck of France through the state in which it now was, desiring that we should grant all his demands, said openly that without great advantages he would refuse a peace; and his proposals were so hard that it was impossible to think of any agreement.

Therefore the Dutch, who wished to quit us, having signed their treaty, the Duc de Longueville found himself wholly useless at Münster for the public good. He thought also of his private interests, and asked permission to return to France; which was granted readily, and he appeared at Court with the sole advantage of having seen the Dutch make peace with Spain, which was likely to be damaging to us. The minister made the queen receive him with evident marks of good-will. I remember that on the evening of the day he arrived, as she was undressing she said to us much good of this prince, treating him almost as a father to the country, although he had already been twice opposed to the king. He was given a place in the Council; which at that time was a favour not as easy to obtain as it has been since. This prerogative had really been granted to him before he went to Münster, up to which time none but princes of the blood had enjoyed the privilege; but the malicious said that such caresses were given only to oblige him to keep the secret of the rupture of the peace, and the difficulties the minister had produced to prevent its conclusion.

The parliament inconvenienced the Court by its delays. Some among its members began to talk loudly; and the queen, who did not like to meet an obstacle to her power when the authority of the king was concerned, was annoyed by the slowness of its proceedings. She sent to ask them whether they assumed to have the right to limit the king's will. They took opinions on this point, and some of them

advised consulting their registers in order to make the queen
an answer authorized by examples from past centuries;
which would, no doubt, have mightily displeased the minister. But the majority being of a contrary opinion, they
sent their chief president as deputy to the queen to assure
her of their obedience and fidelity, and to let her know that
what they had done to modify the decrees the king had
brought to parliament, and what they were doing in favour
of the masters of petitions were only in accordance with the
king's good pleasure, and without the least intention of
failing in the respect they owed to him as good and faithful
subjects.

These protestations were not followed up; parliament,
continuing its assemblies, did not cease to delay the register-
ing of decrees that were necessary for the service of the
king and the advantage of the minister. Their conduct
obliged the queen to summon parliament to let it know her
resolves. She wished to make it understand that it had no
right, after making its remonstrances to the king and to
herself, to oppose the registration of the decrees. She also
ordered the members to bring the sheet in which their decision had been registered, which contained the statement that
their own modifications would be carried out; her design
being to make them tear it up in her presence. But they,
having assembled, sent a message to the queen, entreating
her to think it right that they should not go to her, assuring
her that they were resolved to pay her all the respect that
was her due.

The queen, having risen earlier than usual to receive
them, held a council to decide how to answer this. It was
resolved that they should be summoned a second time and
received by the queen after her dinner. The *procureur-
général*, who went to them with these orders, did not find

them in session; weary of waiting they had departed; which was thought disrespectful by those who knew the respect due by subjects to their sovereign. They were then summoned for the morrow; and in order that this occasion might be the more solemn, the dukes and peers of France were assembled to receive them, and all the great seigneurs then at Court were invited. As it was known that the queen intended to give them a severe and public reprimand, they came with humility to make excuses to her by the mouth of the chief president, whose harangue was full of submission, respect, and promises to obey her; so that instead of punishment they received from the queen a favourable greeting, joined to a command that they should work steadily at the king's business and make no more delays. She told them that she gave them only eight days to conclude it.

The queen took that week to make a little journey (March 25) to Notre-Dame de Chartres, where, during the illness of the king, she had made a vow to go. On leaving Paris, she reiterated to the president the command she had given to his assembled company, and assured him that she should be but five days on her journey. She spent the day at Notre-Dame de Chartres with the king, whom she took there, also Monsieur, who was removed from the hands of women on this occasion. They gave him as governor the Maréchal Du Plessis-Praslin (César de Choiseul), a great and successful captain, who had acquired much reputation for the battles he had won and the cities he had taken. He commanded the army of the king in Italy, where Cardinal Mazarin had known his merits.

During this little absence the masters of petitions, who had been suppressed, came in a body to see the cardinal, to entreat him to protect them with the queen and to get them replaced in their offices. They made him excuses for their revolt and asked for pardon and favour both. He received them with a grave and stern face, but answered gently that if they were willing to humiliate themselves and obey the queen's will, he would do them good service with her.

This action was happiness to the minister. He despatched a courier to the queen with the news, and fully believed that this visit meant that the masters of petitions had resolved to submit to the creation of twelve more offices, which at first they resisted. But they who had made this advance only to succeed in their ends and make the cardinal plume himself on the glory of doing them a service, were not satisfied with his reply and continued in their former determination. So that it was finally decided in council to order the counsellors of State to report all cases of private persons, in order to let the masters of petitions know that the king could dispense with the services of their body. By this punishment many families in Paris were thrown into great distress and fear lest they should lose their offices. As persons of the long robe are for the most part bound together by ties of parentage, this affair seemed to them of great consequence, for it concerned all the sovereign courts.[1] They therefore wished to make known that they would not permit that favourites and ministers should annihilate, in the name of the king, such important officers; and one and all they united to sustain the masters of petitions, intending in that way to save themselves from a like peril.

---

[1] *Cours souveraines*, or *compagnies souveraines* — supreme courts : these were, as given here, the court of parliament, the *cour des comptes*, the *cour des aides*, and the grand council ; when these separate courts met for consultation it was by delegates from each, who held their sessions in the chamber of Saint-Louis, at the Palais de Justice ; hence this united court is called the Chamber of Saint-Louis. — TR.

The Prince de Condé began his campaign this year by a stay of eight days at Chantilly, where he went, with all his court, to spend Holy Week; and the Duc d'Orléans was destined to be the queen's supporter in the events which it was foreseen must arise on the parliamentary side. At this time the two princes seemed to have good intentions to serve the king well, whether in peace or war. The queen spent the holy days as usual, and, to employ them worthily, she ordered public prayers for peace; which were not efficacious, because men are not worthy of the gift that God by His Gospel gave at this time (Easter) to His apostles, saying, when He appeared to them, " Peace be unto you !"

Towards the end of April a gentleman belonging to the household of Mademoiselle, named Saujeon, was arrested. His sister was maid-of-honour to Madame, and the Duc d'Orléans did not hate her. But the inclination he had for the sister did not prevent the disgrace of the brother, because the reasons for it were strong, and the matter itself seemed delicate.

At first, a great secret was made of the affair; the queen alone, her minister, the Duc d'Orléans, and his favourite knew it; and the Court people employed some days in finding out the truth, because adventures which are thought to proceed from the cabinet cause more curiosity than matters of any other nature. The prisoner was secretly interrogated during a little journey which the Duc d'Orléans made to Limours; and though the above-named four personages. kept silence religiously, Comminges, a relative of Saujeon, who was a friend of mine, told me the story; but in relating to me the matter of Saujeon's interrogation, he begged me to keep it secret for a certain time.

Every one began to suspect the truth, but no one knew it wholly. We saw its outburst one Thursday evening, after the council, which was held that day in the little gallery of the queen's apartment. The Duc d'Orléans sent for Mademoiselle to come to that place, where they remained alone, the queen, Monsieur, Cardinal Mazarin, and the Abbé de la Rivière. As she entered, the favourite of her father, whom she hated, told her in a low voice that she was about to receive a reprimand from Monsieur her father, and that the only thing to do was to humble herself to him and to the queen.

The gist of this affair was that Saujeon, perhaps with Mademoiselle's consent, wished to marry her to the arch-duke.[1] His crime was to have had an understanding with a burgher at Furnes, and this burgher had another with a person of quality who was at the court of the archduke. This person, instead of working for the success of the affair (whether by consent of his master or as a spy paid by France to betray him), warned the cardinal of the negotia-tion; and the minister, not being pleased with Mademoi-selle, blackened her to the queen and spoke of this collusion as semi-criminal and deserving of her anger. The queen, who really thought Mademoiselle guilty, spoke of it to Monsieur with such resentment that, in spite of his being her father, he dared not excuse her.

The young princess, who had felt the coming storm, con-sidered that she had better hide her uneasiness and appear to fear nothing; so that on the previous day (last of April) entering the chamber of Madame her step-mother, at the Luxembourg, she remarked, laughing, that it was said that Saujeon was a prisoner for her sake because he wanted to marry her to the archduke; as for her, she thought it amus-

[1] Mademoiselle relates this affair at great length in her Memoirs. She treats Saujeon as a visionary, and denies all direct participation in the project of a marriage with the archduke. — FR. ED.

ing, but as she knew nothing about the matter she could take no part in it except to pity him. However, here she was, called before the council, and much disturbed by the advice the Abbé de La Rivière had whispered in her ear. She found the queen irritated; accusing her of having private understandings with the enemies of the State, of wishing to marry without her consent or that of her father, and of wanting in respect towards both of them; then, having rigorously treated her, she turned her over to the Duc d'Orléans, who confirmed the anger of the queen and himself, and did not refrain from saying everything that could serve as a punishment for her fault.

Mademoiselle, finding herself thus openly attacked, gathered strength from her weakness and sustained herself bravely against these two persons, whom, for so many reasons, she had to fear. She maintained boldly that she had not done wrong and had known nothing of the negotiation. On the contrary, she reproached Monsieur because he might, if he had chosen, have married her to the emperor; and she made it plain to him that it was shameful not to protect her now when her fame was attacked.

The queen, who listened to these words with astonishment, did me the honour to say to me that evening that if she had had a daughter who treated her as Mademoiselle had treated her father she would have banished her from Court forever and shut her up in a convent. We heard the noise of the accusations and the defence; and though none but those three persons spoke (the minister not wishing to show that he had any share in the reprimand), the uproar was so great that we who were in the adjoining cabinet were full of the desire to know the details and the upshot of the quarrel.

Mademoiselle came from the gallery with a face more haughty than ashamed, and her eyes were full of anger rather than repentance. In passing, she stopped before the Abbé de la Rivière and then went away to her own apartments, keenly hurt to see herself abandoned by him from whom she had the right to hope for support and consolation. The next day the Abbé de la Rivière went to see her on behalf of his master, to forbid her to see any one whomsoever until she had confessed all she knew of the affair. The abbé, who perhaps would not have been sorry to please the minister by confounding this criminal, who he knew hated him, did all he could to make her admit the truth of the intrigue; but she continued firm and steadfast in denying it.

She was greatly distressed by many painful things, and this distress gave her a fever; she even fainted from grief when they took away from her one of her women whom they suspected of having aided her to have long conversations with Saujeon. This gentleman had wished to serve a princess who deserved help; but he belonged in duty to the king, and was therefore blamable. His fault, nevertheless, was more imprudent than criminal, for the motive was perfectly innocent. Apparently, Mademoiselle wished to marry, and in this purpose she had doubtless no intention of failing in the respect she owed to the queen and Monsieur; but her conduct was blamable when considered by the axioms of the State, which forbid all private intercourse with enemies and foreigners.

Personally, I had at that time no reason to be pleased with the princess except for the share she gave me of her civility to everybody; and I cannot be suspected of ardour in all that I may say of her; but as I make profession of perfect sincerity I am obliged to render her this testimony. I even had the equity, though she never knew it, to maintain to the queen on the day of this affair, that Mademoiselle was right not to acknowledge she was looking for a husband

through secret intrigues ; and I told the queen that I thought
— whether this were true or not — that Monsieur did wrong
to abandon her and to try to make her publicly confess a
thing which was more shameful to acknowledge than to do
— for a girl is not to blame for thinking of her establishment, but it is not proper that this should be known ; nor
should she appear to be working for that purpose.   " Fathers,
Madame," I said to her, " are accustomed, when proposals of
marriage are made, to keep to certain conventions in order
to protect the fame of their daughters, which always seem
smirched when they seek that which it is perfectly allowable
to wish for."

The queen, who always did me the honour to receive
kindly whatever came from a heart that she knew to be
faithful to her, was displeased by the sentiments which I
had on this affair, because she herself totally disapproved
of it; and that was why in her displeasure she told
the Duc d'Orléans what I had said, and he, without considering the motive which made me speak, complained to
me and said he was astonished that I blamed his course,
because he had always thought me more his friend than that
of his daughter.   Instead of justifying myself to him, I told
my sentiments to his favourite, who was sometimes reasonable enough to receive them well.   I advised him to try and
heal the quarrel, and said that I could understand that Monsieur should complain of a princess who wished to marry
without the concurrence of a father like himself, and that
the queen had also reason to be angry with her.   But I
insisted to him that Monsieur ought not to force her to confess a thing of that nature, and that he himself ought not, out
of compliance, to embitter Monsieur against her.   And I
said that if he did not endeavour to end the quarrel he would
be blamed by everybody for not making his master recognize

the true interests of Mademoiselle's reputation, which were really his own, inasmuch as she was his daughter. I concluded the conversation by telling him, in presence of Mademoiselle de Beaumont, the princess's woman, that while it was true she was wrong and had perhaps risked too much, her fault was legitimate, and that the old age of the archduke, his big ears, and his stern piety ought to justify her before all the world.

This little harangue had its effect. Shortly after, Monsieur learned the truth. Mademoiselle got some one to speak to the cardinal and beg him to change the queen's mind as to the accusation she made against her. Several persons spoke to the Abbé de La Rivière on her behalf, and the minister, who was very glad to lay claim to some merit with her, expressed a desire to serve her. Monsieur's favourite followed this example; and, comprehending that it was right that his master should show pity, he forgot his own little resentments in order to serve her; so that finally, on the eleventh day of her captivity, after great conferences which it was necessary to have with the queen, the Abbé de la Rivière went to take to Mademoiselle a few words of kindness from Monsieur, accompanied by strong lessons and respectful reprimands about her conduct.

The princess had given various subjects of annoyance to Monsieur; and the Comtesse de Fiesque, her governess, made many complaints against her, accusing her of imprudence in her actions, and particularly in not endeavouring carefully to obtain the good graces of the minister. She blamed her for being too much carried away by her friends and against her enemies; and by wise and politic speeches she often drew upon the princess little paternal punishments, gentle or severe according to the mood in which the prince happened to be. But, after all, he tenderly loved Mademoiselle, and always lived on good terms with her; he treated her kindly, and I have several times heard him say that his daughter fed him; that he was a beggar, while she was rich, and without her he should sometimes have wanted bread.

He told the truth, for Mademoiselle having the property of her mother, who was heiress of the house of Montpensier and that of Joyeuse, he had always enjoyed the use of it; not giving her more than was needed to maintain her establishment. This inheritance he paid to her later, in consequence of the suits he had with her, when, growing older, she avenged herself upon him, and insisted on having her property, — with signs of a soul that was rather too hard for love.

The same day, after this mollifying, Mademoiselle went to see the queen, who received her coldly. She told her that she ought not to plume herself on having stood out against her father and her sovereign, not confessing the faults she had committed; that those who counselled her gave her, no doubt, high praise, but that she ought not to allow herself to be deceived by them, for they did not advise her well; and that she ought rather to believe that her fault was great, because she saw it was disapproved by so kind a father as hers and by herself, who had always treated her as her own daughter.

Some days later peace was entirely restored by a visit she received permission to pay to Monsieur, who, after a private conversation, forgave her all her little faults. After that the Court busied itself about other matters, this one being already too old to talk about. Saujeon was sent a prisoner to Pierre-Encise, whence he issued soon after, in May. About this time the little Monsieur, brother of the king, was baptized, and named Philippe, by the Queen of England and by Monsieur, his uncle and that of the king.

X.

1648.

AN event which caused the affair of Mademoiselle to be
the more quickly forgotten was the arrival of a courier sent
by the Prince de Condé to the queen, to let her know he was
beginning to march upon the enemy with a very fine army.
This news made the minister resolve to take the Court to
the frontier, that it might be well placed to assist at the
grandeur of France through the downfall of its enemies;
which could readily be hoped with good troops and a general like the Prince de Condé. But the queen was detained
in Paris by a new embarrassment in the king's affairs, which
proved in the end to be of no small consequence to the
State.

The *paulette* was again given to all the supreme companies on condition that their salaries for four years be with-
held.[1] But to content parliament separately, as the most
important body in the kingdom, and therefore the most
to be feared, it was given to that body without the four
years' forfeiture. The Chambre des Comptes, the Cour des
Aides, the grand council, and all the officers of France, who
found themselves hampered by this treatment, complained to
parliament, and asked its assistance to maintain their right
against the oppression which, they said, had been put upon

[1] Fiscal duty invented by Charles Paulet, secretary of the king's chamber. By paying this tax at the beginning of each year the titulary to an
office (whether judicial or financial) secured its inheritance to his heirs.
If it were not paid, the office, in case of death, reverted to the king.—
FR. ED.

them. They pointed out to parliament that it ought to fear being some day involved in this ordinance; that their humiliation ought to make it apprehend that its own power would be diminished; and that if the courts did not sustain one another they were all equally threatened with total ruin; because favourites, having no more formidable obstacle than the power of parliament, if parliament stood alone by itself, nothing would be easier than to diminish what power remained to it, and put it on a par with the other assemblies of the kingdom.

Parliament was moved by these reasons, by a fear of like treatment, and also by the desire, which at that time ruled the chief minds in that great assembly, to rise higher. It assembled, and it murmured; nearly all its members declared that if they abandoned their brethren the latter would have the right to complain of them; and if they were ill-treated it was to be expected that all would have their share of woes. In short, on May 13, the Chambers having assembled, they gave a decision whereby a union with the other courts [*compagnies*] was agreed to, in which it was said that " they forbade the reception of any new officers at a time when, the *paulette* not being granted to all, the offices would revert to the king, and the widows and heirs be left non-content."

On this decision the queen ordered the chancellor to summon parliament and declare to it, from her, that, having gratified that body especially, her Majesty had believed it would be grateful to her; but, recognizing from its proceedings that it took her favour in another way, she no longer promised to exempt it from the payment of the four years' salaries which she had thought proper to retain from the officers of the other companies; and she would now leave matters as they had been; but she begged them to consider the necessities of the king's affairs, and to consult as to other means of obtaining money.

This answer was too gentle for an offended master; it appeared to come from the spirit of the minister, always ready to come down when resisted, and to force too much when he thought he could do so. But it had a double meaning; the cardinal's thought was to leave the parliament in the condition in which it was, and revenge himself by letting its members languish in uncertainty lest each in dying should lose his office.

The queen sent to the registrar's office (May 18) an order forbidding the reception of any money from parliament, revoking the gift she had made it of the *paulette*, and replacing it on the same footing as the other companies. This course was approved by able men, and would perhaps have succeeded had the minister been able to sustain it. But as parliament now felt itself engaged in a great enterprise it believed that it ought to push its resistance farther, and, in order to come safely out of the affair, to give birth to an opposition to Cardinal Mazarin which would embarrass him. It sought its means carefully; and the bad disposition of the minds at Court, the misery of all France, the public hatred which was beginning to openly declare itself against the minister, gave it such support that without some special protection of God over the kingdom, it is to be believed that parliament might then have overthrown the monarchy.

The queen, who had not tried to gratify parliament willingly, said, in speaking of this affair, that she believed it would repent of what it had done; and that she was not sorry to be compelled to revoke the favour she had shown it against her will, treating it more kindly than it deserved. As the blood of Charles V. made her by nature haughty, she had never supposed that any creature, any servant, could or would dare to defend himself against the will of the king; so that in all these affairs with parliament, whose rules and quibblings she did not understand, she always wanted to overthrow it, and believed that whatever was ordered in her council was to be executed by that assembly.

About this time (May, 1648) the Duke of York, twelve or thirteen years old, escaped from England under orders sent to him by the queen, his mother, and went to Holland. He has since related to me himself how he had kept this plan in his heart for a whole year, without being able to execute it. He made use at last of one of the servants whom the queen his mother sent to him.

His governor had already had the same design, and thought of executing it; but he had been made answerable for him to the English parliament, which, suspecting some such purpose, threatened him that if he ever thought of it the prince would be sent to the Tower of London. The prince related to me what he had suffered, without allowing any thought of escape to show itself. At last, one day when he saw his guards amusing themselves by playing games, he slipped out by a little back door into the park, where the servant who helped him was waiting with women's clothes. He put them on and went to a house in London, where he stayed some days dressed as a girl. Then he embarked with his equerry in a vessel which sailed for Holland; and as he was very handsome the sailors suspected that he was not too virtuous.

When his flight was discovered in London he was pursued by an English vessel, and came near being captured in sight of Flushing. The port where he wished to land was dangerous on account of the wind which was then blowing; so that the prince, divining that the vessel that followed them

was after him, quitted his borrowed sex to threaten the
pilot and force him to put him ashore at the peril of his
life. When the master of the vessel, who did not want to
go to land, resisted, he took the sword of the man who was
near him and made as though he would run him through
the body, in order to make him put him ashore where he
wished to go. The master obeyed under force; and he thus
escaped the persecutions which the barbarous subjects of his
father intended for him.

He came to France, where the king and queen received
him kindly and with the affection due to the grandson of
Henri IV. and the son of a great and unfortunate king. He
left in England the Duke of Gloucester, his younger brother,
with his governor the Duke of Northumberland; also a
princess, his sister, about eleven or twelve years old. These
two children alone received the last blessing of the king
their father when, a few months later, he was put to death.
Then the parliament sent the little prince, who remained in
their hands, and whom they never treated as a prince while
in their power, to the queen, his mother. The daughter died;
she had seemed to feel deeply the misfortunes of the king
her father.

On the 25th of May the queen, seeing that the parliament
was determined to hold out against her will and to favour
public rights, sent to order it to come to her. When it came
the chancellor spoke to it for her, and he spoke strongly.
After this discourse she gave the members a sharp reprimand
herself, telling them that, as their company abused the
favourable intentions she had had to benefit them, she would
never in future do them favours; and she forbade them
absolutely to assemble, or to communicate among themselves
by deputies. The president wished to answer her; but she,
her face severe and threatening, forbade him to speak. Two

days later all the other supreme courts were summoned, — the Chambre des Comptes, the Cour des Aides, and the Grand Council. The same things were said to them, but with even more rigour, because they were less thought of than the parliament; and as the minister judged it necessary to make the anger of the queen feared in some stronger way than by mere words, which do no harm, several of the Grand Council were dismissed and eight from the Cour des Aides, who were all exiled to different parts of the kingdom. Parliament showed much resentment at this petty chastisement; and the courts one and all resolved to assemble in spite of the queen's command.

On the day of Pentecost, the first of the month of June, the Duc de Beaufort, a prisoner for the last five years at Vincennes, escaped from his prison about midday. He found means to burst his chains through the cleverness of friends and some of his family, who on this occasion served him faithfully. He was guarded by an officer of the Gardes du corps, and by seven or eight of the Gardes who slept in his chamber and never left him. He was served by officers of the king; not one of his own servants was about him; and above all, Chavigny, who was not his friend, was governor of Vincennes.

The officer who guarded him, named La Ramée, had taken to Vincennes, at the request of one of his friends, a certain man who, under pretext of a duel that brought him under the law on account of the king's edict against duelling, desired this asylum by which to save himself. It is to be believed, however, that he was put there by the followers of the prince, and perhaps by consent of the officer; but I am ignorant of these particulars, and am only convinced by appearances.

This man, at first, to play the good valet and show that he

was not useless, busied himself more than all the others in carefully guarding the prisoner; and it was told to the queen, in relating the story to her, that he even went so far as roughness. Whether it was that he went there to serve the Duc de Beaufort, or allowed himself to be gained over by him, the duke used him to communicate his thoughts to his friends and obtain knowledge of the plans they had made for his release.

When the time came for executing their scheme, they expressly chose the day of Pentecost because the solemnity of that festival occupied every one in divine service. At the hour when the guards dined, the duke asked La Ramée to let him walk in a gallery where he had obtained permission to go and amuse himself at times. This gallery was lower than the place where he was lodged, but still very high up, on account of the depth of the moats which it overlooked on two sides. La Ramée followed him on this walk and remained alone with him in the gallery. The man won over by the duke pretended to go and dine with the rest; but, counterfeiting illness, he took only a little wine and left the room locking the door upon them, also several other doors between the gallery and the room where they took their meals.

He then went to find the prisoner and the officer who guarded him, and entering the gallery he locked that door also and put the keys of all the doors in his pocket. At the next moment the Duc de Beaufort, who was of commanding figure, and this man who was secretly his, flung themselves upon La Ramée and prevented him from crying out. Then, not wishing to kill him, although it was dangerous not to do so unless he were really won over to their side, they gagged him, bound him hand and foot, and left him. After which they fastened a rope to the window and lowered themselves,

one after the other, but the valet first, as he would certainly
have been rigorously punished had he failed to escape.
They let themselves slip into the moat, the depth of which
was greater than the length of their rope; so that, dropping
from the end of the rope the prince ran the risk of injuring
himself, which really happened. The pain made him swoon,
and he continued a long time in that state without recover-
ing his senses.

Coming to himself after a while, four or five of his friends,
who were on the other side of the moat, and had seen him
lying half dead with terrible anxiety, flung him another rope
which he fastened round his body, and in this way they
dragged him by strength of arms up to them; the valet first,
according to the promise the prince had made him, which
was faithfully kept. When he reached the top, he was in a
bad state, for besides the hurt he received in falling, the
rope he had tied round his body had tightened upon his
stomach under the joltings he had received in being drawn
up. But having recovered some strength through the vigour
of his courage and the fear of losing the fruit of his pains, he
rose and went to join a party of fifty men who were awaiting
him in a neighbouring wood.

A gentleman of his own family who took part in the expe-
dition, told me afterwards, that on seeing himself surrounded
by this troop of men, the joy of finding he was at liberty and
among his own people was so great that he was cured in a
moment of all his pains, and springing on a horse that was
held ready for him, he disappeared like lightning, enchanted
to breathe the air without restraint and to be able to say,
like King François I. when he set foot in France on returning from Spain, "Ha! I am free!"

A woman who was gathering herbs in a garden at the edge
of the moat, with a little boy, saw all that happened of this

mystery. But the men who were in ambush had so threatened her to force her to be silent that, having little interest
in preventing the prince from escaping, she and her son stood
quietly looking on at all they did. As soon as he was gone
the woman went and told her husband, who was gardener of
the place, and they both went to notify the guards. But it
was then too late; men could not change what God had
ordered; and the stars, which sometimes seem to tell the
decrees of that Sovereign, had already revealed to many persons, through an astrologer named Goïsel, that the Duc de
Beaufort was to leave his prison on that very day.

The news at first surprised the whole Court, particularly
those who were not indifferent to it. The minister was no
doubt disturbed; but, as usual, he did not show it. The
queen, who formerly regarded the prince as a friend, and who
now hated him more for reasons of State than from inclination, consoled herself readily for the little annoyance this
escape had given her; and doubtless a great many persons
rejoiced at it. For, besides the fact that the prince was
loved and had a great cabal taking part in his interests, the
enemies of the cardinal hoped that, being at liberty, the duke
would make a party in France and bring about a change in
the government. No one doubted that he had great desires
for revenge upon his enemy, and that the bad disposition of
many minds would easily give him means to obtain it.

The queen and the cardinal talked kindly about the
escape, and laughed over it, saying that M. de Beaufort had
done well. Chavigny alone was blamed, for not having
taken care enough to guard the prisoner; and the queen
blamed him loudly for leaving the exterior of the prison
without sentinels who would have seen the plot. But
Chavigny, though driven from the council by the Duc de
Beaufort and receiving him at Vincennes with joy, not being

now so well treated by the cardinal as he had a right to expect after the rout of " the Importants," no longer cared to guard this enemy, whose ruin had done him no good. When the prisoner escaped Chavigny had gone to spend the festival at the Chartreuse, where he often went for consolation in default of human favour; and in justifying himself to the queen and cardinal he alleged no other reasons except that he considered he ought to leave that duty to the king's officers who were answerable for it, and not he, to whom no special order for watchfulness was given.

The Duc de Beaufort had lived religiously in prison; for it is customary with men to seek God when in trouble and forget him in prosperity. This very thing happened to the prince, who, penitent enough in the forest of Vincennes, thought only of revenge and diversion as soon as he was out of it.

Before this good luck happened to the Duc de Beaufort the cardinal was warned that a plot was preparing to set him at liberty. He wrote to La Ramée about it; ordering him to take especial care to prevent such a thing from happening. The officer answered that unless the prince became a little bird capable of flying out of the window, it was impossible that he could get away; and that very thing having happened, the cardinal showed the letter to the Maréchal d'Estrées, uncle of the Duc de Beaufort, who was astonished to see that an all-powerful minister, so well warned, was unable to avert what destiny decreed for the prisoner, namely, to leave his prison for the accomplishment of great events about to happen in which he was to have so large a share.

The cardinal felt some uneasiness as to the place of the Duc de Beaufort's retreat. He was afraid he might go to Brittany, where his principal estates lay, and would there raise a faction and disturbances.[1] But one of my friends, to whom the cardinal communicated his thoughts on the subject, reassured him completely, and told him that the prince, having neither fortresses nor money, could do nothing against the State or against him — against the State on account of his powerlessness; against him, because the cardinal could pay those who guarded him higher than the duke could pay those he might employ against him.

The queen, doing me the honour to speak to me of all this, said that the Duc de Beaufort was not in a condition to raise a party in France; and, in regard to the cardinal's person, she added that the prince had taken the sacraments too many times in his prison to still retain in his soul the intention to murder. And on my saying that perhaps he would seek to be reconciled with her minister and would ask him to restore him to her good graces, she answered that the cardinal would be foolish to do that and that she should never advise it, knowing well that M. de Beaufort was incapable of making good use of a return to favour.

June 3, the queen went to visit the Queen of England, who had come from Saint-Germain to spend two weeks in Paris for the purpose of gaining the jubilee.[2] Our regent, after visiting also the Duc d'Orléans, who had the gout, began herself the stations ordained to receive that sacred liberality of the pope, who had granted it to Christians from good motives, though it has since served in Naples to further the interests of the King of Spain. France wisely took a spiritual part in it, which was preferable to that taken by foreigners. The queen visited thirty-seven churches, though

[1] The Duc de Beaufort hid himself in the Vendômois, from house to house, until the day when he could come to Paris, and go to Prudhomme's house. — FR. ED.

[2] Plenary indulgence granted by the pope at certain times and on certain occasions. — TR.

she was obliged actually to visit but one; and by this exemplary piety she induced us to do the same, and quit repose for toil in order that by this toil we might acquire true rest.

The evening of the day on which she had gone through such fatigue, both devotional and civil, she went, to refresh herself after the heat she felt in the streets, to walk in the garden of the Palais-Royal, where she spent a good part of the night; for her health was such that she could not bear excess of any kind. Five persons — Mademoiselle Beaumont, my sister Mademoiselle Bertaut, commonly called Socratine on account of her wisdom, M. de Chandenier, M. de Comminges, and myself — had the honour of accompanying her on this promenade. The conversation was agreeable and free, and capable of bringing us some profit. We spoke of what we owed to God by obligation, and what we gave to creatures from inclination. We considered to how many great things that obligation, bound us, and to how many evils that inclination exposed us. After examining those two points, we found that we gave nothing to Him to whom we owed everything, and all to those to whom we owed nothing.

The two men who were in our little group admitted, through equity and a sense of justice, a part of their wrong-doing, recognizing its injury; and we, out of sincerity, candidly avowed, in the name of our sex, that the too great love we felt for ourselves brought us over-much praise and applause; and that often flattery, which we ought to hate, made us too sensitive to the love of human creatures. And we concluded, to our shame, that the wisest and most virtuous of women, at the age when she pleases herself and desires to please others, has moments when she is neither Christian nor virtuous; for, instead of rendering to God the homage that she owes Him, she desires the adoration of others, and would like to have over men the empire that the Creator alone should possess.

Neither is she virtuous; because true virtue proceeds from the heart and the sentiments of the soul, and it is easier to keep the body exempt from corruption than the soul without licentiousness, vanity, or weakness. In short, we judged the human race on this ground, namely: that defects of the spirit are worse by far than the external faults which are seen of men; and that the most virtuous, whether men or women, who call themselves earthly sages, are not so at all. After this general confession, we followed the queen, who went to bed; and when we left her Aurora was just beginning to show, as the poets say, that soon she would enrich us with her pearls; which made us extremely lazy on the following day.

Monday, June 5, parliament assembled, against the orders of the queen; but the chief president, wishing to sometimes do his duty, prevented the members from speaking, and would not open the session; so that, after being all assembled in the great chamber until ten o'clock without saying a word, the members were forced to separate. But they did not do so without great complaints against their leader, nor without muttering loudly against him.

The next day the same thing was done; and President Mesmes, after the chief president had spoken, told them they did some wrong in showing tumultuously so little respect to the queen's orders; for subjects should always testify obedience and submission to their sovereign; but that, nevertheless, he freely admitted they had good reason to apprehend harsh chains because of the iron shackles they had seen put on others; and that he was of opinion that the assembly ought to employ itself in finding a remedy. On that point he blamed the neglect of the Chamber, as much as he blamed its impetuosity in other ways; and he advised that parliament should assemble on the Monday following to consult as to the means of satisfying the queen, and of preventing their robes from being torn from their backs like those of their neighbours and colleagues, who were the first to be maltreated, and were a sign of what would sooner or later happen to themselves.

This speech was blamed by the cardinal; and the queen spoke of it that night, while undressing, to Mademoiselle de Beaumont, a friend of Madame de Mesmes. She complained of that president as a man who seemed to have bad intentions, and said that in talking of respect and submission he doubtless intended to foment the spirit of sedition and revolt in the souls of his colleagues, and that she saw plainly that he wanted to avenge himself on the cardinal, who was the sworn enemy of his brother, Comte d'Avaux. These opinions were inspired in her by her minister in order to get them repeated to that lady, and by that means have them reach President de Mesmes and induce him to correct himself in future and change his conduct.

June 8, the king's lawyers were summoned, and the chancellor spoke to them at the council in presence of the queen, in relation to the resolution of parliament to meet in defiance of the prohibition. He told them that the queen, in forbidding them to assemble, had no intention of opposing the privileges of their body, but only to prevent the union of the other courts with theirs. After which he enlarged upon their rebellion, their want of respect, and upon the claim the king made that it did not belong to them to protect the other courts against his will.

The cardinal, on his side, sent for several members of the Grand Council and the Cour des Aides, and spoke to them humanely, as they said, but very weakly. He assured them he wished to oblige them, said that he thought their reasons very good, and better than he had supposed them; advised them to address themselves to him, as devout men to saints in regard to God, in order to obtain their pardon from the queen, as much for themselves in general as for those of their number who had been exiled; and he promised to exert himself for them, begging, nevertheless, that they would obey the king, which was necessary to maintain the due order of the State.

These mild words, in a period of revolt, had no other effect than to cause great contempt for the minister and produce much ridicule of the weakness and inconsistency of his conduct, which was sometimes too haughty and sometimes too humble. This story went the rounds, even of the ladies' *ruelles*, and gave occasion for all France to say that the minister was incapable of governing or of guiding the country.

June 12, the queen, whose piety was always sacredly occupied, in order to honour the festival of the very Holy Sacrament, ordered to be set up on this day an altar (*reposoir*) in the first courtyard of the Palais-Royal, on which she placed the finest tapestries of the king and the richest ornaments a great queen ever possessed. She ordered, for this purpose, a closed crown, to place upon the altar where the Saint of saints was to rest, made of the finest crown jewels, so rich and splendid that it would have been difficult, if estimated, to put a price upon it.

After having adored Our Lord on that spot, where she awaited the procession, she accompanied the Host on foot through great heat to Saint-Eustache, taking with her the king and the little Monsieur; and the people, as they saw her pass, gave her many benedictions, though already they seemed a little alienated from the love they had formerly borne her.

That evening she sent for the lieutenant of police, and ordered him to release from prison a man whom President Mesmes had sent there because he was found before his door writing down the names of all who entered. This man had declared on being arrested that he was there by order of the Court and belonged to the provost of l'Isle. The next day, on leaving prison, he went to see the queen and complained to her of President Mesmes, saying that he had received great outrages from his servants. When going to bed that night the queen told us, laughing, that she meant to avenge him for all the wrongs he had suffered. And she did, in fact, avenge him so well that she ordered the grand provost to arrest all the servants of the president of whom the man complained.[1]

President de Mesmes, seeing clearly that he did not stand well at Court, thought himself obliged to act with prudence; he left the game; and the next day sent his excuses to his colleagues, saying that he was ill, and needed change of air. He absented himself for some time, in order to avoid the two accusations to which he saw himself exposed, namely: that of weakness if he spoke in parliament in favour of the king, which he was accustomed to do when his duty obliged him; and that of wishing to avenge himself if he said the least word that might seem contrary to the king's service.

He was blamed by those he wanted to satisfy; they murmured against him at Court, and his friends on the other side said that he was very wrong to abandon his associates at this conjuncture, when they were entering into conflict

---

[1] Omer Talon relates the same fact, and lets it be understood that the man was a spy of the queen. "All this," he says, "irritated the public mind extremely, as a species of inquisition."—FR. ED.

with the king, and consequently had great need of assistance as strong as that of a man like himself.

Five treasurers of France were put in prison for having written circular letters to their colleagues, exhorting them not to pay over the taxes that the king demanded, and to pay themselves from the sums that passed through their hands. The man who wrote the letter was named Frotté, a man of worth and zealous for the public good. When he learned what had happened to his five colleagues (a misfortune from which his friends, without his knowing it, had saved him) he presented himself to d'Émery [superintendent of finance] and complained to him that he had not been imprisoned with the others, as if it were a great affront to him, declaring that his fame and honour were affected by his being separated from his colleagues. He continued steadfast in these sentiments, and, shortly after, the prisoners were released, because the minister was always inclined on his own account to gentleness and pardon.

June 15, parliament assembled again to discuss the protection it wished to give, and claimed that it could give, to the other sovereign courts [*compagnies*]. It chose to deliberate also on the annulling of its decree of union with those courts by the order that had been brought to it from the king; and it finally determined that its said decree should be maintained in spite of the one by which the king in council had annulled it. It further resolved to meet the next day in the Chamber of Saint-Louis for ample deliberation, and that deputies from the other courts should be received there. Several members on that day made fine harangues in support of their opinions, which all went to break up the government and blame the conduct of the minister, publicly accusing Superintendent d'Émery of extortion and robbery.

This was a mortal blow to the prosperity of France, and

made her enemies hope that these intestine wrangles would replace them in the fine position from which they were driven out by the able leadership of Cardinal Richelieu and the fortunate success of the regency. That this hardihood displeased the queen and her minister, it is impossible to doubt. After the council held in the cabinet on this affair, it was resolved to annul once more this action of the parliament. The queen commanded Du Plessis, secretary of State, followed by Carnavalet and a few *gardes de corps,* to go to the Palais de Justice and bring to the king that decree so pernicious to the public peace. But the clerks at the Palais assembled and cried out in such a way against him and his posse, declaring that they would be killed first, that he was compelled to return bringing nothing.

On the 16th, parliament was summoned in a body. It came, as usual on foot, to the Palais-Royal. To receive it legally, the dukes and peers, the marshals of France, and all the officers of the crown were assembled. A dais was placed in the great cabinet with a platform beneath it, on which were the king and queen, seated on a species of throne surrounded by all the great seigneurs of the Court. The queen's face was stern and full of grave majesty which marked a threatening anger.

The chancellor made the members a long discourse in the nature of a reprimand, without, however, saying anything to affront them. Then, having ordered their edict of union to be read aloud, he pointed out the fault they had committed in uniting themselves like factious persons with the other courts. He made them see how by so doing they had fomented rebellion and disobedience among the subjects of the king, whom they were, on the contrary, bound to maintain in respect for the laws and order. He also ordered to be read aloud the decree of the Council annulling theirs, and

proved to them that the king, in order to maintain his authority, was forced to do as he had done.   And then, coming to
their edict of the previous day, in which, without regard to
the king's command, they re-affirmed that union, he enlarged
upon their action, representing the great and injurious consequences which would follow it ; and said that, even were
it accompanied by good and innocent intentions, it could
only produce much evil to the State, very bad effects upon
France, and give great hopes to her enemies.

He concluded by the reading of another decree given by
the king that same day.   This last contained a long argu-
ment on all the past and present points, and annulled both
the edict the parliament had given for the union of the companies and the one of the preceding day.   He ordered the
members in the king's name to employ themselves in future
solely in administering justice to his subjects, and commanded them not to meddle again in the affairs of State.
He told them that the king alone could claim that right as
his inheritance, together with the power to govern as he
chose, either by himself or by his ministers.   He said that
the votes in their assemblies had been counted, but not
weighed; that there were many wise men in their body;
that his Majesty was grieved to be unable to separate these
from the others, to praise them publicly and worthily reward
them on this occasion; but that he would mark that difference when the time came to do so; and then he gave orders
to the clerk on the spot to bring to the queen the record
of the last edict within twenty-four hours.

The chief president attempted to reply ; but the queen interrupted him, and told him he could make no answer;
that, for her part, she knew his good intentions, and that
sufficed; and with regard to the factious persons who were
troubling the peace of the State, she assured them that if

they did not obey the commands of the king they would be punished in their persons, their property, and their posterity.

In spite of this ceremony, as soon as the parliament returned to the Palais the members assembled and forbade the clerk with one voice to take their edict to the queen as she had commanded. Moreover, they notified the delegates from the other companies, who were waiting in the Chamber of Saint-Louis that they could not assemble with them until they had first deliberated among themselves over the orders that were given them from the king.

Politicians, arguing in the cabinet over present affairs, all said that the little respect shown by parliament for the prohibitions of the queen would compel the minister to punish it, and to employ against it, in order to maintain the king's authority, all the means which vigorous justice could furnish for such occasions. But, besides the fact that many persons to whom the power of the favourite was displeasing did not altogether disapprove of the course taken by parliament, those who seemed to counsel punishment did not really wish the cardinal to follow their advice. Even if such a course had been a certain remedy for the evil, they would not have desired it; for they all wanted the minister's ruin, and would have been in despair had he done the right thing to prevent the misfortunes which they hoped would lead to it. So that the minister, lacking true counsel and, as every one thought, firmness, let pass all occasions to arrest the torrent at the beginning of its flow; and as this tolerance greatly increased the audacity of parliament, it continued to assemble on the following days, and to testify by its unity a great and firm resolution to maintain its interests against the king.

The minister, who did not wish to push things to extremities, took the part of gentleness and humility, just as the other side took that of force and arrogance. Matters could not go on thus, one side threatening and doing no harm, the other side offending, but with nothing to fear. It was necessary that either their boldness should frighten the minister, or that he, not willing to be frightened, should send terror to their souls by the effects of the sovereign power. But he did not take this course; he laid down his arms and followed, in spite of all ordinary maxims of policy, a system of tolerance and gentleness.

Parliament, on its side, did not send the record it had been ordered to convey to the queen; the members openly declared that their edicts should pass and those of the king should be null, and they voted to still assemble, in spite of the queen's prohibition, in the Chamber of Saint-Louis. There they murmured loudly, and made known by their speeches not only their own interests (the annual tax for themselves and that of the officers justly exciting them), but they declared that they meant to take cognizance of the administration of the finances and concern themselves in the reform of the State, which they insisted was not well governed.

The attorney-general [Omer Talon], wishing in some degree to do his duty and, as the king's lawyer, to represent to parliament its excessive boldness, said that they were getting so forward that either the royal authority would be degraded, or that of parliament annihilated; and he advised, as a wise man, that moderation should be given to their passion.

He was treated as ridiculous by all the youth of the assembly, as though he had uttered the greatest nonsense; and he who on so many occasions had shown such partiality for the interests of parliament and the public was ill-treated at the first word he said in behalf of the king's authority, and forced to silence. They all retorted that he was wrong in making such remonstrances; that they were as good servants of the king as himself; that what they were doing was for the king's service; that they sought only to reform the abuses of the State, and especially the bad management of the treasury.

The cardinal, finding that the mutineers held firmly against him, resolved to go to them and to win over their sullen spirits by smooth words and appeals to their interest.

The queen, who had threatened as a sovereign and feared nothing, believing that exile and imprisonment would put an end to such revolts, could with difficulty bring herself to follow the wishes of the cardinal. She said to those whom she thought his friends that he was too kind, and would spoil all by trying to acquire the good graces of his enemies.

She had a great contempt for the robe, and could not imagine that that portion of the king's subjects could disturb or bring change into his affairs. Moroever, she was ignorant of the great events which, from such small beginnings, had overthrown the most powerful monarchies and ruined the best established empires; so that, knowing nothing but her own grandeur and the external pomp that environs kings with guards and suites, that very splendour (though her virtue made her despise it) rendered her incapable of conceiving that her regency, which she saw accompanied by so much glory, could have any revolution by such low means. This was why she proposed punishment as a remedy which must indubitably arrest the revolt at its source; which sentiment was altogether in accordance with the good sense and advice of the ablest of her Court. She often said to those familiarly about her that she would never permit that *canaille* (meaning the men of the robe) to attack the authority of the king, her son; so that her minister, who had not expected their audacity to reach a point at which he was compelled to yield, now regretted much that he had embittered her mind against parliament.

The queen, who could be gentle and kind, had, nevertheless, an unparalleled firmness, which showed plainly that, if she had been sustained, she would have followed the sternest precepts with force and vigour on this occasion, when it was a question of punishing servants of the king who sought to oppose his authority. She was excusable in having this sentiment and this severity, so long as it was limited by the reason and kindness which always seemed to overrule in her her opposite qualities. It is to be believed that the exile of a few persons now would have saved great evils; for their punishment would no doubt have been followed by acts of her kindness, which always urged her to do harm to none, and to leave every one in the enjoyment of his property and office, as in the past. But she was fated to follow the will of her minister, and was forced to consent to what he desired to do on this occasion.

He resolved, therefore, with the Duc d'Orléans and the Prince de Condé, to offer to parliament all it demanded. He perceived that he had pushed the sovereign companies too far, and he meant that his present gentleness should be the remedy. The princes and the cardinal were of one opinion on this point, and one day, as they were talking together of the queen and her firmness, the minister said that while he desired greatly to pacify all things, the queen was valiant, like a soldier who is brave because he does not understand the danger.

According to this last resolution all the seniors of both Chambers were requested to assemble at the house of the Duc d'Orléans, who spoke to them cordially, assured them of his protection with the queen, promised to intercede for them, and made them hope that the annual fee should be again granted to them. They were requested to no longer protect the masters of petitions, and they were given to understand that if they would only make a show of behaving properly the latter would soon be restored; also it was promised that if they abolished that name of union, nothing should be asked of the other courts whose defence they had taken up; and, finally, that the exiled members should be recalled. The chancellor exhorted them with all his might to receive with a good grace the favours which the queen granted them at the instance of Monsieur, the king's uncle.

The cardinal also made them a great speech, which contained the same things and concluded by begging them to consider that, being offered all they could desire of the queen's kindness, they would, if they refused these favours, be guilty towards the people of whatever evils might happen, for which they would have to answer before God and man, and bear the stigma to posterity.

This done, it was hoped that matters would be settled; for the presidents, who are always more for the Court than the councillors, had made the cardinal hope that by means of these concessions the assembly would become reasonable. But they were not correct in this judgment, nor was the policy of the minister advantageous to the State; which shows plainly that the corruption of men is such that, to make them live according to reason, they must not be treated reasonably; and in order to make them just, they must be treated unjustly.

Until now parliament had had some right to oppose what was done to the supreme courts; and to tell the truth, the public had need of such protection against the sovereign power, which might sometimes be alarming in the hands of ministers if it did not have the limitations that kings themselves have given to it by the intervention of parlia-

ments. If this celebrated assembly had only taken care to
accompany its actions and words with more submission to
the orders of the king and queen, its intentions would have
been laudable and its humble remonstrances would have
found their justification in the rules of equity, in the laws
of the State, and in the opinion of men of worth.   But, by
scorning the kindness that the queen consented to show to
them on this occasion, they became criminal and proved
plainly that the passion, injustice, and self-interest of cabals
into which this body of men had entered, were the motives
that made them act, and not the public good.

It must also be said that the cardinal was blamed for
using these means, because his success was attributed to
weakness.   He would have shamed tyrants by this action
had it been met by virtuous men whose intentions were upright; and far from being despised, he would have deserved
eternal eulogy, — because rigour is, in itself, evil; and if
the malignity of inferiors did not oblige those who govern
them to use it, those who are most opposed to such precepts
would be the worthiest of respect and their fame the most
estimable.

This day, however, dishonoured the minister, because he
had been prodigal of his king's favour, and, by such prodi-
gality had brought about, through the refusal of parliament,
a great diminution of the royal power; but, in truth, it was
more shameful to parliament than to him, because it marked
plainly the iniquity of the latter.

The next day, June 22, the Chambers assembled as usual;
and, far from showing themselves content, their deliberations
went to thanking the Duc d'Orléans for the care he took of
their interests; expressing the desire to refuse the favours
the queen offered them; and requesting that demonstration
be made to her that it was not in their own interests that

they claimed the right to assemble, but because, as good servants of the king, they desired to labour in reforming the abuses of the State; and they entreated that for this cause her Majesty would not think it ill that they should keep to their first resolution.

Besides this, they requested that the decree issued against them be annulled, and their own decree held good and valid. This hardihood gave keen annoyance to the minister, who, having gone to bed that day earlier than usual out of vexation at these ill-adventures, said to one of his friends with much irritation that the chancellor and the superintendent [of finances] had let him fall into this confusion, and they should repent it.

About this time news was received of the death of the King of Poland, which caused no other grief to the queen than that of having to wear mourning. She was not so well pleased with the widow, on whose head she had placed a crown, that she cared to take part in her interests; in fact, had she done so there was more to rejoice at for her sake, than to grieve over. The Polish queen had lost a husband who never treated her well, who was hateful in his own person, and who left the kingdom for a brother, who, according to all appearances, did not hate her. The latter intended to marry her in case he was elected king in place of his elder brother. His birth, his friends, and the assistance of the Queen of Poland, who had both money and influence, gave him reason to hope for that good fortune; and all these things happened not long after, to the satisfaction of every one.

To return to the parliament, whose actions now became the sole preoccupation of the Court. After several deliberations their last decision was to thank Monsieur and to send deputies to the queen, justifying their decree of May 13, and the sincerity of parliament, complaining of the insulting things read to them in her presence from the decrees of her council, demanding the freedom of the prisoners, and assuring her Majesty that nothing would be done in the Chamber of Saint-Louis that was not for the good of her service.

The fear that was felt of worse made this conclusion tolerable. It was supposed that the deputies, when they came, would make protestations of fidelity and duty to the queen which would bring matters to some sort of settlement. The next day the queen received them in her little gallery. With her were the Duc d'Orléans, the cardinal, and the other ministers according to rank, and the doors were left open in expectation of some meekness from the deputies; but the contrary of what was hoped for happened. The address of the chief president was so strong and so bold that it surprised the auditors and seemed to offend the queen. I shall insert it here, in order to show clearly to those who read these Memoirs what was the spirit of this parliament and the audacity of its undertaking. Here are the principal points, which I noticed myself, having been there and heard the speech : —

Summary of the harangue of the chief president. — His speech turned on the thought that sovereigns ought to reign more by love than by fear; that justice was the chief bond between the sovereign and the people; that this justice, rendered by the ministry of officials and through them distributed to the people, was to-day hampered on all sides. That parliament and its members had always believed that time was the sovereign remedy of evils; but, on the contrary, those they had to complain of grew worse with time, and they must now believe that their continuation would soon undermine the authority of the king and the good of the

State. That nothing was left for parliament to do but to serve as barrier to prevent the disorders into which that authority had fallen. That his Majesty had been persuaded that they had not the right to assemble, whereas it was a usual thing to do so. That the word " union " had so shocked the minds of those who gave him pernicious counsels (the counter-blow of which seemed to shake the royal authority), that they had tried to represent parliament and its members as factious and seditious persons. That these accusers deserved that title much more than they who had never had other intentions than those which their innocence and their respect for the king inspired in them. That they were obliged to let his Majesty know that these same persons had concealed from him the precedent of 1618, when they assembled for public affairs, and even for the *rentes des aides ;* that the king had then approved all that they had done, knowing that it was intended for the good of his service. That when they thought of the grandeur of that throne before which, a few days ago, the chief parliament of France had made honourable amends, but in presence of which their edicts of May 13 and June 15 had been publicly read and then annulled by decree of the council, and defamed by guilty accusations against innocent persons, accusing them of divers crimes ; and when they considered all the other insults which had been offered to them publicly, — they were forced to make his Majesty understand that they were well assured such insults did not proceed from him ; that they were far too sure of his virtue, his piety, and his extreme sentiments of kindness. Therefore they doubted not he would be soon disabused of the evil impressions those persons had given him, and in a short time he would see reason to trust parliament. And, in conclusion, that he (the chief president) was charged by parliament to make

known to the king the justice of its decrees; to entreat
him very humbly to be willing to suppress the decree of his
council of June 8, given against it; to consent that the parliamentary decrees should remain upon the register as having been issued with *power and justice,* and that it would
please him to make a declaration of the innocence of parliament, which had been accused and insulted without just
cause. A promise was given that nothing should be done
in their assemblies that was not for the good of the king's
service, and that of the public, and for the peace of the
State. And finally, they conjured him very ardently to continue to them the honour of his good-will, with many
protestations that they were his very humble, very obedient,
and very faithful servants.

After this harangue was ended, the queen, quite amazed,
had the king's lawyers called up and told them that in the
course of a few days she would make known her will to
parliament.

The state of France was such that it was no longer a time
to attempt rigorous measures without running the risk of a
great revolution. Parliament had usurped too much authority. By refusing the offered favours, it had shown to the
people that it sought only the public good and the cure of
the evils of the State.

The people were overwhelmed by taxes of all kinds; the
kingdom was impoverished by long wars; every one was
discontented. The courtiers hated the minister; all wanted
a change, more from unruliness of mind than from reason.
The minister being despised, each took the liberty to follow
his own caprice; it seemed to all quite just to shout against
the tax-brokers, who appeared, in fact, to be the only ones
who triumphed from the public misery. Men of worth,

without considering that this is a sometimes necessary evil,
and that all ages in this respect have been alike, hoped
through disorder to attain to some greater order; and that
word " reformation " was as pleasing to them in the light of
a good principle, as it was to those who wanted disorder
through the excess of their madness and their ambition.   So
that all, from different motives, raged against the queen and
against her minister, without considering that it was not
right to allow parliament to take upon itself the authority
to reform the State as it chose; and that such reformation
would, in consequence, bring with it the destruction of the
monarchy, through the overthrow which such an abnormal
combination, so opposed to our laws, so fatal to royalty,
would cause to the State.

Those laws contain in themselves, no doubt, the necessary
rules for the guidance of the people and for their happiness;
they are equitable; justice is their basis; and the royal
authority is, and ought to be their supporter.   But it must
also be understood in observing them, as we are bound to
do, that they subject us, by God's command, to the supreme
and single will of our kings, without permission under
any pretext to fail therein.   If parliaments have the power
to correct the faults of kings and their ministers, we do not
know that those who compose them may not commit greater
ones, or banish virtue from the throne merely to seat vice
upon it; or whether the ambition and the passions of the
many may not be more dangerous than those of the one.

By the cardinal's docility and the offers he had made to
parliament, the latter must have seen that if it had really,
in good faith, discovered disorder in the finances and asked
modestly for their reformation, it would have been granted.
If its members, with fidelity, had served the king usefully,
and if by their very humble remonstrances the people had

obtained relief, they would have earned the reputation of being judges and subjects without reproach. They would indeed have deserved that fame, and kings themselves would in future years have esteemed an integrity which had made them act so skilfully for the good of the public and the happiness of the State.

But they were far indeed from such sentiments, and their unbridled audacity made the minister believe that the best way to treat them was by dissimulation. He resolved, therefore, to make the following answer to parliament, which was infinitely blamed by both sides. June 29 parliament was informed by the king's lawyers that "the queen had so good an opinion of their fidelity that she could not believe their assemblies could be by their own will in any way prejudicial to the service of the king; that being so, she permitted them to assemble, provided that all their deliberations should end within a week."

On the evening of June 30 the cardinal told the queen that he had just received letters from Flanders which informed him that the enemy were taking heart from the news of the proceedings in parliament; that the tale had been so commented on that they now believed Paris was in arms; which rumour, though false, was having a bad effect on the affairs of the king and exciting foreigners to take decisive steps.

As he felt himself battered by the tempest, he affected such humility that he told Madame de Senecé the same evening, when she spoke to him of his nieces who were still with her, that he begged her to bring them up as ordinary young ladies, for he did not know yet what would become of them, or of himself either. And as he knew he was accused of taking money, he showed, as far as he possibly could, that he was disinterested, saying that he did not desire either favour or fortune except for the good it enabled him to do to his friends.

The deputies of parliament and those of the other sovereign courts assembled in the Chamber of Saint-Louis, according to their own will and the consent of the queen. They had extorted that permission from her, of whom they made little account, either as her favour or that of her minister. The first propositions which they now laid down were bold, seditious, and all in favour of the public and the people, for the purpose of gaining popularity and of giving themselves strength by that which makes the strength of kings. These proportions were: —

1. To remit to the people one quarter of the *taille*-tax, with which the tax-gatherers now paid themselves.

2. To remit to the people what they had owed for the last few years, which they could not pay on account of their insolvency.

3. To revoke entirely the office of provincial intendants, — who profited by such employments from the mass of the people, — and to make the treasurers of France, the elected and other officers appointed for the purpose, responsible for the king's revenues.

4. That no person should be kept in prison more than twenty-four hours before being examined by parliament, which in future was to take cognizance of the cause of each person's imprisonment.

5. That no fines or taxes should be imposed upon the people without the decrees being duly examined.

6. That a chamber of justice should be convened, composed from the four sovereign courts, to judge supremely the abuses and malversations committed in the finances.

Those were the principal propositions made by parliament, which had agreed to work solely for the service of the king.

The queen in this extremity, to prevent parliament from re-establishing the masters of petitions by its own authority, did this herself without request. After having indicted and sentenced them with her own lips, she was forced, in spite of the contempt shown for her favours, to replace them in their former offices. And, as if to cover royalty with shame, Monsieur, the king's uncle, at a complimentary visit which some of the parliament paid to him to thank him for having shown that he favoured them, again offered to work for them, and they on behalf of the parliament, accepted his offer.

July 6, the Duc d'Orléans went to parliament and, in a great speech, endeavoured to show the members that their proceedings gave false hopes to the enemy, which might turn into true ones, against their intentions, if they did not take the side of the king as well as that of the public; that, notwithstanding the dangerous consequences of their conduct, the queen did not object to the desire they showed to remedy the evils of the State; but she wished it to be without injury to the grandeur and happiness of France, and she therefore begged them to suspend the edict they had given against the provincial intendants. In conclusion Monsieur offered them a conference on all their propositions, promising his protection and entire sincerity in all matters there treated, as a prince who, never having deceived any one, would surely not begin with a company for whom he had much affection — ending his speech with a few complimentary words.

That same day, the masters of petitions came to the Palais-Royal in a body to thank the queen for the favour she had bestowed in restoring them. Her Majesty received them in her great cabinet, with her usual company, namely, the Duc d'Orléans, the cardinal, the chancellor, and the four secretaries of State. Their harangue was humble and full of gratitude. They then went to Monsieur, and afterwards to the cardinal.

July 7 and 8 were spent in conferences at the Luxembourg. These took place in the great gallery. The Duc d'Orléans sat in his arm-chair opposite to Cardinal Mazarin; beside him was the chancellor, then came the chief president and the other members on simple stools. The latter all expressed much satisfaction with the Duc d'Orléans and the kindness he had shown to them in their conferences. Deputies from all the chambers and sovereign courts were present, and the matters proposed in the Chamber of Saint-Louis were discussed. The cardinal addressing them praised their zeal for the service of the king; and the very men who, a few days earlier, were treated as rebels in the queen's presence, and who, in very truth, were quasi destroying the royal authority, were now called by the minister restorers of France and fathers of the country.

This inconsistency of conduct gave to the spies upon his defects a fine subject on which to ridicule and despise him and treat him as a weakling, — reproaching him for having none of the heroic virtues that great men ought to practise in the guidance of great States; for it is a general precept that kingdoms must be governed by laws, maintained by firmness and by uniform control.

During these conferences certain members of parliament were fomenting intrigues against d'Émery, the superintendent of finance. His office, which they desired to obtain, was the real cause of the complaints that now burst forth against him.[1] They made a pretext of no longer being able to endure that the man who had attacked them should continue

---

[1] Montglat, in his Memoirs (Fourteenth Campaign), relates the exactions of d'Émery, who "ruined every one to find money with which to carry on the war, and also to satisfy the greed of the cardinal, which was insatiable." — FR. ED.

to control the finances of the country. They therefore proposed to the minister to dismiss him. Every one became eager for his ruin, — some from self-interest, others from mere caprice. The man seemed loaded down with public hatred, and those whose interests were against him made the cardinal hope that by his dismissal all other things would be made easy for him. D'Émery's friends at Court, seeing from afar the storm that was preparing to burst upon his head, worked to support him with all their strength; for, as he paid them well, they served him well in return. But the cardinal, imagining that he could buy his own tranquillity by d'Émery's ruin, resolved to sacrifice him to the public good, and to his own in particular.

During these days, when the fate of this man was uncertain and there were still favourable moments for him in the mind of him who was master of it, and then again very bad ones in which the minister looked upon the ruin of the superintendent as the source of his own prosperity, it happened that one of d'Émery's friends proposed, in the Chamber of Saint-Louis, to make inquiry as to the moneys which were sent out of France. Certain friends of the minister warned him of this, and several of the members of parliament put aside the proposal, because they saw that it went direct to him personally. They did not like him, but they had found him so docile and accommodating that they judged it was now a good time to use his apparent softness to attain their ends; they determined therefore to begin with the superintendent before going on to other works.

The cardinal, knowing that the person who had proposed the inquiry into the exported moneys was one of d'Émery's friends, believed that the superintendent had instigated that proceeding in order to entangle him and involve him in his own conduct, thus making him either his defender or his accomplice. This proposal having had no effect against the minister, it had, necessarily, a very bad one for the superintendent ; inasmuch as it gave cause to the cardinal to abandon him more readily to the public wrath; and even to do this with some justice, because he could accuse d'Émery of having tried to ruin him. The affair being in this state, on the evening of the 8th, after the conclusion of the conference at the Luxembourg, his dismissal was arranged by the queen, the Duc d'Orléans, and Cardinal Mazarin ; which solved a question they had been discussing for a week among themselves.

The next morning, about midday, Le Tellier went to see d'Émery on the part of the queen, and commanded him to retire from Court within two hours. It is to be supposed that this embassy was not agreeable to the superintendent. He beheld his misfortune, not without foreseeing and apprehending it, but certainly without having fully believed in it, because he had always hoped his friends would save him. The Abbé de La Rivière, on whom many things turned in consequence of the greatness of the man he ruled, had given d'Émery the hope that he would serve him. The Maréchal de Villeroy and several others worked for him, but neither the abbé nor any one else could succeed in maintaining him.

He had always flattered himself with the belief that the minister would never abandon him, and never give such advantage to parliament, because, if he did, he himself in all probability would be the next to suffer ; for, no longer having this object of hatred before their eyes on which to expend their maledictions, and the spirit of revolt not being likely, according to all appearances, to cease with his ruin, it was to be expected that on his disappearance the minister himself would be attacked, and therefore his own interests

would oblige him to maintain him.   D'Émery was mistaken
in his reasoning ; but this is not surprising ; men usually
think differently on the same subject, because they themselves have different ideas and different interests.

The king's governor [the Maréchal de Villeroy] went to
visit d'Émery a quarter of an hour after he had received the
order, and was as much surprised to find his friend exiled
as he was mortified at knowing nothing about it.   Two
days earlier the queen had treated me with more confidence ;
for she did me the honour to tell me, speaking of the superintendent, that he was certainly much hated, and it seemed,
as every one wished his dismissal, that it would have to
take place.   By which I judged that his affairs were going
badly, and that this witty and vicious hog who despised
us [1] — because men of business care only for those who have
influence with a minister — I judged, I say, that this man,
whom the world regarded with some envy on account of his
wealth and the luxuries of his living, was about to become
an object of compassion, an example of the vicissitude of
the things of this life, and to teach us more strongly than
ever that "the fashion of this world passeth away."

They sent immediately for the Maréchal de La Meilleraye,
grand-master of artillery, and gave him the superintendence
of finance, as being a man whose heart seemed superior to
the greed of riches, having, by reason of his great establishments and fortune, no need of them.   This seigneur, who,
in the days of Cardinal Richelieu had shown his courage on
many signal occasions, had a noble soul and professed openly
to love virtue and honour ; but with all his fine qualities, he
was judged not fitted for this office : first, because his health
was bad ; next, because he knew more of war than of money ;
and lastly, because his temper was violent.   Moreover, he

---

[1] D'Émery was very fat. — FR. ED.

was suspected of wishing to marry his only son to one of the cardinal's nieces, and that reason alone sufficed to make him hated by the silly populace.

As he was an honest man and much esteemed, the Court was glad, and men of honour felt that they had gained a support and that the new superintendent would consider the merit of persons rather than their favour. In fact, during the short time he remained in office, though it was an evil time and full of wretchedness, he satisfied every one by his honest way of dealing and retained all his friends; instead of the thieves who had hitherto ruined others by taking everything for themselves, this man took nothing for himself and let all go into the coffers of the king, — drawing down upon his head the benedictions of those who saw his integrity.

As soon as he was settled in office he sent the *procureur-général* to say to parliament that his intention was to satisfy it by his conduct of affairs; that, being disinterested and faithful to his master, he believed he could hope to please parliament by serving him well, and in that he would willingly employ the remainder of his life. But certain of the parliament, who no longer set limits to their audacity and lawlessness, laughed at him, and treated him as a weakling. In truth, he deserved it for having made them a submission he did not owe to them. He was blamed for having gone against his nature to do ill, for he was never suspected of being too humble. They gave him as assistants Morange and d'Aligre, who signed all documents under him, — men of integrity, who could not be suspected of peculation, or of allowing it in others, who apparently hated the tax-jobbers as heartily as the most jealous of the parliament; but men, nevertheless, of more virtue than capacity; I mean by that the capacity which finds means to enrich kings without impoverishing their subjects.

XI.

1648.

SUPERINTENDENT D'ÉMERY being ousted, it seemed as if
the troubles would now be appeased; fate had overtaken
him, and public safety would, it was hoped, be found in his
ruin. But minds were not satisfied with this one victory.
The facile concessions of the minister greatly increased the
hopes of the rebels, and parliament henceforth began to
attribute to itself so excessive a power that there was reason
to fear that the evil example it saw in that of England
would make an impression upon it, and that those of the
assembly who had good intentions would be misled by the
others. The kingdom was getting more and more impoverished daily; domestic peace was disturbed and France was
in a state to fear civil war. The queen was forced to
borrow money of private persons and to put the crown
jewels in pawn. The very kitchen of the king was un-
supplied, and in order to pay the servants the minister was
obliged to pawn some large diamonds and get certain of his
friends to lend him what more was needed for this purpose.
The Princesse de Condé lent the queen 100,000 *livres;* the
Duchesse d'Aiguillon offered her money, and many others
did likewise.

So, in bringing order into the State nothing came of it
but disorder; and the worst of all was that the greater part
of the king's subjects did not desire that this evil state of
things should cease. The people, hoping to save themselves
from taxes and tithes, aspired to nothing but trouble and

change, and appeared to confide in parliament for protection. Each counsellor seemed to them an angel descended from heaven to save them from the tyranny of the cardinal, which they imagined to be greater than it really was.

The conferences of the ministers and parliament held at the Luxembourg, Monsieur's residence, ended in resolving that the king should issue a declaration which should amount to the same thing as the decree given by parliament against the provincial intendants, in order to save by this ruse the royal authority, and let the measure seem to have come from the will of the queen. In this declaration the king excepted only three departments of justice, at which parliament murmured loudly; for it wished there should be no exception.

The Duc d'Orléans made several visits to parliament, during which new propositions were made in his presence. One of them was found to be, under present necessities, very convenient for the king, namely: to put an end to the *partisans* [companies for the levying of taxes] and to keep back the money of loans made by private individuals. Such persons had lent to the king on the faith of brokers and superintendents, and from these loans they were drawing high interest. Nearly all the families in Paris were enriched in this way.[1] It was not legitimate. Stern casuists assert that it is forbidden by the gospel; it is, moreover, long known to be very injurious to the State and to the king's affairs; because such great usury ate up his revenues and emptied the coffers of his treasury. It was therefore

[1] Omer Talon, relating this shameful proposition, says it was President de Novion who chiefly defended it. Cardinal de Retz, in his Memoirs, declares that the courtiers, who had nearly all invested their money in loans made to the king at immense usury, uneasy at the bankruptcy with which they were thus threatened, urged Mazarin to take decisive measures against parliament. — FR. ED.

advantageous to the king to have a pretext to make bankrupt many persons of all conditions who had put their property into loans. But as all families, whether of the Court or city, had interests in this, a great outcry arose in Paris at the proposal. It seemed unjust, and displeased individuals as much as it pleased the minister, who saw the king usefully relieved in this way of a heavy burden.

President Mesmes, who had now returned, often gave the sternest advice, but always for the good of the State; so that there were days and moments when the cardinal believed that perhaps these disorders would end in a better regulation of the king's affairs and that he should reap the benefit. His policy was to risk nothing himself, and try to draw some advantage from the schemes of parliament and the ruin of the *partisans;* but at the same time it was evident to others that he would finally be forced to change that method, which could not possibly succeed.

The Duc d'Orléans returned to parliament July 13; and because the first declaration of the king, excepting the three departments of justice, was not agreeable to the assembly, it was thought best to produce a second, establishing a Chamber of Justice such as parliament had desired, in which it would be permitted to work at the reformation of abuses committed in the finances.

Parliament, as usual, deliberated; and it was ordered that Monsieur should be very humbly entreated to induce the queen to send a revocation of the order against the intendants because the one that had been sent included only the jurisdiction of the parliament of Paris. Also, in regard to the *taille* tax, to bring the queen to remit to the people the payment of all arrearages up to the year 1646; and for those of 1647, 1648, and 1649, that the queen be entreated, if her affairs permitted, to remit one quarter. Also that the declaration as to the Chamber of Justice be registered; and that her Majesty be entreated by the Duc d'Orléans that there should be no commissioners in it but those from the parliament, the *chambre des comptes*, and the *cour des aides;* and that the fines and confiscations ordered by the said Chamber should not be diverted or given away, but employed solely in meeting the most urgent expenses of the State.

The evening of that day the queen said to us, speaking of her affairs, that what had taken place in the morning was not of much good, for it merely marked the power that parliament was assuming in the State; but nevertheless, since they had shown a desire to further a scheme for reforming it, without directly offending the king, she hoped some advantageous results could be reached regarding his finances, and that what they were then doing would bring many millions back to the treasury.

Nothing was comparable to the satisfaction parliament showed at the behaviour and fine qualities of the Duc d'Orléans. He spoke with kindness and eloquence in their public and private conferences, showed that he acted with judgment, and answered all their difficulties with intelligence and gentleness; and as these matters were all produced by the immediate occasion, his answers could be attributed to none but himself. The queen also had reason to be satisfied. She was so, and seemed to be grateful to the duke for the care and affection he showed for the good and the peace of the State, and for her repose in particular.

July 14 the duke went again to parliament. The deliberations did not then turn to the advantage of the king, and the courtiers said that the State was afflicted with intermittent fever. That same day the queen said to us, with much vexation, that she no longer understood anything; that things had always to be done over again, and she was tired of hearing every day, " We will see what they do to-morrow." Certainly this great princess felt the blood of her illustrious forefathers boiling in her veins, and could not endure the empire assumed, little by little, by this mutinous crowd. I know that one day, at the council, in presence of the Duc d'Orléans, she seemed to wish to blame her minister, and told him that she did not approve of his conduct.

In consequence of that, when the duke had gone and the cardinal was alone with her as usual, after receiving with humility all that the queen was pleased to say to him, he answered, driven by distress and perhaps by fear: " In short, Madame, I see that I have displeased your Majesty. I have ill-succeeded in the purpose I have always had to serve you well. It is just that my head should answer for it." On which the queen, who was gentle and always kind to him, being persuaded of his good intentions and his disinterestedness, told him that she would not punish him for his misfortune, and that he ought to be convinced that he could never lose through those qualities either her confidence or her affection.

Another day, at about the same time, wishing to extol to us the excellent nature of the king, she did us the honour to relate how the cardinal the preceding evening, had warned her to be careful of her health, saying that she did not look well ; and on her replying that she did not mind dying, considering the miserable state of her affairs, the king, overcome by grief, began to cry tenderly and she had much trouble in soothing him. This indifference to death was a sign in the queen of discontent ; and the sentiment gave comfort to everybody ; for it seemed then as though it would be advantageous for herself and the State if she had been even more uneasy, so that, seeing the evil, she might have striven to remedy it. That remedy would have been in allowing herself to be less governed and in acting more in accordance with her own sentiments and her own ideas, which certainly seemed to be instinctively opposed to the policy of her minister.

The cardinal in those days (July, 1648) had moments of fear. Those who enlarged before the queen on the harm that parliament did the State were suspected by him of wishing to make her quarrel with him and thus do him evil offices. D'Émery's friends were taxed with this purpose more than others, and were accused of talking in this way with malicious intent contrary to his interests. The Maréchal de Villeroy suffered much from this; but as he was very adroit, he smothered the rumour which was spread against him with so many fine appearances, carefully assumed, that he not only saved himself from danger, but also from angry glances, which are always annoying to such as he.

The cardinal complained to the Marquis de Senneterre, who told me about it a few hours later. He told him expressly (intending to make him by implication the same reproach) that d'Émery's friends had blamed his conduct and begged the protection of the Abbé de La Rivière, not thinking his power sufficient to save them. On which Senneterre replied that it was true d'Émery had sought the friendship of that man to serve him, in union with other friends, with the Duc d'Orléans; but that they had no intention in so doing of caballing against him, the minister, or of supporting d'Émery against him; that they were too clever courtiers to have any such chimeras; and that if they had wanted to attack his authority there were much better means than that, such as persuading the Duc d'Orléans by their friend La Rivière, to listen to the proposals that were daily made to him to become regent. So far from doing that, the cardinal had been so well served by all of them that Monsieur, like Germanicus, had rent his garments at the mere proposition.

The star was now terribly against kings; and here is a proof of it. On this very day, July 14, Mademoiselle de Beaumont and I went to see the Queen of England, who had retired to the Carmelite convent, to soothe the grief she felt at the departure of her son, the Prince of Wales, who had gone to Calais, intending to sail for Scotland, where he hoped to touch the hearts of his subjects by his presence.

We found her alone in a little chamber, writing and making up despatches, as she told us, of great importance. They were just finished, and she then described to us the apprehensions she felt as to the success of this voyage, and confided to us her present necessities, greatly increased by those of our king and queen. She showed us a little gold cup from which she drank, and said she had no other gold, of any kind whatever, except that. She told us, moreover, that after the Prince of Wales departed, all her servants came to her demanding money, telling her they should leave her if she did not pay them; this she could not do, and so had the grief of knowing herself unable to remedy the wants of her officers, who now overwhelmed her with their miseries. She added that the officers of her mother, Queen Marie de' Medici, had done much worse, and that being in England at the beginning of their troubles, and she and the King finding themselves unable to give them money as punctually as before, these officers presented claims upon her to the English parliament, which had caused her great distress.

This description moved us to compassion, and we could not wonder enough at the evil influence that seemed to rule over these crowned heads, victims of the two parliaments of France and England, — ours being, thanks to God, very different from the other in its intentions, and different also in its effects.

July 17 the Duc d'Orléans went again to parliament to carry to it the declarations of the king containing all that parliament had demanded. There had been many disputes in council as to the more or the less, but all was finally done according to the good pleasure of parliament; and the king might esteem himself fortunate that it was willing to receive, under an appearance of his name and authority, that which it had already ordained for his State.

On the following days parliament put forward other points, among them the following: it being publicly notorious that the king's farms were let at a cheap price, and no bids received for them, nor any awards made in due form, other auctions should be held; and the court of parliament ordered that an article to that effect be included in the written representations to be made to the queen.

Parliaments have certainly the power to make remonstrances to our kings, telling them the truth in the strongest manner in which they can explain it without failing in the respect which subjects owe to their sovereign. They are, after the States-general, the most violent remedy which up to this time sovereign companies have been able or have dared to apply to the ills of the State. But, thanks be to God, we were now living in an age when, by the virtues of the queen, by her kindness and upright intentions, we had no need of reformations which excess of evils and perils render useful and necessary. She wished that all under her reign should enjoy a sweet tranquillity, occupied only in serving God and the king. What the minister wanted to do against the masters of petitions and the parliaments had alarmed her, and with some cause; but the clemency of the queen at their first appeal, and their public sorrow, would easily have disposed her to give them better treatment; and the cardinal let it be seen, on this occasion, that he was not, as I have elsewhere remarked, incapable of giving himself a lesson to prefer the public good to his personal feelings.

That is why so many remonstrances and such clamour were neither just nor necessary, because the queen, with a spirit of wisdom and piety, preferring gentleness to severity, and the relief of the people to the pleasure of being implicitly obeyed, had followed the advice of her minister and her own disposition to seek as far as possible the welfare of the king's subjects — though it is true that this last indulgence, inasmuch as it might pass for weakness, caused her pain. She made no secret of this; she acknowledged it freely to herself.

We must acknowledge, to the shame of our nation and in order to correct its faults, that the rebellions made by the people in this country have nearly all been unjust and ill-founded. Our kings, issuing from the greatest race on earth, before whom the Cæsars and most of the princes who formerly commanded many nations are but *roturiers*, have given us saints of their blood; while none of them have deserved the name of "wicked" as some we find in other monarchies, who, in their epoch, have been execrated by their peoples and are still the objects of horror and wrath to those who read their lives.

Our great monarchs have had defects, and some have committed crimes which have been blamed according to their magnitude, or excused so far as they deserved to be, but we have never seen in France a Christian II. as in Denmark, a Pedro the Cruel as in Spain, a Henry VIII. as in England, with many others who are dishonoured for their abominable actions; but we have had a Charles V., the wisest

prince that ever was, who, as dauphin, was nearly crushed
beneath the unjust rebellion of his people.   Henri III. suffered another which, as a king, he did not deserve, for he
was valiant, kind, learned, and able, and if, as a man, he
was a sinner while wishing to appear devout, God alone, and
not his subjects, should judge him, to punish or to pardon.

I do not speak of the war which, after the death of this
prince, was made under Henri-le-Grand.   We owe greater
faithfulness to God than to a king; and those who, from a
true motive of conscience and religion, took part against him
were excusable in refusing a heretic king.   We can blame
only the ambition of the princes of the League, who, under
a noble pretext, were visibly endeavouring to usurp the
crown.   But God, no doubt, made use of their unrighteous
desire to preserve France from the evils of heresy.

Kings, according to the obligations imposed upon them
from on high, ought to will that their subjects should find
protection in them and in the officers and judges of their
kingdom.   All wise princes must desire that the good should
not be oppressed, and that the wicked should be punished.
The parliaments of France were instituted to labour at this
great work; and sometimes the kings themselves have
found in their regulations assistance and succour against
their own disorders.   But parliament, in the present instance
had encroached upon the royal power, and chosen to do that
which the king alone had the right to ordain; and as, un-
fortunately, our king was then too young to exercise that
right, and his minister under the minority had not power
enough to enforce it, it was impossible that this ill-regulated
state of things should lead to good order in France.   For, after
all, these reformations were being made by mischief-makers,
whose sole object was the ruin of the cardinal, the grandeur
of the princes through the attachment many of the parlia-

ment felt to them, and the elevation of certain individuals
It is easy, therefore, to judge by all these things that what
was now doing tended towards the ruin of the State, and
that God would not bless the labours of these men, whose
iniquity was visible; for "the wisdom of man shineth on his
face, and wickedness will not save the wicked."

The other parliaments, following the example of that of
Paris, rebelled also.   Ours in Normandie demanded the revocation of the *semestre*, declaring that it was unjustly established in the time of the late king and Cardinal Richelieu,
who never allowed them to lift their heads.   Thus all
things in the internal affairs of France were in a bad
condition.

The Prince de Condé, impatient at being with the army,
doing nothing, and perhaps a little jealous of the reputation
of the Duc d'Orléans, wanted to take part in the affair of
the parliament.   He wrote of it to the Maréchal de Gramont, one of his friends, and begged him to go to Court and
secretly propose his return.   The cardinal, who was very
glad to balance the power between the two princes, consented willingly, on condition that the prince would take
the queen by surprise, and that she should not appear to
have listened to his proposal.

Immediately after this consent, about the 20th of July, it
was known that the Prince de Condé was about to return
from the army; and this return astonished the whole Court.
The queen, Monsieur the king's uncle, and Cardinal Mazarin
had often determined together that if they were constrained
to use open force against parliament, the Prince de Condé
should be sent for at once.   But as this determination was
still indefinite, and the minister had, so far, followed a
course of great gentleness and humility, the return of the
prince had been delayed, and the Duc d'Orléans now felt

Mignard

Cardinal Mazarin

much surprised on hearing it was about to take place. He could not believe that the queen and cardinal knew nothing of this intention, and he was angry, saying openly that he had cause to complain of the queen, who, without a word to him, called another to her assistance who could not serve her better than he was doing, or with more affection.

The Abbé de La Rivière, from whom I heard all these particulars, came to see the queen, and made her his master's complaints, promising that he would try to smooth them, but declaring also that he was very angry and he doubted if he could pacify him. The queen and her minister told him that they had known nothing of the prince's return; and that the Maréchal de Gramont had doubtless, on a few words carelessly said, and possibly without thought, given rise in the prince's mind to the desire to return to Court. To this the abbé replied that his master desired that the Prince de Condé, who was expected to arrive in one hour, should be sent back, inasmuch as he came without orders.

The cardinal, troubled by this little storm, got into the abbé's carriage and went to see the Duc d'Orléans. To him he protested his ignorance and tried to soothe his vexation by all the finest words his eloquence could produce. The Duc d'Orléans was not to be appeased in that way, and the cardinal returned to the queen, to seek with her some means of satisfying the duke, to whom she was really under obligations for his fidelity; for it may be said that up to this time he had lived with her in a perfectly praiseworthy manner. To find a remedy for his complaints it was resolved, after a long conference between the queen, the cardinal, and the Abbé de La Rivière, that the queen should ask Monsieur to be willing for her to receive the Prince de Condé, on the promise that she would send him back to the army as soon as she could.

The prince, on his arrival, was received by the queen with a smiling face; and he, in his heart, was pleased and content; for he had been warned about Monsieur's vexation, which was joy to him, emulation being natural to persons of his birth. He stayed an hour with the queen and her minister, and then went to his own house, where all the people of quality flocked to do him homage. The next day Monsieur and he dined together at the cardinal's, where they seemed good friends, and according to all appearance, thought of nothing but laughter and good cheer.

The same day, by a special piece of luck which gave the queen a chance to keep the promise she had given to Monsieur, news was received that the enemy's army gave signs of advancing with certain designs upon ours. So that the next morning, Sainte-Madeleine's day, the prince took leave of the queen and returned hastily. He had had thirty-five thousand men under his command; but with that army he had not prevented the taking of Courtray, a very important place. For sole exploit, he had taken Ypres in a week, a large town, the taking of which was of little importance to us. His army after that second-rate exploit was diminished. This general, destined for great actions, not being at liberty to act as he wished, but compelled by the queen's orders to undertake nothing, was deprived of certain victories, which without the troubles in Paris that diminished the royal authority, he would certainly have won.

The Maréchal de Schomberg, not standing well at Court, had been constrained to take command of the army in Catalonia, which General de Sainte-Cécile, brother of Cardinal Mazarin, had resigned in disgust. The Maréchal went there with little money, little favour, and few men; and those who make it a business to laugh at others said satirically that whoso wanted to go into perilous places should follow the marshal; by which they meant that his adventures would end in serenades to Spanish ladies; for though he was not young, he was still gallant.   But a courier presently arrived from him, July 26, informing the queen of the taking of Tortosa, which he had besieged for a short time. As he knew that the enemy were marching in great haste to relieve the place, he took it by assault and cut every one to pieces.   A general massacre took place, with such resistance that the bishop of the city was found among the foremost killed in the breach, with a pike in his hand.   This prelate had gone himself to defend the walls, accompanied by all the priests and monks of the city, who followed his example on this perilous occasion.

The Maréchal de Schomberg received all the glory he deserved for so fortunate, bold, and fine an enterprise; but his favour at court was not increased by it: it is not always virtue or noble actions which give that.

July 28 the queen had the *Te Deum* chanted at Notre-Dame.   The king went on horseback, with a little buff-leather collar, and all the Court followed him in good order, with much embroidery, plumes, and ribbons.

The enemy took advantage of the Prince de Condé's little journey to Paris.   They besieged Furnes in his absence, a place in no wise strong, which the prince had taken two years before in three hours.   It was not of much consequence to us, but was near to Dunkerque, which the enemy apparently intended to attack, for they regretted the loss of it.   La Moussaye brought the news to Court and charged Maréchal de Rantzau with not having taken sufficient precautions, of neglecting the place to preserve a little fort called the Knoque, between Ypres and Furnes, and of not observing the orders he had received from the Prince de Condé before he started for Paris.   To finish this news of

war, Maréchal Du Plessis, who was in Italy with the troops
of the king and the Duke of Modena, besieged Cremona.

July 29, the deputies of parliament came to make their
statements to the queen on the disorders they complained
of in the government, and also on the remainder of the
propositions drawn up in the Chamber of Saint-Louis. The
latter chamber the queen and cardinal wanted to put an end
to ; but in spite of the three declarations the Duc d'Orléans
had taken to parliament, it insisted on continuing that
assembly with new propositions.

After many councils held on the subject, the queen resolved to take the king to parliament in order to end the
contest by granting all demands. She even wished to give
them something more, in order to win over the people to the
king. A declaration was therefore drawn up in which she
loaded them with favours ; and at the same time forbade
them to assemble, intending to use the utmost rigour if they
disobeyed this order; she herself saying so openly, that it
might be told throughout Paris and that none of the members could ignore it.

She said to us that she was going to parliament to fling
roses on their heads ; but if after that they were not good,
she should know how to punish them ; adding that if
she had been believed at the beginning of the revolt she
should not now be seeking means to end it; and that she
ought to have taught them their duty on the first day they
abandoned it; but that now she had at last conquered the
cardinal's gentleness, and made him resolve in open council
to endure no more.

She said to us, moreover, that, for her part, she laughed at
the consequences the council were always apprehending;
that revolts were not so easy to make in Paris; that the
regiment of the Gardes would suffice to repress the first up-

rising of the populace; and at the worst, twenty or thirty houses pillaged would be the expiation of their disobedience. She added that she should be sorry for this, but that such an evil was less than that of the ruin of the State; and that in the council they had all made war upon her for the joy she felt at being on the eve of punishing those mutineers; telling her that she feared she might be obeyed because she should then have the vexation of losing that joy. She showed us, in truth, a great desire to avenge herself upon those who had attacked her authority. She was stung by the lowering of the royal dignity, and felt the contempt that parliament had shown for the gentleness, reason, and good-will she had wished to show in its favour.

The queen went to parliament, as proposed, on the 30th of July, in the usual order, for the purpose of doing favours to all, or of punishing those who did not receive those favours with the gratitude and respect they owed to her. It had been resolved in council, in order to acquire the good-will of the people, that instead of the half-quarter rescinded on the *taille*-tax, by order of parliament, the whole quarter should be yielded up to them, so that this liberality should seem to them to proceed from the will of the king only. We shall see, by the effects which this declaration will produce in course of time, what good reason the queen had to expect opposition and to wish to punish the ingratitude of both parliament and people.

This declaration read, the *procureur général*, Talon, made an harangue, which was fine. The chancellor then took the opinions, and there were members insolent enough to answer that they would inform him the next day of what they should do. Finally the said declaration was received and passed, with very little gratitude for the favours granted. The chancellor turned to the queen and spoke to her; then to Monsieur and the cardinal; after which he sat down, and at once announced to the assembly the gift the queen made of the annual fee without commission to the four sovereign courts to wit: the court of parliament, the *chambre des comptes*, the *cour des aides*, and the grand council, for a period of nine years.

The queen, on leaving the great hall, said to the chief president that she expected him to obey the orders of the king, and henceforth prevent the parliament from meeting again. She said also to President de Bellièvre that it was his place to begin and hold his Chamber in the Tournelle. They answered respectfully that they would obey her; but they could not do so.

That day the king looked handsomer than he did on his first visit to parliament. The stiffness of his face had passed off, it was no longer swollen; but he had lost the delicate beauty which made every one admire him; the roses and lilies had left his complexion, but only to leave him another skin more suited to a warrior than a lady; which was beautiful enough, however, to please all fair ones if his age had allowed him to desire it. It was remarked that on this occasion the people did not shout as usual, *Vive le roi!* and seemed to show a coolness towards him.

That evening the queen, speaking of all that had happened, told us she awaited with impatience what would be done on the morrow; which, however, was like the other days; parliament called upon its members to assemble, which they did tumultuously, grumbling against the king for having forbidden them a thing which they maintained was their right. But they said no more about the Chamber of Saint-Louis, which was the sore point; and the chief president, wishing to please the Court a little, kept them waiting so long that the hour struck at which they ad-

journed; but they did so crying out that they were determined to deliberate on the declaration of the king, and if
they were prevented they would not bear it.

The minister, to whom all these wrangles were most
displeasing, had strongly wished that parliament might not
force the queen to extremities.   In spite of her impatient
feelings, which could not brook that which showed contempt for royalty, he had restrained her in order to see
if there were no means of bringing these sullen spirits
to some agreement.   Moderation was the cardinal's familiar spirit; he would risk nothing, and always desired
to avoid by negotiations what might lead to civil war,
which he dreaded for the State, and still more for his own
private interests.

In spite of all his prudence the mischief did not end;
this self-willed body insisted on assembling, and on August 4
Monsieur was constrained to go to them again.   They spoke
out boldly before him, declared they were not satisfied, and
concerned themselves very little about the orders of the
queen.   They declaimed against their head president, who
had prevented them from opening their session and deliberating as they chose on the king's declaration, and
Monsieur returned to the queen very ill-satisfied.   They
voted that day to continue to assemble until the Chamber
of Justice which they demanded was established, and to
deliberate constantly over the declaration, and also over the
rest of the propositions made in the Chamber of Saint-Louis.
They no longer spoke of continuing that Chamber, which
the queen had forbidden; but the present one was of the
same consequence.   About all these troubles we did not
fail to see many councils at the Palais-Royal, which produced nothing efficacious as a remedy and such as the state
of these disturbances demanded.

In the midst of these troubles came a little affair of small
notoriety, which was nevertheless vexatious on account of
its results. The Duc de Beaufort was then living at a
country-house belonging to his father, the Duc de Vendôme.
He gave good feasts to his friends while awaiting with
impatience till the present wrangles should become sufficiently strong for him to profit by them ; and when he discovered that the cardinal had spies about him he boldly
drove them away. The Duc de Vendôme had sent one of
his retainers to Paris to offer to the parliamentarians his
services and assistance. This man had been arrested by
order of the queen ; and to increase the vexations of the
day, a request was brought before the assembly from this
prisoner while Monsieur was present, requesting to be released and examined according to the will of parliament.
The assembly had already shown signs of intending in future
to take cognizance of all persons whom the king caused to
be arrested, as proposed in the Chamber of Saint-Louis, and
that evening this prisoner was hastily transferred to the
Bastille in the wood of Vincennes, lest the king should no
longer be master of his person.

Monsieur returned to parliament, August 5, to be present
at the deliberations.[1] As the members saw that they
would wholly embitter the queen's mind if they did not
obey her, and their destiny not being as yet ripe for accomplishment, their decision on this day was to obey the
king, and to concern themselves until the middle of August
solely with affairs of individuals. They deputed four commissioners to examine the points of the deliberation, intend-

---

[1] It was at the deliberations of August 4 and 5 that Broussel made the
propositions which began to alarm the Court. The Duc d'Orléans half
rose as if he would leave the assembly ; but the presidents entreated him
to keep his seat, assuring him that *parliament would not fail in its duty.*
(Memoirs of Omer Talon.) — FR. ED.

ing to assemble and deliberate over it again when they
should see fit.

Meantime things were as much embroiled in the provinces
as in Paris; everywhere could be seen and heard a horrible
letting loose of curses against the government and an
unbridled freedom in speaking ill of the minister. Murmurs
arose against the queen ; she was openly attacked and hated
on account of the man whose greatness she upheld. In
their blindness and ignorance truth was stifled; for, after all,
the cardinal did not deserve such great hatred, nor did the
queen deserve blame to the extent to which they gave it.
She owed her protection to a minister established by legitimate power which she was bound to respect. And as she
had accepted him of her own choice in the ministry where
the late king had left him, she felt that she ought to give
him strength to meet the vexatious events which were likely
to arise in the course of a long regency. Beholding in herself the source of the authority with which she sought to
clothe him, she imagined she could easily resume it, and
that she would not diminish her own power by the share of
it which she gave him, because it was given only to put
him in a position to serve her better.

According to what came of this course, the queen appears
to have deceived herself; and by it (as I have remarked)
she drew upon herself the scorn of the people and the
blame of those who envied the excessive power of the
minister, which, did, indeed, seem too great. But in thinking herself obliged to maintain him, she had regard primarily
to the glory of the crown, which seemed diminished by the
attacks of parliament. The opposition of that body strengthened her in the desire to resist it, and we shall see her
continue in that course with steady steps which no obstacle
whatever was able to turn aside. She did not believe that

the minister was the cause of the revolt; neither did she wholly blame his conduct for the misfortunes of her regency, although she often thought it weak. His mildness, which she supposed to lie at the bottom of it, seemed to her praiseworthy; as a Christian she could not blame in him the desire to succeed in satisfying all the various parties who opposed his favour; and she saw clearly that, if his sentiments were judged by souls that reasoned, their value would be understood.

She was also too equitable to forget the first placid years of her regency, which made the courtiers say they were tired of so much happiness; and although she now knew all that the malice of the populace invented against her upright intentions and the innocence of her life, the consciousness she had within herself gave her strength to bear all without uneasiness; moreover, the trust she had in God made her hope for His protection. She acted according to her feelings and her lights, comprehending that, whatever she did, she would never be exempt from the evil interpretations which are always given to the actions of princes, nor from the hatred that the people are wont to feel to ministers.

The queen's piety was at all times remarkable. I know from Madame de Senecé, her lady-of-honour, who told it to me privately, and afterwards in the queen's own presence, that when very young and in the days of her greatest beauty, as she had not enough money to do all the alms she wished, she robbed herself of jewels and chains, pretending she had lost them accidentally, in order to give them to the poor. She hid this from Madame de Senecé, then her lady of the bedchamber; and when she saw her looking for these things and troubled, and could not pacify her by merely telling her they were lost and that she need not worry herself, she then owned she had taken them to give to those she could not help in other ways; but she told this with as much shame as if she had done a bad action; and urgently requested her to say nothing about it to any one.

During her regency her heart must have found some satisfaction in the good works that she did throughout France; and even Christians in all parts of the world received some portion of her liberality. It happened, nevertheless, that, as she did not have the use of the king's treasury, having placed it in trust in the hands of the cardinal in happier times, now, when she might have been mistress of all favours, and when the minister, the superintendent, and the finance officers were profusely using it to their own profit, she was frequently in a state of need which did not allow her to do what she would have liked to do. She did not pay her debts, and never had enough to satisfy her generosity, either in regard to the poor or to those about her for whom she had an affection. She was persuaded that there was never enough money in the treasury; and though she had about her persons bold enough and faithful enough to tell her the contrary, her indifference, which made her neglect too much the knowledge of the truth, deprived her of this means of exercising usefully the moral and Christian virtues of which her soul was full — the only happiness that can render crowns desirable.

On the day of Notre-Dame, in August, the king went to hear vespers at the Feuillants, and the cardinal was with him. It is the rule that in any place where the person of the king is, the captain of his body-guard is to hold the keys. It is also the rule that no other guards than the body-guard shall be on duty. A procession was to be made with the king through the cloister; the Marquis de Gesvres, captain of the body-guard, was therefore the master of it. Information was brought to him that the guards of the grand provost were al-

ready in that place with one of the provost's lieutenants.
The Marquis de Gesvres ordered his lieutenant, named de
L'Isle to go and turn them out.   De L'Isle went; and being
wise and cautious, he first pointed out that the other guards
had no right in the place, and ought to leave it, because
otherwise he had orders to turn them out.   The guards answered insolently that they would not go; and their anger
against de L'Isle was so great that he judged it was necessary to use violence.   But, before doing so, he returned to
his captain for further orders.   De Gesvres told him to make
them go in any way he could.   De L'Isle returned and, wishing to obey, he was forced, by the resistance of the provost's
guard, to take sword in hand.   In the scuffle two of the
guards were maltreated; one was killed, the other wounded.
De L'Isle, who was a worthy man, did his best to prevent
this misfortune, but it was not possible to control the matter,
for the Suisses seconded the body-guard and together they
made the uproar.

It is a crime of *lèse-majesté* to take sword in hand in the
king's house, or in any place where he is.   As the rumour of
the affair spread, everybody was troubled.   Jarzé, friend of
the grand provost, spoke out against the Marquis de Gesvres,
taxing him with having been too hasty.   Cardinal Mazarin
was displeased in his soul that the marquis had given these
orders in his presence without asking his advice as to what
he ought to do; nevertheless he did not show it, but concealed his vexation.   The king having returned to the Palais-
Royal, the minister pacified the quarrel between Gesvres and
Jarzé and sent at once to the queen (who had gone to sleep
at the Val-de-Grâce for the feast-day) to tell her of the mis-
adventure.   The next morning, in consequence of the Marquis de Gesvres having caused blood to be shed in presence
of the king — but really because he had not shown due re-

spect to the cardinal — Le Tellier was sent to order him to give up his baton and place it in the hands of the Comte de Charost, another captain of the body-guard like himself.

The Comte de Trêmes, father of the Marquis de Gesvres, went to the minister and complained to him of the treatment his son was receiving; he said he had not failed in his duty, but had maintained the rights of his office; and, moreover, if he were forced to give it up, the Comte de Charost was not the man to take his place, but he himself was; inasmuch as his son only served the king in reversion to himself, who was the veritable captain of the Guards, and they could only take the baton from him with his head. Besides this, he informed the Comte de Charost that he would disoblige him if he received the king's order, and said that as they all owed support to one another, he begged him not to accept the command.

The cardinal now declared that he had reason to complain of the Marquis de Gesvres for having given orders in his presence without informing him of them; and said that being prime minister and intrusted with the education of the king, de Gesvres had failed in the respect that was due to him. Through the resentment he felt to the son he would not consider the prayers and the rights of the father, and therefore induced the queen to persist in declaring that the baton was to be given to the Comte de Charost. She said the command was issued, and must be obeyed, although had she known that the Comte de Trêmes was in Paris she might perhaps have ordered him to take it; but that now, as he had opposed her orders and her will, she should not listen to him. She said aloud that she willed that Charost should serve, if only for two hours, to show the obedience which she declared was her due.

Beringhen, first equerry, a wise and prudent man, exhorted

Charost to do as the queen desired, and he resolved to obey.
The cardinal himself urged him and even prayed him to
oblige him ; so that Charost promised him to take the baton.
With this intention he went down to the room of the captain of the guards, where was the Comte de Trêmes, who
had taken possession of the baton, declaring that he should
hold it till the queen came back from the Val-de-Grâce and
he could receive her orders from her own lips. Charost,
who had just left Cardinal Mazarin, told him he had pledged
himself to take the baton, and asked him for it. The Comte
de Trêmes answered that he could not give it to him, for his
honour was concerned in not seeing it in another man's
hand, while he had committed no wrong that deserved its
loss.

The Comte de Charost, a man of real worth, who approved
of his colleague's resistance and felt he would have done the
same in his place, answered that he never wished to take
the honour from him, that it was only by force he was led
to accept it, and that now, seeing him determined not to
give up the baton, it was all right that he should keep it,
for his own intention was, as far as in him lay, to do harm
to no man. Charost then, not venturing to see the cardinal
again, went off to his own house, preferring to let him hear
of the matter from others than himself.

The queen had heard at the Val-de-Grâce that Charost
had resolved to serve, and the rest of the day passed without
either her or the cardinal knowing aught to the contrary.
That evening, on her return, the king having run some distance to meet and embrace her, she noticed that the captain
of the Guards was not with him, and asked the reason.
They told her that the Comte de Trêmes would not allow
Charost to serve as he intended, and that, seeing this resistance, the latter had not liked to oppose it and had gone

home. The queen, seized with a little rush of anger, and touched with keen resentment at the general state of her affairs, which this piece of boldness recalled to her mind, exclaimed aloud: "Ho! God be thanked, I have reached the point where every one makes it an honour to disobey me!"—meaning by those words both the parliament and the people of the Court.

The cardinal came to her at once, and she soon after ordered to be brought before her the four captains of the guards (except Villequier, who was not in Paris), namely: the Comte de Trêmes, the Comte de Charost, and the Marquis de Chandenier, — [1] the Marquis de Gesvres being in reversion to his father, and the only culpable one, did not appear. She gave them a reprimand on their disobedience, which at first was rather gentle, wishing by such treatment to make them repent of their fault. But when they wished to present their reasons and showed that they intended to support one another, she was angry and turned them out of her cabinet, telling them that she wished never to see them again, and would find others who would obey her better.

The whole Court was now divided on the affair. Some approved of the queen's course at a time when her authority was only too much disregarded; others disapproved of it, saying that she had not shown sufficient regard to the rights of the Comte de Trêmes; and the latter were possibly right. Now the queen, of her own inclination, would doubtless not in any way have resisted granting him the baton, if she had not been led to do so by the cardinal's passion. Continuing, however, to sacrifice to him her own kind feel-

---

[1] Madame de Motteville has forgotten to say that as soon as the Marquis de Gesvres received orders to give up the baton, the cardinal sent for Chandenier and offered it to him; but he refused it out of delicacy. See Memoirs of Montglat. — FR. ED.

ings, she ordered that Chandenier be brought before her, a
last unfortunate remains of the "Importants," whom she
had considered and treated as one of her most faithful servants. He remained at Court only by enforced tolerance on
the part of the minister; consequently he was chosen by
him on this occasion to be the victim of his policy.

The resolution was already taken to exile Charost. They
wished to punish him for the compliance he had shown to
the Comte de Trêmes, and give an example of severity which
should pass from the Court to the parliament. He had some
original sin in regard to the false divinity adored at the
Court, which rendered him suspected by the minister. He
was brother of the Comte de Béthune, great abettor of the
"Importants" and friend of the Duc de Beaufort, who was
beginning to live again after his escape from prison, and to
give back some lustre to the annihilated cabal.

Chandenier was in worse case still; the minister had
great reason to hate him, for, besides what I have just told,
he was found at the beginning of the regency to be a relative of Des Noyers, Cardinal Mazarin's enemy, who, in the
days of the late king, had driven the minister from Court.
Chandenier, having therefore no protection but that the
queen owed to his goodness, confided himself to her; and
as soon as he saw the cardinal in a position to make himself
feared, he entreated her to take pains herself to put him in
the good graces of one she had raised to the power of preserving or destroying. She meant to do this; but, whether
she did it feebly, or whether the minister could not endure
a semi-favourite, it happened at last that Chandenier was
dismissed from Court instead of being well-treated.

As he knew he must find help in other ways, he got friends
to speak to the cardinal for him, and by that means he returned to Court. He stayed but a short time, for the min-

ister felt that he hated him. Chandenier was deficient in the behaviour necessary to preserve a good-will which, being feebly given, required great care to strengthen it; and the native distrust of the minister could at last no longer endure a man whom he had no reason to love and had sufficiently ill-treated to fear. However that may be, it is certain that never did he show him any further good-will, and Chandenier stayed on at Court, kindly treated by the queen, but ill-satisfied with her minister, and little considered; for he was not thought able, although esteemed as a man of honour and integrity, blamable only in being somewhat ostentatious about it.

The solid virtue that a man should have is opposed to display and notoriety, and he who possesses it, if he wishes to receive true praise, should not ask for praise. As such persons are usually too impatient of the faults of others, he had often blamed those of the minister; and when it was known that the queen had sent for him, no one doubted that, having joined with his colleagues in refusing to serve, his revolt would be made a pretext by the minister to get rid of him. He was a friend of mine, and I did what I could to make him think carefully of his answer to the queen before he appeared before her, because on that moment his future depended. But, knowing the engagement he had taken, which bound him to great fidelity to the interests of his colleagues, he having owned to me that he had himself advised their resistance, I was reduced with his other friends to pity him and hope he might still come safely out of the affair, without being able to divine in what manner he could save himself from the danger.

He went before the queen; and to tell the truth, he appeared with a very tranquil countenance. When she saw him she said that, having always believed he put more affection into his service than many others, she had also supposed him the most ready to obey her; for that reason she had sent for him; that the king was left without service; and that she desired him to take that duty as a proof of his fidelity. He answered that he very humbly begged her to consider his engagement towards his comrades; that if he obeyed her commands he should declare them guilty, and thereby become himself the most infamous of men; that he had reason to complain, because, being and always having been her faithful servant, she had chosen him on this occasion to order him to do a thing by which he should lose his reputation if he obeyed her. On which the queen, who did not wish to ruin him, offered, to satisfy this chimera of honour, to command him openly and before all the Court to obey. But, seeing that he still persisted in refusing, she raised her voice before us who were present at the conversation, and said quite sternly, " Enough, Chandenier, enough ! " He retired; and the next day an order was sent to him and to Charost to retire from Court, and go to their country-houses. The same order was sent to the Comte de Trêmes, and their offices were given to others. That of the Comte de Charost was given to Jarzé. The latter had birth and stood well at Court; but his mind was more brilliant than prudent, and its frivolity in many passages of his life will show how necessary wisdom is to man. He took the oath from the hands of the queen, and a promise was given to the Comte de Charost to reimburse him for his office.

The next day the same treatment was given to Chandenier,[1] but, no doubt, it was intended by the minister to be quite other than that of Charost. His office was given to

---

[1] The pathetic close of his life and history is told in Saint-Simon's Memoirs. — Tr.

the Comte de Noailles, who had already deprived him of much property, having, by the help of Cardinal Mazarin, married Mademoiselle Boyer, a rich young woman whom Chandenier was seeking. De Noailles took his oath of fidelity; and, as some persons are born for the misery of others, he kept his office much longer than Jarzé kept that of Charost.

Thus in one day we saw driven from the king's household three of his most important officers, without the cardinal appearing to have any part in it, the queen taking upon herself all the odium of this action to save her minister. It seemed that these captains of the Guard ought to have obeyed the king, and that they were wrong to so obstinately oppose his sovereign will; for, after all, it is right that our masters be obeyed, even in matters in which they may not have reason on their side. In vain would they be called by the great names of monarch, king, all-powerful, if their subjects could resist them on the slightest occasion. But it is just and right that these very kings should enter into the interests of individuals, hear their reasons, and take care to satisfy them, when they respectfully ask to be treated with equity.

The queen never of herself failed to follow these noble precepts; such virtues are the ones which appeared in her with the greatest glow, and drew to her the admiration of the public. Her ears were never weary of listening to the plaints of the unfortunate; her heart received without repugnance the importunities made to her by those who suffered oppression. She was incessantly exposed to this through her kindness and humanity; and her will, always disposed to right action, never refused to do justice to those who asked it of her. But on this occasion, when the corruption of the air about her made her more sensitive to disobedience, she could not endure this instance of it; and all the more because the cardinal's private animosity was hidden from her by a veil of policy. For this reason she contributed, without any design, to the misfortune of her old servant, Chandenier, and abandoned him to the resentment of her minister.

After the festival was over, parliament once more began to deliberate on the king's declaration. They examined it article by article. On some they voted remonstrances, on others they gave decrees. They complained that it was captious, declared that it only half favoured them, and then with bad intentions. Their chief complaint was about the article on the *taille*, which they maintained was not explained, and they demanded on behalf of the people that the quarter granted by the king should be exempted from costs.

August 20, Monsieur having gone to parliament, the discussion ended by asking him for a conference at the Luxembourg. It took place on the 21st with the same good success as before, and Monsieur on his return told the queen that all was going well; they had regulated the tariff on the number of taxes which parliament consented should be levied; which number was to be posted in the streets that the people might not be deceived or forced to pay more than they ought. Nevertheless, parliament did not put an end to its assemblings; so that, in point of fact, it scoffed at the king's order, at the authority of the queen, and at that of him who governed the State; whose strength was beginning to diminish as that of parliament increased.

On the same day an uncertain rumour came to give joy to the queen, for, if true, it would cure all her troubles, or at least give her comfort for a period of time. A man arrived from Arras with the assurance that a battle had been fought and cannon had been heard. No one, he said, had returned, — a proof that the battle had been won, because no fugitives had appeared on the frontier; apparently they were all busy in pursuing and despoiling the enemy.

The queen spent the whole day in great impatience to know what had happened, and at midnight, as she was undressing to go to bed, the Comte de Châtillon arrived, sent by the Prince de Condé immediately after the battle [of Lens]. We heard afterwards that this noble courier had done wonders that were worthy of himself and his race. He assured the queen of her good fortune, and told her that all she could have hoped for had happened; that victory remained with the French, after wringing it from the enemy at the cost of lives and blood; cannon were taken; General Beck and his son were prisoners, also the Prince de Ligne, and the Comte de Saint-Amour, general of artillery; three thousand dead were on the field, besides an incredible number of wounded, and five thousand prisoners were taken.

This battle had been desired by both sides. The archduke had orders from the King of Spain to give it at any price; the king believing, with reason, that if he won it, France, in the state in which she then was, would fall a prey to his ambition. For this purpose the archduke had sent all his baggage into Flanders; and the Prince de Condé, on his side, had done the same; these two great princes having the same intention, namely, to fight to the death. Both therefore did great deeds. The Prince de Condé, as usual, was everywhere. The Comte de Châtillon related to the queen how, for all speech to his soldiers, the prince had said: " My friends, have good courage. We must fight to-day; it is useless to hold back; for I tell you, brave men and cowards, all shall fight, willingly or by force." The preceding evening he gave an order to the whole army to watch their marching, in order that the cavalry and infantry should advance on the same line, carefully keeping their distances and intervals; and to charge at a walk [*au pas*] only, and let the enemy fire first.

Our army had then only 14,000 men, that of the enemy 15,000 or 16,000. The Prince de Condé asked for a marshal's baton for the Comte de Châtillon. But this was refused on account of the number of applicants, who embarrassed the minister.

The king, hearing that a battle had been won, cried out with a great exclamation that parliament would be very sorry for the news. He had heard so much said of that body being his enemies that he immediately came to this conclusion. Their proceedings, differing from their intentions, which I desire to think more innocent in fact than in appearance, deserved that the king should think them traitors; for they had brought France to such a state that had the battle gone against us, the monarchy might have seen its end, through causes which, in their beginning, seemed of little consequence.

After the first emotions which this victory caused in the soul of the queen, her reason and her kind nature made her wish for peace, and policy played its usual game. She knew that her minister was blamed for not making it; for this reason she affected to say pointedly before the whole Court that after this battle she hoped that Spain would wish for peace, for if it did she believed it would indubitably come.

XII.

1648.

THE queen, wishing to have the *Te Deum* chanted at Notre-Dame, to render thanks to God for the great victory, and to carry to the church the banners conquered from the enemy,[1] wished also to use this day of triumph to bring some remedy to the rebellion of parliament and to punish it for its last disobedience, which had seemed, in the eyes of every one, to hide a criminal audacity under a false appearance of fidelity.

To do this, in full agreement with the Duc d'Orléans and her minister, she commanded Comminges, lieutenant of her guards, to arrest President Blancmesnil, President Charton, and, above all, a man named Broussel, counsellor of parliament, who had constantly raised the standard against the king and opened all discussions that tended to destroy the royal authority; he had made himself the mouthpiece of the people, showing on every occasion the spirit of a man born in a republic, and affecting the sentiments of a veritable Roman. This day was chosen by advice of the cardinal, because the ceremony of the *Te Deum* gave occasion to put the whole regiment of the guards under arms; it being usual to line the king's way and the neighbourhood of Notre-Dame, where Broussel lodged. As there was some reason to fear that the populace

---

[1] These flags to the number of sixty-three, were borne to the choir by the Suisse guard. The members of parliament were present in great numbers at the ceremony, to remove all suspicion that this victory was not agreeable to them (Omer Talon). — FR. ED.

would rise in his defence, it was necessary to have a certain amount of force ready against that *canaille,* and thus prevent it from gathering sufficient strength to resist the name of the king and the glory of the successful victory.

The queen, having given her orders to Comminges, he gave his for the execution of the enterprise confided to him. He sent two of his lieutenants, — as he told me himself with every particular, — one to President Blancmesnil, the other to President Charton, reserving for himself the most dangerous affair, that of seizing Broussel, the friend and protector of the people.

The queen, after the *Te Deum,* and after committing this matter to the Sovereign of sovereigns as a severity forced upon her and necessary for public tranquillity, left the church, saying in a low voice to Comminges, " Go, and may God assist you; " well content with herself, as she told us afterwards, in being able to hope that she should be avenged on those who had despised her authority and that of the king her son.

Le Tellier, secretary of State, also said to Comminges at the same time that he could go, for all was ready ; meaning that the three men were in their homes.   Comminges waited a short time at Notre-Dame with a few guards until he knew that an order he had given was executed.   As it is usual for the officers of the body-guard never to leave the person of the king, notice was immediately given to some of the parliament who were still in the church that the lieutenant of the queen's guards had remained there, which seemed to threaten the liberty of some of the individuals of their assembly.   On receiving this warning they all took to flight, and the church, to their thinking, had not doors enough to let them get out as fast as they wished. The populace who filled the space about the church, having come there to see the king pass, hearing this rumour, collected in groups, and began to watch and listen for what it might mean.

Comminges had sent his carriage with four of his guards and one lieutenant to the end of Broussel's street, which was short and narrow, with orders to the officer as soon as he saw him, Comminges, approach the house on foot, to bring the carriage to the door, with the curtains raised and the steps lowered. This he ordered, so he told me, that in case he was attacked in the carriage with his prisoner, he might see all around him and give his orders. Accordingly he went to the house on foot and knocked at the door. A little foot-boy opened it without delay; he seized the entrance, and leaving two guards there he went up to Broussel's apartment with the two others. He found him just finishing dinner, with his family around him. Comminges told him he brought an order from the king to seize his person; but, if he wished to spare himself the trouble of reading the *lettre de cachet*, which he showed him, he had only to follow and obey him.

This man, over sixty years old, was alarmed, in spite of the courage he had shown in parliament, at hearing the king named in this way, and showed that the visit distressed him greatly. He replied that he was not in a state to obey, having taken medicine that morning, and he asked for time. An old woman of the house began to scream to the neighbours that her master was being carried off, begging them for succour, and telling Comminges with a thousand insults that he should not be obeyed, that she would prevent him from doing harm to her master. At the woman's noise, the populace collected in the little street; the first who ran up called to others, and in a moment the street was filled with *canaille*. When they saw the carriage full of arms and

men, they began to shout that their liberator was being
carried off. Some wished to cut the horses' reins, others to
break the carriage; but the guards and a little page of
Comminges defended it valiantly, threatening to kill all
those who attacked it.

Comminges, hearing within the house the noise of the
populace, and seeing the riot which might happen if he
delayed any longer in his purpose, seized Broussel by force
and threatened to kill him if he refused to walk. He
dragged him from the house and the embraces of his family,
and flung him into the carriage whether he would or not;
the guards going before to push back the people, who threatened to attack them. At the sound of this uproar chains
were fastened across the streets, and at the first turn Comminges found his way stopped; so that, in order to escape,
he had to have the carriage turned round often, and gave a
sort of battle to the populace, whose numbers increased the
farther he advanced on his way.

He arrived at last opposite to the house of the chief-
president, where his carriage was upset and broken. He
would have been lost if at this very place he had not found
soldiers of a regiment of Guards, who still lined the street
with orders to render him assistance if needed. He had
sprung with his prisoner from the overturned carriage, and
seeing himself surrounded by enemies who wanted to tear
him in pieces, and having only three or four of his own
guards, who were not enough to save him, he called out,
" To arms, comrades! to the rescue!" The soldiers, faithful to the king at all times of the regency, surrounded him
and gave him the necessary assistance.

The populace also surrounded him, with very different
intentions; and there ensued a combat of fists and insults
not less dangerous to the State than those of guns and

blades. Comminges remained in this position until one of his guards brought up another carriage, which he had taken from some passers, turning the ladies out with threats, and, in spite of their remonstrances, compelling the coachman to serve the occasion. This carriage also was broken at the corner of the rue Saint-Honoré, and these various accidents made known this action of the government to the whole city of Paris, and stirred to compassion a vast number of persons who thereupon fomented sedition.

Finally another carriage arrived, which Guitaut, uncle of Comminges and captain of the queen's guard, sent to meet his nephew, foreseeing that he might need it. It came most luckily; he jumped into it, his prisoner with him, and reached a relay which was waiting for him near the Tuileries, where Mademoiselle was then lodged. This relay took him to the château de Madrid, thence to Saint-Germain, according to his orders from the queen. She intended to have Broussel taken from there by a sub-lieutenant to the place where she had determined to send him, which was, I think, Sedan.

When the Parisians lost sight of their Broussel they were like madmen, shouting through the streets that they were lost, that they would have their protector restored to them, that they would die, every one of them, cheerfully in his behalf. They assembled, they stretched chains across the streets, and in a few hours they erected barricades in every quarter of the town.[1] The queen, informed of this disturbance, sent Maréchal de La Meilleraye through the streets to pacify the people and speak to them of their duty.

The Coadjutor of Paris [Jean-François-Paul de Gondi, afterwards Cardinal de Retz], who, from inordinate ambition,

[1] Omer Talon says that twelve hundred and sixty barricades were counted in Paris. — Fr. Ed.

had inclinations that were far from wishing to endeavour to remedy these evils, was also sent. But, wishing to conceal the tendency of his mind, which was to desire a change, he went out on foot with his hood and rochet ; and mingling with the crowd he reproved the people, shouted peace to them, and pointed out the obedience they owed to the king, with every sign of disinterested affection for his service. Perhaps he may even have acted in good faith on this occasion, for, as his sole desire was to play a part in great affairs by any or every means that offered, if in this way he could enter the good graces of the queen and make himself necessary to the State, his ambition being satisfied he would have taken no other course.

The populace replied to what he said to them with respect for his person, but with audacity and anger against the idea of what they owed to the king. They demanded their protector, with protestations that they would never be pacified until he was returned to them ;[1] and without considering the respect they owed to the Grand-Master, the Maréchal de La Meilleraye, they flung stones at him, overwhelmed him with insults, and, in threatening him, uttered horrible imprecations against the queen and her minister. Against the latter they launched such insolence as deserved the gibbet if the king had been master, or if the queen had been capable from private vengeance of putting any one to death.

The two men returned to the Palais-Royal to consult as to what should be done at this crisis, when words seemed too feeble a remedy for so great an evil. But, as it was thought best not to embitter the people still further in their first heat, they were sent back to expose themselves once

[1] Broussel was an old army officer, sixty-three years of age, popular for his benefits, and for his zeal against the new taxes. In the Chamber of Saint-Louis, he had played the rôle and taken the attitude of a party leader (Omer Talon). — FR. ED.

more to stones and insults. They went with a good grace, although the Maréchal de La Meilleraye had the gout and could walk only by the aid of a stick, and the health of the coadjutor was feeble. Soldiers were also sent, to see if a show of arms would not frighten the furious groups. But after a few blows which dispersed them for a moment, their anger increased and their rage became more violent. This medicine, given only from necessity, to try if an appearance of force would not cure the evil, not having any such effect, they ceased to administer it; it was thought that the best plan would be to do nothing extraordinary, for fear of letting the Parisians know the danger to which their folly was exposing France.

All this day was spent in hoping that the tumult would subside, but with many a fear that it might increase. The council was held at the Palais-Royal as usual; and we all sat peacefully laughing and talking, as usual, of a thousand frivolities. For, besides the fact that no one on such occasions likes to say what he is thinking of, or to appear to be afraid, none of us wished to be the first to prognosticate evil. Many persons, in fact, came to see the queen, and told her, with levity and on false assumptions, that the affair was nothing and that matters would soon be pacified. Kings flatter themselves readily; our regent did so, and being born with intrepid courage, she ridiculed the emotions of the populace and could not believe they would ever do her any serious harm.

That evening, the coadjutor [ecclesiastic who aids a bishop or archbishop in his functions and succeeds him] returned to see the queen on behalf of the people, being forced to accept their commission to ask again for the release of Broussel, they being resolved, they said, if this request were refused, to recover him by force. As the queen's heart was not susceptible of weakness, and she possessed a courage that might shame the most valiant, and as moreover the cardinal did not find it to his advantage to be always defeated, she scorned the proposal, and the coadjutor returned to the people without an answer. One of his friends (slightly one of mine), Laigues, who perhaps, like himself, was not, in the depths of his soul, in despair at the bad position of the Court and who had never quitted him all day, whispered in my ear that all was lost; that we must not amuse ourselves by thinking the affair was nothing; that there was everything to fear from the insolence of the people; that already the streets were filled with outcries against the queen, and that he did not believe the matter could be easily pacified.

The night that followed dispersed the crowds and confirmed the queen in her belief that there was nothing to fear from the tumult of the day before. She turned the thing into a joke, and asked me, as she left the council and came to undress, if I had not been in a great fright. She was continually making war upon my cowardice; and she did me the honour to tell me gaily that when at midday, just after her return from the Te Deum, they came to tell her of the uproar the people were beginning to make, she had instantly thought of me and of the fright I should have on hearing the terrible news and those big words " stretched chains " and " barricades."

She guessed rightly, for I thought I should die with the shock when they told me that the populace were up in arms; never supposing that in this Paris, the abode of pleasures and delight, war and barricades could exist except in the history and life of Henri III. The queen's jest lasted the whole evening; and as I was certainly the least valiant of the company the whole shame of that day fell upon me. I laughed myself, not only at my own terror, but also at the advice Laigues had so charitably given me a few hours earlier. It was not without wondering at how differently things can be viewed, according to the diverse passions and desires of men.

The same day the chief president came, on hearing of the banishment of his colleagues, to ask the queen for their release; but she sent him away without an answer. The people, who suspected him of being in collusion with the Court, went to his house; rascals full of fury shouted that he was a traitor and had sold his colleagues. He was compelled, in order to pacify them, to go out into the streets on foot to address the rioters and justify himself to them. Had he not done this firmly, they might perhaps have gone still further in their insolence; but his gentleness calmed their fury, and they received his justification on condition that he returned to the queen and demanded Broussel. This he did, with as little success as before.

The next day, as resolved in the council of the preceding day, the chancellor, Séguier, had orders to go to the Palais de Justice and preside there, so as to calm the minds of the members and prevent any disturbance which might arise on pretext of this affair.[1] The sedition had terrified every one, and the friends of the chancellor told him that this occasion seemed to them very perilous for him. He saw the danger to which he was exposed with the same eyes as theirs; but his soul, too attached to favour, was not as much attached to love of life. He preferred the advantage of doing an action which was out of the common; and as the queen thought it a necessary one, he wished to perform it without giving any sign of weakness.

[1] It was thought also that he was to forbid parliament; but I have no certain knowledge of this. I saw at the time no sign of it, and I did not hear of it until long after. (Author's note.)

He started at five in the morning and went to the Palais, or rather, he left his house with the intention of doing so. The Bishop of Meaux, his brother, insisted on going with him, and his daughter, the Duchesse de Sully, young, beautiful, and brave, sprang into his carriage in spite of what he did to prevent her. When he was on the Pont-Neuf, three or four tall scoundrels came up to the carriage and insolently demanded that the prisoner be given up to them; telling him that if this were not done instantly they would kill him. These desperate fellows having begun the tumult, others came up and surrounded him, threatening the same thing.

He, not knowing how to escape peacefully from this *canaille*, ordered his coachman to drive on, and go towards the Augustins, where the house of his friend the Duc de Luynes stood, intending, if compelled by the crowd, to enter the courtyard, or else, for greater safety, to go by the Pont Notre-Dame to the Palais; for he thought that the worthy burghers would not let him be maltreated by these rioters. When he arrived at the Augustins, the crowd had begun to scatter; so that he resolved to leave his carriage at the Duc de Luynes, and go on foot to the Palais. But he had hardly taken three steps when a tall ruffian, dressed in gray, came up shouting: "To arms! to arms! Let us kill him, and avenge upon him the evils from which we suffer!"

On this the tumult grew hotter and hotter; and the chancellor was forced to take refuge in the hôtel de Luynes in order to save his life. He was received by a good old woman who, seeing the chancellor asking for help, took him by the hand and led him to a little closet made of pine boards at the end of a hall. He had no sooner entered, he and his party, than the *canaille* arrived with furious shouts, demanding to know where he was, and declaring, with many oaths, that they meant to have him. Some said: "Prisoner for prisoner; we will exchange him for our dear protector." Others, more malignant, said he ought to be killed and quartered, and the pieces hung in the public squares to show their resentment by their vengeance. They came at last to the little closet in search of him, but as the place looked deserted they contented themselves with giving a few kicks against the planks and listening if they could hear any sound; after which they went to seek him elsewhere. It is to be supposed that the chancellor while this was going on was not at his ease, and that he felt himself human. While in that closet he confessed to his brother, the Bishop of Meaux, and prepared himself to die.

He had sent to the Palais-Royal for help, and as soon as the peril he was in was known the gendarmes and the light-horse were sent to his assistance. The Maréchal de La Meilleraye started to find him with two companies of Swiss guards; and the illustrious prisoner was saved at last by the coming of the grand-master. The latter took him by the arm to lead him to the Palais-Royal, for in the confusion the carriage could not be found, and all things were now safe except for exposure to the fury of the populace. The Comte d'Offremont also came to the chancellor's aid, and, meeting him on the way, he put him into his carriage with his daughter and the Bishop of Meaux. As they passed before the Place Dauphine in the middle of the Pont Neuf, the populace, angry at having lost their prey, fired upon him, killing several of the soldiers who surrounded the carriage. The Duchesse de Sully received a shot in the arm, from a ball that was nearly spent, having been fired from a distance; consequently the wound was only a bad contusion. One of the king's lieutenants, who was in the suite of the chancellor, was killed by this *canaille*, and so was one of the guards.

They arrived at the Palais-Royal, much alarmed by their adventure; and the chancellor stayed there several days, not daring to return home lest the angry populace should attack and pillage his house. After he returned there I went to see him in his chamber, and he told me himself of the state of mind in which he was during this affair; and when I asked him whether the image of death was not horrible to him, he told me he had suffered that which, according to humanity, no one is exempt from feeling, but that God had shown him great favour, having entirely filled his mind with the care of his salvation and in asking from Him the forgiveness of his sins.

Thus passed the morning of the second day, which was no better than the first. At the queen's waking, about nine o'clock, the news was told to her. She was infinitely angered; not only at the treatment given to a person of such quality, who, for her service, had been two hours in the hands of scoundrels deserving of a rope, but also because of the affront to her authority, which would certainly have dangerous consequences to the State, and produce bad effects through the noise it would make in foreign countries. She knew the latter would recover strength from this news. A chancellor of France, without respect in Paris, threatened with death in the streets, his king being present in the city, was a sure sign that the royal power was diminishing and the love of the subjects to their sovereign extinct.

After the queen had received this blow, which showed her, in spite of her firmness in not allowing herself to be shaken by anything, that she had everything to fear, she was forced to rise and receive the parliament, which came on foot to demand the release of the prisoner. She spoke to them vigorously, with good sense and without anger, for on this occasion she acted according to her own feelings and of her own monition. Among other things that she said, these words remained in my memory and seemed to me worthy of remark: That it was strange and very shameful for them to have seen, in the days of the late queen her mother-in-law, the Prince de Condé in the Bastille without making any remonstrance; but that now, for a man like Broussel, they and the people made many; that posterity would regard with horror the cause of such disturbances, and that the king, her son, would some day be able to complain of their proceedings and punish them.

The chief-president said little, and President de Mesmes, interrupting him, took speech and addressing the queen, said: "Shall I dare, Madame, to tell you that, in the state in which the people are, a remedy must alone be thought of; and that your Majesty ought, it seems to me, to avoid the pain of having the prisoner set free by force, by granting his freedom to us of your own will and with a good grace?" The queen replied that it was impossible to do that wrong to the royal authority, and to leave unpunished a man who had attacked it with such insolence; that parliament ought to see by the mildness of her regency what her intentions were; that, for herself, she was always disposed to pardon them; but they knew very well that kings were compelled to a certain severity, in order to control the people by some fear.

After this sort of dispute she left them, and the head-president, running after her, conjured her to think well what she was doing. To which the queen (instructed here by her minister, as she admitted afterwards) replied that on their side they had better do what they ought, and show in the future more respect for the king's will; and when they did that, she, on her side, would do them all the favours they could justly claim from her.

The chancellor, who was present, explained that this answer was meant to let them know that if they would promise not to discuss the king's declaration any longer, and cease absolutely from assembling to discuss the affairs of the State, she would release the prisoners; inasmuch as the only reason which had obliged the queen to act as she had done was their rebellion, and the censure they gave daily to that declaration which crowned them with favours and showed them plainly the kindness of the king and of his minister.

On this proposition the members decided to return to the Palais and assemble to discuss their answer. They went out from the queen in the same order in which they came, and when they reached the rue Saint-Honoré the populace stopped them at the first barricade and surrounded them, shouting a demand for Broussel. Several approached the chief-president and putting a pistol to his throat, insulted him and threatened that if he did not cause M. de Broussel to be returned to them they would kill him. They showed, in fact, a strong desire to maltreat him; but he escaped by his own steady firmness; assuring them he intended to work for that result with all his strength; and on those words they gave him his life with the condition that he should go back at once to the queen, and signify to her that if he did not obtain Broussel they would cut him into a thousand pieces.

The whole assembly, therefore, returned upon its steps, much astonished to find the anger of the people turned upon them. They knew themselves to be the cause of these disturbances, and yet they could not remedy them had they wished to undertake it; for when the people meddle with the work of commanding, there is no master; each man for himself wants to rule. The famous republic of Rome, which made itself the mistress of nearly the whole world, learned by experience how dangerous it is to let the people have part in the government; and that illustrious, all-conquering community, in which each citizen counted himself a king, no doubt felt, through its noble illusion, the love of liberty, how hard and cruel and grievous a thing is popular fury.

France, which is accustomed to a beautiful and honourable duty to sovereigns, regarded the power that the people were trying to seize in Paris as a great malady in the State; even parliament was startled. I entered the king's room shortly after the return of the long robes to the Palais-Royal, and I saw them pass from the queen's large cabinet over the terrace which separates the two main buildings of this palace, on their way to the grand gallery of the king, where they were to do what they had proposed to do at the Palais de Justice, namely: seek for means to remedy the evil. They had eaten nothing all day, and it was now late. Out of pity, rather than kindness, the queen had taken care to send them bread and wine with a few dishes, which, as I thought, they ought to eat with shame, seeing that they were the cause of these disturbances, of the anxieties of the queen, the capture of Broussel, and the revolt of the people.

After their repast, the Duc d'Orléans went to them to take his usual place. The chancellor was also there to preside; which he did with great presence of mind, although the images of death and danger which he had so recently escaped pursued him. The cardinal went in for a moment; intending to conjure them to think seriously, with sincere intentions, on the remedy for evils that might grow out of these beginnings of rebellion. He had much cleverness of mind, and spoke our language fairly well, and he wrote it in

a way to be admired; but as the accent of his own country
stayed by him, he had no charm of speech, nor any facility
to express himself elegantly. He merely told them that he
thought they had good intentions, and the queen thought the
same; and that being so, it was easy to agree. One of my
friends who was in the assembly told me he repeated these
few words over and over again, confusedly; so that his little
harangue only made those laugh who did not seriously think
of doing as he advised. Which ought to make us see that
the heart of man is naturally perverse, and that justice is
often banished from it. If it were not so, men would value
things that are reasonably said, from whatever lips they
came.

All this day, in spite of the barricades, many persons
visited the queen, who remained in the circle with the
Queen of England and several princesses, awaiting the decision of parliament. The cardinal was not without anxiety,
and during this period of waiting he shut himself up in the
queen's little cabinet with the Abbé de La Rivière, who was
not as troubled as he, for he hoped that the decline of the
minister might lead to his own elevation.

This anxiety did not appear on the cardinal's face. On
the contrary, when he showed himself in public he assumed
great tranquillity, and, as I have said elsewhere, he was more
humane and gentle in misfortune than in prosperity; he did
not fly from those who wished to speak to him with the same
harshness as when he was satisfied and content. For this
reason, the Court people always wished him some ill-luck
in order to humble him; for it is natural to men to rule
their feelings by their interests, and the most virtuous man
is not virtuous when he desires some benefit which is refused to him with every mark of contempt and rudeness.
In spite of the cardinal's apparent gentleness, he did not

often show that quality in his behaviour or in his words, which were nearly always harsh, and very different from his promises, which were never fulfilled, or seldom, unless he was compelled by the manœuvres of claimants. They nearly always wrung his benefits from his weakness, not his kindness.

Parliament, having ended its deliberations, came to see the queen, who went to receive it in her little gallery, taking no women with her. The chief-president, in the name of the Assembly, protested their fidelity in a rather brief compliment, and then rendered to the queen an account of their proceedings, in which they promised to postpone all further deliberations, except those on finance and tariff, until after Martinmas.

This decision was of no good. Beneath that promise was seen the intention of beginning anew when the specified time had passed, and of assembling at their pleasure to discuss all matters. Nevertheless, in consequence of this postponement, the queen, forced by the state in which Paris then was, granted the release of the prisoner and gave them, then and there, a *lettre de cachet* to bring him back in the king's carriages, which were ordered to go for him with all diligence.

This concession, extorted solely by an apparent but transitory obedience, was, properly speaking, a victory won over royalty which distressed the queen, and must have done the same to the cardinal. It caused regret in the souls of honest Frenchmen, the number of whom was small; for those who composed the Court had ulcerated it with hatreds, or were filled with the desire to see the fortunes of the minister change. Thus it may be said that while the troubles of the queen were great, few persons took heed to them.

Here, then, is the prisoner Broussel, whom the queen is

compelled to surrender; the parliament is victorious; it and
the people are masters.   The burghers had previously taken
arms (by order of the king, fearing that the insolent *canaille*
might become too absolute), and the colonels of quarters and
the companies of the city are now mounting guard with such
order that it may be said that disorder was never so well
ordered.   A sedition so great and impetuous would seem
likely to cause more evil than it really caused.

But the burghers who had taken arms very willingly to
protect the town from pillage were no better than the populace, and demanded Broussel as heartily as the rag-pickers.
For, besides being all infected with the love of the public
good (which they held to be their own in particular),
devoted to parliament, and hating the minister, they were
filled with joy at the thought that they were necessary to
some purpose.   They believed they had a share in the government because they were guarding the gates of the city;
and each man over his counter discussed the affairs of the
State.   They did not make as much noise as the others, but
they demanded Broussel gravely, and declared that they
would never disarm until they saw him free with their own
eyes.

After parliament had had its audience the assembly left
the Palais-Royal, and returned as triumphant as the queen
was humiliated.   The populace and the burghers surrounded
the members to ask what they had done for Broussel; to
which they replied that they had obtained his liberty; and
one of his nephews showed the *lettre de cachet* and promised
that he should be in Paris the next day by eight in the
morning.   This promise gave them some comfort and
calmed them a little.   But, at the slightest doubt occurring
to their minds, they began once more their imprecations,
and in the midst of their anger the great exasperation that

they showed against the person of the queen and of the minister was startling. They did not hesitate to say that if deceived they would sack the Palais-Royal and drive out that foreigner; and they shouted incessantly: "Vive le roi tout seul, et M. de Broussel!"

The night was troubled, for with such a state of things there was much to fear. The alarm was great in the Palais-Royal; the queen herself, with all her firmness, was uneasy. The burghers were firing incessantly, and they were so near the king's house that the sentinels of the regiment of the Gardes and those of the rue Saint-Honoré could look at each other. The threats made by the people were not concealed from the cardinal, and in spite of the gaiety he affected in public, he did not fail to take the precautions of a frightened man. He sat up all night, being booted and ready to mount a horse in case he was compelled by the fury and madness of the people to fly. He had a body of soldiers in his house, a guard before his door, and in his stable a great pile of muskets for defence if attacked. He kept cavalry in the Bois de Boulogne to escort him if obliged to fly, and the persons who were attached to his service never left him at all that night. An Italian among them, who had as much cowardice as wit, and little tenderness for his master, said to me the next day, "For the whole kingdom of France, I would not pass another such night as that."

The next day the rioters, while awaiting Broussel's arrival, continued their threats saying openly that they should send for the Duc de Beaufort and place him at their head. Their insolence increased when they heard of the cavalry being stationed in the Bois de Boulogne. Unable to divine what this really meant, they imagined there were ten thousand men held in ambush in order to chastise them for their revolt.

When eight o'clock sounded and the prisoner had not arrived, the shouts redoubled, with such terrible threats that the state of Paris at that instant was something awful. At last, about ten o'clock, this tribune of the people having reached the city, the joy was unbounded; the street chains were let down, the barricades broken to allow of passing through. Never was triumph of king or Roman emperor greater than that of this poor little man, who had nothing to recommend him but his obstinacy for the public good and his hatred of taxes; which is, in fact, a praiseworthy thing if regulated by good and prudent conduct, and if its virtue is quite aloof from the spirit of cabal; but I know that during the whole war factious minds, acting solely from self-interest, had much intimacy and long conferences with him. That is why his good qualities were not pure, nor free from corruption. He was taken to Notre-Dame, where the people wanted to have a *Te Deum* sung for him, but the man himself, ashamed of the uproar, escaped from their hands, and getting out by a small door of the church fled to his home, where many of the Court people went to see him out of curiosity.

After Broussel's return it seemed as if the disturbances ought to cease; but the burghers, showing no submission to the orders and will of the king, would not lay down their arms nor remove the barricades except by order of parliament; and they said openly that they recognized no other master or protector. The same morning, in presence of Broussel, the Assembly, masters of the life of the king and of the city, issued a decree in these terms: —

"The court this day, the Chambers assembled: The provost of the merchants of this city, in view of the orders he had given in consequence of the excitement of the day before yesterday, yesterday, and this morning; hearing also that the *procureur général du roi* has ordered that the chains and barricades employed by the burghers be unloosed, demolished, and taken away; enjoins upon the people to retire to their homes and return to their vocations.   Done in parliament, August 28, 1648."

The result of this decree was that every one obeyed it so promptly that within two hours it was possible to go about Paris as in peaceful times; and matters so calmed down that what had just happened seemed like a dream.   But as it takes very little to disturb the minds of a populace already excited, ill-luck would have it that two caissons of gunpowder for the regiment of the Guards were brought into Paris through the Porte Saint-Antoine.   The sight struck the imagination of the people with a thousand terrors, and made the burghers believe, like criminals fearing the gallows, that the queen was intending to punish them.   On which they rushed to the carts and pillaged them, crying out, as before, " To arms ! "   The magistrates of the city went to the spot to pacify them and assure them they had nothing to fear; but they were not to be persuaded.   The fire of this new rebellion flared up with such rapidity that in less than half an hour it communicated its heat from one end of the town to the other; and Paris in an instant resumed the same aspect it had had in the morning.

On this information reaching her the queen took counsel with the Duc d'Orléans, the cardinal, the grand-master, and others.   It was resolved to send back to their quarters all the Guards stationed before the gates of the Palais-Royal, in order to remove the suspicions excited in the public by the sight of the caissons; this was done immediately.   Popular emotions in Paris, which is a world rather than a city, are furious torrents, that spread themselves out with such impetuosity that if allowed to swell they would be capable of making ravages such as posterity could hardly believe even from their terrible effects.

Finally the provost of the merchants was sent for, to whom the queen said that she was amazed at the rumour; that the powder which had so terrified the people was merely intended to supply the king's guard-house which happened to be without any, and in order to show that she had no intentions which could disquiet any one whatsoever she had sent all the companies of the Guards to their several quarters. She assured the provost that none were left in the guard-house but the king's usual guard, and she requested him to make known these truths through the streets in order to reassure everybody.

He obeyed the orders of the queen; but he was not listened to, — reason and truth not being within range of such a populace. The queen's assurances were received with insolent remarks, and rejected as wrongs against which the furious crowds had a natural antipathy. Incredulity was increased by a remembrance of the cavalry they had heard of in the morning as being ambushed in the Bois de Boulogne; and out of all these chimeras a fable was made in which the populace had more faith than in the truth. The terror they gave to themselves had such force upon their imagination that some were silly enough to say that the queen of Sweden was at the gates of Paris to help the queen, simply because they had heard that that princess was warlike, and they knew from her late ambassadors that she had contracted an alliance with our queen.

However, by dint of shouting to them that there was nothing to fear, there came moments when their passion seemed about to subside; and at seven in the evening messages were brought to the queen that the people were apparently willing to quiet down; which allowed her to prepare to go to bed. She needed rest after the fatigue and the cruel anxieties she had felt in spite of her usual tranquillity.

She was scarcely seated at her toilet-table before the up-roar of the rue Saint-Antoine which had spread over Paris, began again in the rue Saint-Honoré, with much more terror for the Court than that of the previous day; for at night things seem more dreadful and cause more anxiety. There were persons wicked enough to scatter notes about the streets and public places urging the burghers to take arms, warning them, charitably, that there were troops in the neighbourhood of Paris, and that the queen was about to carry off the king and then have the city sacked as a pun-ishment for their rebellion.

The alarm was great everywhere, and the Palais-Royal had its share of it. They came to tell the queen frankly that she was not in safety in that house without moat or guards. They told her there were troops of burghers min-gled with the *canaille* who declared openly that they wanted the king, and meant to take him into their own hands and guard him themselves in the Hôtel de Ville; also that they wanted the keys of the city, fearing that the queen would carry him away; and declaring that if they once had him out of the Palais-Royal they did not care what happened, and would set fire to it themselves very willingly.

On hearing these horrible threats we all began to fear both for her and for ourselves, for her person and for ours, and for our houses, which, being close to the Palais-Royal, ran great risk of being pillaged. Every one then spoke to her of the peril in which she was and of the insolent things that the people said against her; for though kings are flattered to the last extremity, when the mask is raised no

one spares them.   Jarzé, the new captain of the Guards, said
to her ostentatiously, "Madame, we are a handful of men
who will die at your door."   But as such offers had more
beauty than force, she received them more as signs of the
danger in which she stood than as a remedy capable of
supporting her under evils she had reason to fear.

She was forced to find support in her own firmness; for
the cardinal was so full of trouble and fright that she received no help from him.   She now saw clearly all that
might happen to her.   She felt it; and the colour which
flushed her face at Jarzé's words let us see it.   But I must
render her this testimony: after having observed her sentiments, her speech, her actions, I saw no sign of weakness in
her.   On the contrary, she continued equable, firm, and
steady, appearing at this crisis very worthy of her great
forefathers, and speaking like the granddaughter of Charles
V., who added piety in his last retreat to his heroic virtues.
To those who told her dreadful things she replied in these
beautiful words, which I shall remember all my life:
"Fear nothing, God will not abandon the king's innocence;
we must trust in Him."

When I heard her speak thus I was ashamed, I own, for
having thought that her tranquillity was sometimes caused
by ignorance of danger.   I had suspected this, because, in
truth, kings never see their misfortunes except through a
thousand veils.   Truth, which painters and poets represent
naked, is always dressed for kings in a hundred ways, and
never does worldly beauty change her fashions as often as
Truth when she enters the palace of kings.

On this occasion a great queen cannot be accused of blindness.   She felt the position in which she was so strongly
that she was well-nigh ill of it.   But her soul, stronger than
her body, supported her with such firmness that she scorned

to show the suffering that nature made her endure. And this honourable pride of hers was so great that it kept her from giving to her griefs any witness save the darkness of the night. In our presence she contented herself by asking with untroubled manner for the news which arrived from time to time; without neglecting, however, all that care and foresight could do to remedy the present extraordinary evils, under which she had no advice or help of any kind whatsoever, not even from her minister, who thought then that he should be forced to leave France.

It is true, in fact, that he dressed himself in gray to be ready to start; his horses were bridled all night, and his people kept ready to follow him. He even went to visit the burghers' guard-house, to hear what the people were saying and judge for himself. But finally, about midnight, the burghers, seeing that the guards were really no longer stationed around the Palais-Royal, where there were but two poor sentinels, and that quiet seemed to reign in the king's house, began to feel reassured. They became so, wholly, after the keys of the city were brought to them by the queen's order, and the magistrates, who walked the streets all night, had sworn to them that there was nothing to fear. The uproar quieted down; so much so that Comminges, having gone about the city to see for himself the state of things, came back to assure the queen that he had met scarcely any one. On which assurance we left her, and went to seek in rest some comfort for our misery.

XIII.

1648.

By August 30th, Paris had recovered an air of peace; no traces remained of the disturbances, nor of the violent excitement of the people. It is to be presumed that the trust the queen had placed in celestial help had, for the present, saved the great city; at any rate, among so many evil-intentioned persons not one would declare himself the leader of the rebellious *canaille*. Either that form of unfaithfulness horrified them, or else their malignity was not yet great enough to wish to ruin France, their country, and their king. Their ambition, envenomed by factious designs, had not yet reached the point to which, for our punishment, God allowed it to be carried; for great evils are not done at a single stroke. Men accustom themselves to crime only little by little, but, to the shame of human nature it must be owned that they do so readily. What gave most uneasiness to the minister was the notes flung about the streets, which he thought must come from a leader holding himself ready to command this body composed of so many different members. All their movements, which the imprisonment of Broussel brought to light, were, in fact, the foreshadowing of an actual evil which came soon after.

The coadjutor of Paris,[1] who had much intelligence and knowledge, and besides that, great courage and grandeur in his soul, feeling bound to employ on this occasion the in-

---

[1] Jean-François-Paul de Gondy, afterwards Cardinal de Retz, born 1614, died 1679. He was appointed coadjutor to his uncle the Archbishop of Paris in 1643. — FR. ED.

fluence that his character and dignity gave him to pacify the sedition, had gone about the streets with the intention of doing all the service of which he was capable to the king and queen; and he imagined that he had done them a sufficiently important one to be in a position to continue to serve them. But he now learned that instead of praising what he had done, the Court people laughed at him; the minister declared he was afraid, and said that when he himself had allowed him to come to his house, Beautru had ridiculed him. He complained aloud among his friends, of whom he had a great number, that he was ill-repaid for the pains he had taken; but it was thought that in order to make known that the evil was greater than was believed at Court, he himself had inspired the insults to the chancellor.

The Duc d'Orléans, who, up to this time, had always seemed affectionate to the queen, could not behold the state in which the Court now was without being conscious in his soul of some hope that the hatred felt for the queen, increasing daily, would replace in his hands the authority he had ceded to her, or at least give him a greater share than that with which he had contented himself. His favourite, who saw this opportunity of increasing his master's power, could not refrain from wishing for it as a means to increase his own; and as it is difficult not to show what we have in our souls, it was easy for the queen to see that in the council Monsieur did not act as strongly for her as he had done. For this reason she did not employ him as often to find a remedy for her troubles, fearing that the physician might make the malady worse. She therefore thought of bringing to her side the Prince de Condé, who was inclined to think, as she did, that Monsieur had profited by his absence to make himself master not only of the parliament, but of the council, the city of Paris, and the whole kingdom.

The war matters were going on in their usual way in Flanders. The battle of Lens, won by us, made us, in some degree, masters. The Prince de Condé besieged Furnes, which the enemy could not relieve.

About this time our little prince, the real Monsieur, fell ill with a continued fever and great pain in the loins, which made the physicians think it the small-pox. Two days later the disease came out in abundance, and as his fever lessened without any serious mishap, the queen was not uneasy. He was left in his apartment, carefully closed, and was lucky enough to keep his beauty, about which the ladies were much troubled, unimpaired.

In the beginning of September the queen was ill; but as she never had for herself any of that effeminate delicacy which is common to our sex, she did not cease to see all the captains of the quarters, whom she thanked for preserving the city from pillage; and, concealing her feelings, she sent for the burghers and the guild of merchants, to whom she said kind things, though indeed she had good reason to complain of them, for they had shown as much passion and fury against her as the most malignant of the *canaille*. When she ceased speaking to them, I, who had the honour of standing near her, said to her that she had just performed a queen's duty, namely, dissimulation; to which she replied, " And the Christian's duty also." I agree with her that the matter was ample enough for that duty too.

September 3, parliament came to the Palais-Royal to renew its persecutions. The chief-president made remonstrances to the queen on the articles of the King's declaration. He requested on behalf of the members, that another should be made to them according to their own forms; they again declared that they wanted one quarter of the *taille*-tax to be exempt from all depreciation [*non-valeurs*]; they demanded that a fund should be formed to pay the salaries of officers, which had not been paid for a long time; that subaltern officers should be admitted to the *droit annuel* without any supplement being asked of them, and that the *rentes* should be paid quarterly, or at least semi-annually. The last thing in the world they thought of was obeying the queen, or even keeping their word to her.

She, losing courage because she had had too much, answered gently that she was very glad that they took knowledge of the affairs of the State, and of the need in which the king now was. That being so, she was convinced of their fidelity and affection, and that they would not ask more remissions for the people in a time when all his affairs were in disorder. Nevertheless, forced by the necessity which was then her guide, she granted nearly all that they asked, except the exemption of the quarter of the *taille* from all charge, which was much more than she intended to grant in the last declaration.

The demands of parliament increased in proportion as favours were granted to them, and they now resolved to ask the queen for permission to continue their sessions during the holidays, which surprised the minister extremely and embarassed him much. He had hoped for the end of parliament as a release from his troubles, for, as the Italian proverb says : *il tempo dava vita* — time gave him life. After various negotiations he found himself constrained to grant what the parliament desired, because its members openly said they were resolved to continue their sessions in defiance of the Court. The State was no longer ruled by the old maxims of duty towards sovereigns; they offended him by their disobedience and served him in spite of himself.

The queen was therefore compelled to send this permis-

sion to parliament by the king's lawyers, but, to defend the
ground a little, it was granted for two weeks only. She
humbled herself to the point of begging parliament to put
an end to the rumours that ill-intentioned persons were putting forth against her, accusing her of a thousand false
things, of which it was impossible for her even to think. It
was told that she had ordered the street chains filed through,
and that certain astrologers had predicted great disorders on
the day of Notre-Dame, when, it was said, she meant to
have a second Saint-Bartholomew. She told them once
more that she knew they were holding certain assemblies in
the Faubourg Saint-Germain, composed of many sorts of persons who were defying her authority, and she requested them
to take notice of this and give orders to apply the necessary
remedy.

These submissive entreaties, so at variance with the sentiments and past conduct of the queen, showed clearly that
there were two wills, hers and another's; and that the first,
to her misfortune, yielded often to the second. On all these
demands of the queen, Broussel said that, in his opinion, they
ought to be enregistered; which was done solely for the
glorification of parliament, as it did not put an end in any
way to its intrigues. To keep up appearances and to satisfy
propriety in some degree, the Assembly issued, a few days
later, a decree against the astrologers and, in general, against
all who disturbed the public peace. But no one took the
trouble to put it in execution; and as for what concerned the
respect due to the person of the queen, it became a subject of
public ridicule.

While parliament was thwarting in this way all the plans
of the cardinal, he, instead of avenging himself on his enemies, was trying to conciliate them. About this time he
received a letter from the Comte de Béthune, father of the

Comte de Charost. This old seigneur, then over eighty years of age, entreated the minister to protect his son under the fault he had committed. In acknowledging this crime, he excused the criminal so wittily that it was easy to see he regarded his son's fault as noble and honourable, and that he was not at all sorry to know he was guilty of it. The letter was much praised by him who received it; copies flew about Paris, exciting admiration for the spirit that produced it, and the minister (very laudable in this) showed a desire to arrange the affair to the satisfaction of all parties.

On September 12 news was received from Furnes which informed the queen that the Prince de Condé had received a musket-shot on the thigh before that place; but fortunately it was only a contusion, because his buff coat chanced to have doubled itself back at that very spot.

On the same day the queen said openly that she thought of making a little trip to Ruel merely to have the Palais-Royal cleaned, for it needed purifying. The people had shown such aversion to allowing the king to leave Paris that it was thought unwise to allow this apparently simple trip to be known before the time of its execution. The cardinal, against whom the populace vomited execrations, was reduced to the extremity of not daring to leave the king's house. He feared the after results of the rebellion, which might be dangerous for him personally. The queen did not refrain from going out, but the bad disposition of the public mind gave her reason to fear many things. Thus the air of the open country, telling of liberty and innocence, seemed as necessary a preservative against the corruption of souls as it was also against that of the body. The dirty condition of the Palais-Royal was therefore a plausible pretext for bringing to a climax certain designs locked up in the breast of the minister, which were of sufficient consequence to oblige him to take all necessary precautions in order to execute them properly.

September 13, without making more stir than the queen's remark about the journey on the preceding day, the king, accompanied by Cardinal Mazarin, a few persons, and a few guards started from Paris at six in the morning; and by this celerity the opportunity was taken from parliament and burghers to oppose his going. The queen remained behind, as being the most valiant, to cover this retreat. Her confessor being ill she arranged to go to the Cordeliers to confess, and then to bid adieu to the good nuns of the Val-de-Grâce, whom she honoured with her particular friendship. Before leaving, she went in to see Monsieur, whom she found well treated for his small-pox; nevertheless, she said nothing of her departure, for fear of distressing him.

The king, as he left Paris, met several groups of rascals who shouted, "To arms!" and attempted to pillage the carts that carried his baggage. This insolence made the minister extremely uneasy on account of the queen, who remained alone in Paris. He sent Estrade back to warn her, and to beg her from the king not to go to the Val-de-Grâce, but to come straight to Ruel, and as quickly as possible.

I had the honour of being alone with her when she received this advice, and I saw her consult within herself. She judged, as she did me the honour to tell me, that nothing ought to be changed in what she had said she should do. Her carriages were already in the courtyard and her coif upon her head; she was ready to start; and she knew, by her good judgment, that if she showed any fear her own officers, through the surprise they would feel, might perhaps rouse the populace. She decided, therefore, that it was better to show security to all than to trust this

secret to a few; and so, without betraying alarm at so
evident a danger, she made her two visits and after that a
glorious retreat. She saw the provost of the merchants
before starting, to whom she promised that the king and
herself should assuredly return in a week.

The queen showed, by this act of prudence and firmness
that the cardinal was much mistaken when he said that
her courage came from ignorance. Mademoiselle did not
accompany the queen on this trip; she was living rather
retired from Court since her last adventure. She often
went to one of her country houses to amuse herself and
show that she did not care for the affront she had received.

The Prince de Condé, after the taking of Furnes, had
expressed an extreme desire to return to the king; and
the queen, who was not as satisfied as usual with the Duc
d'Orléans, willingly consented, in order to have a strong
support against the people, and a second against the Duc
d'Orléans, in case he proved capable of wishing to profit by
the bad state of her affairs.

Parliament and the people, finding themselves deprived
of the person of the king, were alarmed, and this alarm
increased their rebellion and their audacity. They both
knew their own wrong-doing; they knew the power of the
sovereign, and they saw his armies victorious, triumphant,
and faithful. They saw also the two princes of the blood
attached apparently to the interests of an offended queen
and her outraged minister. In such a position, they would,
reasonably enough, have fears; but also they had confidence
in their own audacity, and imagined, with good reason, that
the way to save themselves was to make the minister
afraid.

The queen, on her side, not yet feeling sure of being able
to avenge herself, showed no sign of intending to do so; on

the contrary, she spoke of returning to Paris, without, however, naming the day, and seemed to meditate a little visit
to Fontainebleau, to see from there, in peace and quiet,
what time might advise.   The cardinal, more wily still,
sought to vanquish his enemies by dissimulation.   By
avoiding their blows he hoped, when this first storm was
over, to give them a few on his return, and such as would
insure their defeat.

Many speculative minds declared that the queen could
not, without shame, let Paris go unpunished for the outrages to her person; that as the army of the Prince de
Condé was returning, the people ought to be made afraid by
blocking the entrances to the great city, which, from its
vastness, would suffer in two weeks' time so severe a famine,
that they would find themselves compelled to ask pardon
for their crimes.   Others, fearing a general rebellion of the
whole people disgusted by so many years of war, thought
there was reason to doubt the success of that measure, and
that if Paris were in a state of open rebellion all the
people of the country would follow her example, and the
punishment of one city would drag the whole of France
into the same crime.   But the arguments of persons at
Court do not always accord with the designs of those
who rule there; the queen at this moment was thinking
only of how to maintain peace in all parts of the kingdom,
and the thoughts of her minister went no farther than a
little war against two individuals, by which he hoped to
escape a greater.

Parties, in States, are born usually of some hidden cause
which the passions of men produce; and often the great
movements of the world which make or destroy empires
have no other source than the secret intrigues of a few
persons about trivial matters.   It is to be believed that

parliament was not impelled of itself alone to such great undertakings. It was clearly seen that certain persons must be in collusion with the leaders of this assembly, making them act, and inspiring them with that spirit of rebellion which was doing such harm in France. Châteauneuf and Chavigny were suspected by the cardinal of being the two poles on which these great undertakings hung, and it is to be believed that he was not mistaken.

Chavigny [1] was a man who had always considered that the office of minister was usurped by the cardinal. Châteauneuf was a former friend, irritated and now become the cardinal's enemy; he had worked for the latter's elevation by Cardinal Richelieu, and his friends, at his request, had assisted in placing him with the queen. Consequently, he had not been able to endure that the minister should treat him with so little favour. It was easy to judge that so ambitious a man would not bear such overthrow without avenging it, or without working to protect himself from the evils put upon him. Chavigny was attached to the Prince de Condé, and had many relations in parliament. President Viole, who was among them and his intimate friend, was also one of the bitterest against the Court; and it seemed as though there could be no mistake in accusing him of fomenting the rebellion of parliament. Châteauneuf was protected by the Duc d'Orléans, and he also had many friends attached to his interests, whether in parliament or elsewhere. So that these two men, regarded as party leaders, having the

[1] Chavigny, prime minister of Louis XIII., dismissed by Anne of Austria under the influence of the Vendôme party (*les Importants*), replaced in the council by Mazarin, to fulfil a pledge, and again removed and made governor of Vincennes. Montglat says formally that Chavigny had friends in parliament "whom he stirred up secretly against Mazarin, advising them to name the cardinal openly, and not to be satisfied with the exile of d'Émery, unless that of the minister was also granted to them." — FR. ED.

same sentiments and tending to the same end, though by
different roads and opposing cabals, had both about the
same destiny.

As soon as the queen arrived at Ruel, Châteauneuf received the commands of the king to retire to his own house,
one hundred and fifty miles from Paris, in order to remove
him from a place where he was continually intriguing
against the minister. Chavigny was then (September 18)
at Vincennes, of which he was governor. This same morning, at eleven o'clock, they came to tell him that a gentleman in ordinary of the king asked to see him. After the
battle of Lens the prisoners of importance were ordered to
be placed in Vincennes. Chavigny supposed that the person
who came from the king brought some order in relation to
these foreigners; he sent his lieutenant to him with direc-
tions to do whatever the gentleman commanded. But the
lieutenant returned to say that it was to himself that the
messenger wished to speak. He then made him enter, and
received from him a *lettre de cachet*, commanding him to
start in two hours for Chavigny and to take his wife with
him. When he had read the letter he showed it to two of
his friends who were with him and said: " Messieurs, we
must separate. We hoped to dine together, but you must
return to Paris, and I must go where the king commands
me within two hours." At these words Madame de
Chavigny came to him; they conferred together as to what
they had to do, and resolved that before starting she should
go to Paris and get some papers, and some clothes which
she needed. They did not expect at this moment any
greater misfortune than that which they saw before them,
which was simply quitting Paris. But, just as she was
getting into the carriage, they came to tell her husband
that a captain of the Guards, named Droit, asked to see

him. When the latter entered, he said that he had come to take possession of Vincennes. On receiving this order Chavigny gave him all the keys; and Droit, having received them, placed guards on the avenues and at all the gates of the castle, and then returned to Chavigny, whom he arrested in the name of the king, placing guards in his chamber.

Madame de Chavigny, who was already in her carriage and about to go to her own house, received orders not to return to Paris, but to go to Chavigny alone. She got out of the carriage, and going up, in spite of the guards, to her husband's room, she found him already surrounded. They were not allowed to speak together in a low voice, but as he kissed her, he put into her hand letters from the Prince de Condé which he had in his pocket. She told me afterwards that they were of consequence, and might have injured him. They said a few words to each other and then she was compelled to leave him and obey the order she had just received.

Chavigny's friends returned to Paris. As for him, he was taken to the prison where the Duc de Beaufort and the other captives in his charge had been confined. He found himself humiliated in the very place where he had commanded, and reduced to the hard necessity of suffering through the orders of the one man in the world whom he thought the most obliged to him. Here we see the vicissitudes usually to be found in the fate of men who live by favour. It is almost impossible for such men to continue long in a state of prosperity; the different events of life make those who aspire to the grandeurs of the world feel the extremes of good and evil, — good forever accompanied with some trouble, and evil oftenest without the mixture of any good.

For the last two years Chavigny had been very ill-satisfied
with the Court; he had suffered much, no doubt, at seeing
himself turned out of the dignified office he had held under
the favour of Cardinal Richelieu. But that ill was only a
slow fever that affected his health without danger to his life.
But now he was in the strongest throes and paroxysms of
the disease; most unfortunate if innocent, more unfortunate
still if guilty of having, for his own private interests, contributed to a rebellion which was causing great evils to the
State. He remained some time at Vincennes and was then
sent a prisoner to Havre. But he came from there much
sooner than the minister desired.

Chavigny's friends thought he had great reason to complain of Cardinal Mazarin, and the minister was treated by
them as the most ungrateful of men. But he said in his
own defence that he had returned to Chavigny, when the
latter was in favour, all the benefits to which friendship and
gratitude constrained him. And one day, one of his friends
having reminded him of the friendship that M. de Chavigny
had shown him, he replied that, considering the manner in
which he had treated him, the devil himself would have
loved him; and that later, when, raised to the ministry of
the regency, he had found that M. de Chavigny was disliked by the queen, he nevertheless kept him in the ministry; for though he could not give him back his office
of secretary of State (which the Comte de Brienne had just
received from the queen's own hands), it was partly because
he would not openly thwart the inclinations of a princess
on whom his own fortune depended; and besides this, he
was not capable of doing a violent thing, which Chavigny
ought not to have asked of him. But otherwise he had
treated him well, and fully intended to let him share his
own favour had he shown that he was capable of receiv-

ing it with the same deference he had formerly received from himself.

The cardinal said, further, that having never been able to bring M. de Chavigny to that deference, it was impossible to let him share a good he would only receive in his own way. Finally, dislike having succeeded to friendship, it had now passed into hatred, but he was not the cause of it; and nothing but M. de Chavigny's own audacity had forced him to fail in that which he confessed he owed to him.

The friends of Châteauneuf did not complain on the same grounds; but they were much grieved at the disgrace of their friend; the only consolation they had was in seeing that Chavigny was worse treated. The Commander de Jars, always ready to strongly defend those whom he liked, no sooner knew of Châteauneuf's dismissal than he went to see the cardinal. He told him frankly that he was shocked at this change, which had not been perceived by any of those who made public profession of being their friends; and that even lately he remembered that his Eminence, speaking to him of Châteauneuf, had not shown any sign of wishing to complain of his conduct; consequently the latter's dismissal had greatly surprised him.

The minister, well-used to making smooth speeches, replied that it was true he did not wish to harm his friend, — who was innocent of any crime; but he was willing to tell M. de Jars that, having the intention to arrest M. de Chavigny, who was protected by the Prince de Condé, then triumphant from the battle of Lens, he had judged it best, in order to legitimately refuse him the freedom of this prisoner whom he protected, to be able to tell him that Monsieur, the king's uncle, was also refused the return of M. de Châteauneuf, and therefore it was necessary that he should have a little patience.

The cardinal, however, regarded with precisely the same eyes the banished man and the imprisoned man, and Commander de Jars perceived a sort of coldness towards himself in this reply. In truth, the minister saw with vexation that two fine abbeys which he had given to de Jars did not make him less partial to his friend from whom he had never received anything.

The commander, feeling his position, went to see the queen. As he had entire familiarity with her, he spoke to her in these very words : " Madame, M. de Châteauneuf is sent away. He is a man to whom I can never cease to be a friend. Your Majesty knows the intimacy that I have with him. It is not my intention to let it be prejudicial to your service. But Madame, if you have the least suspicion that it may be, or if M. le cardinal has, I very humbly entreat you to tell me so. For, rather than be regarded by your Majesty with any distrust of my fidelity, I should leave the Court and live in a manner to give your Majesty no ground to complain of me."

The queen, who had much good-will to him, answered that his friend had not been sent away for any wrong he had done, but merely for reasons of State concerning his service; that therefore she could not take it ill if he should continue to be his friend; and that she herself wished him to remain with her and live as usual. That evening, on leaving the queen, he told me the whole conversation, which greatly solaced his heart. For he was a true gentleman, full of honour, though his goodness was sometimes obscured by the violence of his temper, which prevented him from always judging and acting by strict reason. So that, being beset by his own feelings, he was too convinced that the minister was always wrong; and as he did not like him, he never did him justice under any head.

Fontrailles, exiled under the late king [the Marquis de
Fontrailles, who had taken part in the affair of Cinq-Mars],
had returned to Court under the protection of Chavigny.
He was even one of the familiar friends of the cardinal;
for it was no crime with him to have been the confidant of
the grand equerry. Latterly, he had displeased the minister by replying to a gentle reprimand about certain de-
bauches, that it was not for the cardinal to take notice of
such matters; and if he and those who accompanied him
had done wrong, parliament could sue them. As the mere
citing of that assembly at this time was a crime, the minister regarded this speech as a threat, and banished him a
second time.

It was certainly not an unreasonable thing to send away
from Court and from the city of Paris a man who only
cared for making jests, who decried the government, and
infected with atheism the souls of those with whom he was
intimate. For at this time and henceforth the Court was
only too much contaminated by this very sort of free-thinking minds, which are always the cause of great evils. This
man had great charms in society; he was witty, generous,
honourable; and, according to the world's maxims, those
qualities were enough to make his friends weary at not seeing him.

Some one [the Duc de Mortemart] bolder than others
asked the cardinal to bring him back. He answered that
he would willingly do so, but that Monsieur did not wish
it. This friend, with capital craft and making no stir about
it, went to see the Duc d'Orléans and laughingly reproached
him for not letting that poor Fontrailles return to those
who were languishing with grief at his absence. Monsieur,
who had not opposed his return, replied at once that he
asked no better than to have him back, but that the queen

and cardinal did not wish it. The active friend, being thus assured on both sides, though he knew very well from whom came the harm, without saying another word to the minister, sent for Fontrailles and boldly presented him at Court. Cardinal Mazarin was amazed to hear of his return, and demanded the reason of the zealous friend, who coolly replied that, his Eminence having assured him that he was willing Fontrailles should return provided Monsieur was willing, and Monsieur having consented, he had sent for him. The story ending thus the minister received it with a good grace, though in his heart he was not pleased; and the trick played upon him was not forgotten when occasion came.

Fontrailles was one of Chavigny's friends; it was well to punish him for his other sins under cover of this one. They sent to arrest him at the same time that Chavigny was put in the prison at Vincennes. But he, who was accustomed to escape from perils of this nature, having been warned on waking that the king's Guards were before his door and seemed to be awaiting him, ordered horses to his carriage and a fat valet into his bed to fool the soldiers, while he escaped on the other side, and thus preserved his liberty to work at other intrigues.

The dismissal of the two ministers of the late reign made a great noise among those who were interested in their fortunes. The two cabals, which were in a way embodied in the persons of these men, made this matter an affair of State, which was taken up by parliament as being advantageous to it. On the 22d of this month (September) it assembled and would not listen to further discussion of tariff or *rentes*. The speakers complained of the violence committed on the person of M. de Chavigny, a man of worth and honour, saying openly that he was outraged by one who owed to him his fortune, by a foreigner, by a man who was ruining the king and the State, and robbing the treasury to send money to Italy. In short, they said, against the minister and in favour of the prisoner all that self-interest suggests on such occasions to passionate men.

After deliberating on what they should do, they decided to send deputies to the queen at Ruel, praying her to bring the king back within twenty-four hours, and to continue, themselves, to assemble until they had reformed the State and changed the minister. To succeed in this purpose they sent deputies to all the princes of the blood entreating them to be present the next day in parliament, in order that in their presence they might take steps to regulate the disorders and abuses which had crept into the kingdom by the fault of him who governed it. They said openly that their intention was to issue on the morrow an edict like that of 1617, which was given on the death of the Maréchal d'Ancre, decreeing that in future no foreigner, of whatever rank he might be, should govern the State. The chief-president was deputed to go to the queen the same day, and President de Maisons to the princes, entreating them to be present the next day at their deliberations.

The Prince de Condé was in Paris. He had just arrived from the army and had not yet seen the queen. President de Maisons found him and made the request in due form. The Princesse de Condé told me, this same day at Ruel, that her son had replied as follows: that he was just starting to see the queen and receive her orders; that he begged parliament to do likewise, and to resolve to obey her, as he himself intended to do. Some hours later all the deputies arrived together at Ruel, with the excitement that such a deputation was sure to cause in a Court predisposed to prejudice.

I had gone to Ruel very early in the morning to see the queen about these changes; for I had not had that honour since she had left Paris. I found her at her toilet, dressing herself tranquilly, and not knowing as yet what the parliament had done; and I myself could not tell her, because it was still assembled when I left Paris, and my haste had prevented me from learning what the seditious minds of that assembly were doing against her peace. The queen did me the honour to take me aside as soon as she left her mirror, to ask what was being said in Paris. I replied that persons were talking much of the fear of the Parisians lest she should not bring the king back to them for a long time; also of the imprisonment of M. de Chavigny; and, above all, they desired that M. de Châteauneuf should keep his office; and I told her that all these things together made me fear that some tumult would arise, and that she ought to prepare herself for bold enterprises which would surely displease her.

She answered that the people were wrong to suspect her of wishing to punish them; that I knew her, and knew that in truth she only asked for peace; as for M. de Chavigny, whose wife, she knew, was my friend, she assured me she had not resolved on his imprisonment without very strong reasons, and that the cardinal also had had great difficulty in doing so. She added that she awaited with impatience to know what parliament would do that day, foreseeing bad results from their usual violence, the regard they had for the prisoner, and the hatred they felt to her minister. All that she apprehended happened as she said; and soon after they came to tell her of the resolutions passed (as I related), with which she was ill-pleased and her minister much embarrassed.

I went to dine with the Duchesse d'Aiguillon, who kept open house for the honourable persons who came to pay their

court to the king and queen, whom she had the honour of
lodging in her house.   On my return I found the queen in
her circle, with a face apparently set firm against evil, laughing and talking as usual.   With a single glance of her eyes
she made me understand what was passing in her soul, but
towards the public no sign of any change in her mind was
visible.   And yet she was attacked in the person of her minister, whom she saw on the verge of being driven away by the
violence of the populace; she saw her authority trampled
under foot, her person insulted by a thousand outrages; and
she knew she had no resource but the hope that the princes
would not abandon her, — which must surely be a very uncertain hope for a regent, whose fall from power is necessarily
their rise.

About three o'clock the deputies arrived at Ruel, with
an air of pride that looked a little like bravado.   The Princesse de Condé, who liked Chavigny, from whom she had
received a thousand little services in the days of the late
king and Cardinal Richelieu, and who was the secondary
cause of the opposition she had always made to Châteauneuf,
took me by the hand and led me to the window to see these
dotards of the long robe file into the courtyard.   The deputation did not displease her; she thought they all made a good
appearance, and could not help saying — speaking to me as
to a person who had the reputation of knowing how to hold
her tongue — that she approved of the answer her son had
made to the deputies; but she did not approve of his being
indifferent to the imprisonment of M. de Chavigny.

The harangue of the chief-president was short.   He told
the queen that he had come on behalf of his company, to entreat her Majesty to return with the king to their good city
of Paris, among their good and faithful subjects, who complained that the absence of the king had seemed to them

more like an abduction than a journey, he having left the city early in the morning without guards; and, this sun being thus eclipsed, darkness seemed everywhere, and it was to be feared that his continued absence would cause some great disturbance.   He then made complaints on behalf of parliament respecting the imprisonment of M. de Chavigny, offered urgent prayers for his release, and concluded by entreating the queen not to think it ill that they had resolved to continue to assemble and labour for the reformation of the State.

The queen replied that she was astonished to see that kings were deprived of the privilege which all private persons enjoyed; that it was the custom of those who lived in Paris to quit the town at this season to enjoy the last of the fine weather; and it was strange that subjects should wish to prevent their sovereign from living like other men; that she had left the Palais-Royal in order that it might be cleaned of the dirt which always accompanied a Court whenever it stayed for a length of time in one place; and that she particularly desired to ventilate it from the infected air of small-pox which her son had had; that she intended to return to Paris, but it would be when it pleased her; that she was much dissatisfied with their mutinous spirit and the manner in which they censured her actions, for which she rendered an account to God only, and would render to the king her son when he should be of an age to judge them; that she had caused M. de Chavigny to be arrested for good and sufficient reasons; that she did not think their demands just or their assemblies legitimate, and that they must take care to reform them.

President de Maisons then made his harangue to the Duc d'Orléans, in presence of the queen, and entreated him, on behalf of parliament, to be present the next day at their deliberations, which they were determined to continue until they had put the requisite and necessary order into the State.

The Duc d'Orléans replied vigorously that he joined in the interests of the queen to defend the royal authority, which was infinitely insulted by their proceedings; that, their assemblies being held without the royal permission, they could only be contrary to the king's service; and, having the honour to be uncle to the king, he was bound to maintain his authority and to work with all his power to have the queen obeyed; and he repeated more than once that he would have her obeyed and the cardinal maintained in defiance of their seditious cabals. The duke, in spite of the coolness which the queen had noticed in him, answered thus with warmth, first, out of fidelity to the king, and next, from emulation of the Prince de Condé, who he saw was going over wholly to the queen's interests; besides which, he did not like M. de Chavigny, whose imprisonment was not displeasing to him, and he was angry with parliament for making such disturbance for his liberty.

The Prince de Condé, who had arrived that day to visit the king and queen, replied to the harangue which was made to him at the same time, saying that, having learned from the queen's own lips that her Majesty had not permitted them to assemble, except for the tariff and the *rentes*, he was very ready to say to them in her presence that he would never allow their disobedience or their undertakings; that he would spend the last drop of his blood in defending her interests against them; and having the honour to be what he was to the king, he was resolved to die in his service; and that he should never depart from these feelings, nor from the friendship he had promised the cardinal, whose interests were very dear and considerable to him.

The Prince de Conti also made an answer based on the two preceding ones, assuring them that he should not depart from the sentiments expressed by Monsieur and his own brother; that he himself was servant of the queen and would die in her interests and those of the cardinal.

The Duc de Longueville, wishing to figure as prince of the blood, tried to speak to President de Maisons, but, either by order or by chance, he found himself interrupted by the chancellor.[1] Then all together, sometimes one sometimes the other, they talked to the gentry of the parliament, pointing out to them their fault and the disturbances that through such conduct they would cause in the kingdom.

The queen did me the honour to tell me that evening, before I started to return to Paris, that the chief-president, in speaking to her, had his eyes full of tears from pain at seeing himself obliged to be mixed up in such audacious enterprises, so contrary to the service of the king and the public good.

Though the cardinal had not been named by the deputation, he was not ignorant of the way in which he had been treated in the sessions of parliament, and he seemed to desire some public demonstration of the protection of the royal family. The princes had been quite willing to give it to him, not only to oblige the queen, but more because they believed that this minister without power, and who up to that time had seemed weak, was better for them than any other. He himself felt that they were accustomed to his industrious and submissive ways and found them convenient. He cleverly made use of the defects that appeared to be in

---

[1] Omer Talon says that the Duc de Longueville did speak, but with more gentleness, and he exhorted the magistrates to conciliation and moderation. This may be why the chancellor interrupted him as Mme. de Motteville states.— FR. ED.

him in order to impress upon their souls a real desire to protect him, from a belief that by supporting him they would reign more absolutely through his dependence upon them.

Matters being in the state in which they were, the queen resolved to bring the little Monsieur from Paris, where he had been left ill with the small-pox.   In order to cheat the Parisians, who were delighted to have this precious hostage in their hands, she gave orders to Beringhen, chief equerry, to go in quietly and achieve this conquest over them.   He left Ruel and came to Paris, as others of the Court did daily. Having arrived, he got into a carriage with two horses and went to the Palais-Royal to pay a visit to the little prince. He took him in his arms and hid him in the back of his carriage, and then drove to Longchamps.   There he put him into a boat in which to cross to the other bank of the river, where one of the king's carriages awaited them, which took them to Boisenval, close to Ruel.

The queen went to see her son the next day, and took him back with her to the king, intending to change her place of residence and go to Saint-Germain, where the Court would be separated from Paris by three arms of the river, and at a more reasonable distance than at Fontainebleau for working conveniently on the matters which parliament stirred up daily.   Guards were placed at the bridge of Neuilly until the departure of the king, because they feared a surging-up of the people of Paris and the dangerous results of their anger.

The next day, September 23, a declaration was sent to parliament from the king, forbidding it to assemble except for the discussion of the tariff and the *rentes*.   Throughout that night many persons left Paris; many others sent away their property; and all divined, without being astrologers, that we were on the brink of many misfortunes.   The popu-

lace and the burghers felt already in their fears the punishment of their rebellion.   They laid in a stock of wheat;
provisions grew dearer; and all things foretold to them the
anger of Heaven and that of the king.   When the Parisians
became aware that Monsieur had been taken from them, they
murmured loudly and some of the *canaille* assembled around
the Palais-Royal, crying out they were lost, the city would
be sacked now that Monsieur was out of it.   But all this
came to nothing.

Parliament, on its side, deliberated on the last declaration
of the king; on which it was resolved to send remonstrances
to the queen in writing and to enjoin the provost of merchants to take measures for the public safety and provide
that the people should not be left without provisions.[1]
While they were assembled, Choisy, chancellor of the Duc
d'Orléans, brought them a letter from the duke, and the
Chevalier de La Rivière brought them another from the
Prince de Condé.   Here is what they both contained: —

From M. le Duc d'Orléans to the Parliament.

MESSIEURS, — You know the pains I have taken to conciliate present affairs, and that I have always brought to
that purpose all the moderation [*tempérament*] which the
service of the king, my lord and nephew, and the satisfaction of your company could desire; and as I judge that in
the present state of those affairs a conference would be very

[1] This decree, passed by a majority of four votes only (seventy-one
against sixty-seven), cast alarm into Paris, and stopped all business, —" to
such a point," says Omer Talon, " that a cart loaded with furniture belonging to the Baron d'Aigle, was stopped before the markets and pillaged, the rascals saying that, as the covers were red, the property belonged to the cardinal.   Besides which, a carriage in which were eight or
ten thousand silver *livres* belonging to Madame de Bretonvilliers was
stopped near the Île Notre-Dame and pillaged by boatmen, but a part of
the money was immediately recovered." — FR. ED.

useful to regulate all things, I am willing still to write you this letter to beg you to depute some of your body to be in a place where the queen will be to consult on means judged suitable for public peace.   I wish to believe that you will concur with me in this good purpose, and that you will give the same belief to what the Sieur de Choisy, my chancellor, will say to you on this subject.

                    Your affectionate friend,
                                        GASTON.

From RUEL, September 23, 1648.

On the back was written, —

" To *Messieurs les gens* holding the court of parliament of the king, my lord and nephew."

The letter of the Prince de Condé was as follows : —

From M. le Prince de Condé to the Parliament.

MESSIEURS, — Being unable to go to parliament, as you showed to me you wished by your deputation of yesterday that I should do, and foreseeing the inconveniences which may arise if you continue your deliberations without my previously seeing you, I have thought best to invite you, as M. le Duc d'Orléans has done, to a conference at Saint-Germain, at which we can discuss the disorders at present in the State, and endeavour to remedy them.   The zeal that I have for the service of the king, and the affection that I have for your company, induce me to propose to you this method of remedying evils which perhaps neither you nor I can again control if you lose this occasion.   The queen has all the sentiments of kindness that your company can desire and expect.   M. le Duc d'Orléans has sufficiently proved his to you by the care he has taken up to this hour, and by the letter he now writes to you.   As for me, I have no stronger

passion, after that which I have for the good of the State
and the maintenance of the royal authority, than that of
serving you. Show, therefore, on this occasion, the zeal
which you have testified for the service of the king by con-
tributing all in your power for the conciliation of matters,
and give me reason to show to you, by the services that I
shall render with her Majesty, that I am your very humble
and very affectionate servant.

LOUIS DE BOURBON.

From RUEL, September 23, 1648.

And on the fold of the letter, —
"To Messieurs of the court of parliament."

After the reading of these letters and their discussion, it
was resolved to send deputies to Saint-Germain to the
princes, *to confer with them only,*[1] according to their request, on the disturbances in the State and present matters.
These deputies were ordered, before entering on any discussion, to demand of the queen Chavigny's liberty, Châteauneuf's return, and that both be restored to their offices.
On this point President de Mesmes said that it was reasonable to demand their liberty and their return, but that it was
just to leave the queen the choice of her favours and benefits, seeing that our kings could not be forced to employ in
their councils those who did not please them.

Among the different opinions of those who spoke, some
said that, M. d'Avaux having been appointed superintendent
on going to Münster, it was reasonable that he should be
restored to the exercise of that office. And it was thought
from the words of his brother, President de Mesmes, that
the latter, being reconciled with the Court, had wished

---

[1] The formula "with Messieurs the princes only" was used to exclude
Cardinal Mazarin. — FR. ED.

not to give suspicion to the minister that he solicited the votes of parliament to restore the superintendency to his brother. Broussel, speaking of Chavigny, said he was told that he was suspected of having secret understandings with himself and with others in parliament; and he therefore felt obliged to say, in the interests of truth, that for himself he did not know him and had never seen him; and as for M. de Châteauneuf, he had never seen him either since he was twenty years old, when he was counsellor of parliament.

On the 29th, the deputies went to Saint-Germain, where the queen had arrived on the 24th. They went, full of pride and presumption, and had their conference in the Duc d'Orléans' house, from which the cardinal was excluded at their request. The rank he held in the State could not protect him from this affront. It was necessary to yield this point to those who seemed the stronger, and the princes, who protected the minister more for their own interests than from any power they had to do so, abandoned him on this occasion.[1] It was an extraordinary and mortifying affair for him, and showed openly that the princes were not sorry to be masters.

The first demand the deputies made was for the release of M. de Chavigny. The Duc d'Orléans replied that he thought it very strange that, being himself a son of France and exiled in the lifetime of the late king, his brother, parliament had neglected him to the extent of never speaking of his exile, and yet now they made this great talk about M. de Chavigny, who was certainly not of as good a family as himself, but whom they liked better. President Viole said, in relation to this matter, that he had orders from parliament not to

---

[1] Omer Talon relates with more detail the insolence shown by the deputies at this meeting, as they deliberated whether or not the cardinal should be excluded from the conference.— Fr. Ed.

make any propositions until the liberty of the prisoner had previously been granted ; on which the Prince de Condé retorted that previously [*préalablement*] was not a proper term to use to his master ; that President Viole ought to consider the respect he owed to the king and to those who maintained his interests ; that, as for himself, he intended to serve M. de Chavigny as his friend, and should do so by doing him good service with the queen as much as possible ; but it was only putting his liberty beyond all hope by endeavouring to obtain it in ways contrary to the duty and respect that were owed to the king.

He said this, repeating the word *préalablement* and turning it into ridicule in a way that made it plain he did not wish to be suspected of abandoning the king and queen for the interests of Chavigny. As a result of this speech the deputies of parliament, not venturing to say another word on that point, entered upon their demands for the good of all, which were as follows : —

I. That full security should be granted to them in their own persons and to the people in general ; that assurance should be given for the return of exiles and the freedom of prisoners, of whatever rank and condition they were ; that it should not be in the power of ministers acting in the name of the king to imprison any person whatsoever without parliament taking cognizance of the matter within twenty-four hours.

II. That one-quarter of the whole *taille*-tax [tax levied on persons not nobles or ecclesiastics] should, without being subject to diminution, be remitted to the people.

And, in conclusion, they demanded that the king should return to Paris.

These proposals seemed hard, and too bold, and after the princes had disputed each article the conference ended with little satisfaction on either side. But as the princes found their own security in these demands it is to be supposed that they were not altogether displeased by them. However that may be, the conference was adjourned till two days later to allow of an answer to the proposals; and that time having expired, this is the answer that was made to parliament on behalf of the king : —

I. That the setting at liberty of M. de Chavigny being a favour of the queen, it must depend on her; but, in accordance with the kindness of her Majesty, it might be hoped that she would think proper to grant it.

II. That the return of the king to Paris would be at the time of year when persons usually returned there, provided the parliament and people made themselves worthy of that happiness by their submission and their obedience.

The article relating to prisoners and exiles was rejected; that which demanded cognizance of imprisonments within twenty-four hours was also refused and treated as a thing impossible and against the royal authority.

As for the quarter of the *taille*-tax, the queen replied that she was quite ready to grant that, but she should let them see the necessities of the State and the great expenses she was compelled to incur; that after they had that knowledge she was certain they would themselves see it could not be done; but if they judged the contrary she would willingly do it.

By this conference the two parties were only half satisfied with each other, and the deputies agreed among themselves to return to Saint-Germain a second time. During this little interval the Duchesse de Vendôme, seeking to profit by the power of parliament, presented to it a request asking for protection against the persecutions of the minister. This request was received with many marks of good-will, because it gave parliament a pretext for further outcry, which was agreeable to it. It was presented the last of September to the assembled Chambers, and given to Lesnée, but the chief-president, anxious to favour the Court, prevented its being reported. On that same day the deputies who were appointed to return to Saint-Germain were instructed by parliament to treat of all the other articles proposed at the Chamber of Saint-Louis.

INDEX TO VOL. I.

Ingram Content Group UK Ltd.
Milton Keynes UK
UKHW050825190423
420422UK00008B/501

9 781271 560455